The Projected Nation

A volume in the SUNY series in Latin American Cinema
―――――――
Ignacio M. Sánchez Prado and Leslie L. Marsh, editors

The Projected Nation

Argentine Cinema and the Social Margins

MATT LOSADA

Published by State University of New York Press, Albany

© 2018 State University of New York

All rights reserved

No part of this book may be used or reproduced in any manner whatsoever without written permission. No part of this book may be stored in a retrieval system or transmitted in any form or by any means including electronic, electrostatic, magnetic tape, mechanical, photocopying, recording, or otherwise without the prior permission in writing of the publisher.

For information, contact State University of New York Press, Albany, NY
www.sunypress.edu

Library of Congress Cataloging-in-Publication Data

Names: Losada, Matt author.
Title: The projected nation : Argentine cinema and the social margins / Matt Losada.
Description: Albany : State University of New York Press, 2018. | Series: SUNY series in Latin American cinema | Includes bibliographical references and index. | Includes filmography.
Identifiers: LCCN 2017040337 | ISBN 9781438470634 (hardcover) | ISBN 9781438470641 (pbk.) | ISBN 9781438470658 (ebook) Subjects: LCSH: Motion pictures—Social Aspects—Argentina.
Classification: LCC PN1993.5.A7 L67 2018 | DDC 791.430982—dc23
LC record available at https://lccn.loc.gov/2017040337

10 9 8 7 6 5 4 3 2 1

Contents

Acknowledgments		vii
Introduction: A History of Erasures		ix
Chapter 1	National Modernization and the Production of Marginal Spaces in Early Feature Films	1
Chapter 2	The Classical Cinema and the Perpetuation of a National Fantasy	25
Chapter 3	An Inquisitive Gaze on the Nation	73
Chapter 4	Contemporary Cinema and the Neoliberal Social Margins	131
Notes		167
Works Cited		179
Filmography		189
Index		191

Acknowledgments

Looking back from the end of this project, the beginning has become hard to discern. The sources of inspiration are many, including Professors David William Foster, James Gaasch, Rosamel Benavides, Lilianet Brintrup, Ellsworth Pence, David Castillo, Evlyn Gould, Massimo Lollini, Steven Botterill, Mia Fuller, Jeffrey Skoller, Ignacio Navarrete, Natalia Brizuela, and Verónica López. All provided inspiration and lots of help. I'm most grateful—especially when I consider that I completed my doctorate and found gainful employment—for the generosity and warmth of Dru Dougherty, an exemplary professor, adviser, and friend.

I owe a great debt to my excellent colleagues in the University of Kentucky's Department of Hispanic Studies: Yanira Paz, Ana Rueda, Aníbal Biglieri, Haralambos Symeonidis, Alan Brown, Carmen Moreno-Nuño, Moisés Castillo, Irene Chico-Wyatt, Heather Campbell-Speltz, Jorge Medina, Ruth Brown, Brent Sebastian, Dierdre Reber, Susan Larson, and Mónica Díaz.

Although I have not met them, I deeply appreciate the work of the audiovisual preservationists who care for the cinematic past and generously exhibit its films—among them Fernando Martín Peña, Fabio Manes, and Paula Félix-Didier—as well as the efforts of the many other organizers of film screenings and those who attend them. They make Buenos Aires a wonderful place for a cinephile, and this project could not have been imagined were it not for their work. A special thanks to the Museo de Cine, and especially to the generous Fabián Sancho, a treasure of information on all things cinema and culture.

Thanks to those at the NEH seminar in Buenos Aires in 2014 for long walks and stimulating conversations, especially Rocío Gordon, Stephen Silverstein, Patrick Ridge, and David William Foster, to the organizers of the symposium *Film and Phenomenology: Affect, Bodies, and Circulations in Latin American Cinema* at Virginia Tech University, María del Carmen Caña

Jiménez and Vinodh Venkatesh, to Gary Crowdus, founder and editor of *Cineaste*, and friends and cinephiles Pablo Baler, Andrei Dubinsky, Adam Shellhorse, and Chris Eagle.

Much love and appreciation to Gerardo, Carmita, Feña, Vale, Lola, Tato, Fede, Toni, Lucía, and el/la nuevo/a, as well as to Aunt Irene and my cousins lost on Long Island. Many others go unmentioned, though never unloved, but reserved for last is appreciation and love for my mother, Patricia, for Pops and Mike, and for Pepita (you are missed). My deepest love and gratitude to Remi and Mia, who put up with me as I wrote this book and nonetheless managed to make each day a wonderful adventure.

I am very indebted to the reviewers of the earlier versions of some of the material in this book, which were published in journals as follows: a few paragraphs of the introduction, chapter 2, and chapter 3 in a much earlier form in *Chasqui* 40.2 (Nov. 2011); part of chapter 1 in an earlier form in *Hispanic Review* 80.3 (Summer 2012); a section of chapter 3 in a slightly earlier form in *Revista de Estudios Hispanicos* 50.3 (Oct. 2016); and a few paragraphs of chapter 4 in an earlier form in *Romance Notes* 50.2 (2010).

All translations are mine unless otherwise indicated.

Introduction

A History of Erasures

To begin to illustrate the cultural field in which filmic representations of Argentine national space were conceived, I will open this book with a poem written as the cinematic medium had only begun to take on importance in the national culture. "El hermoso día" (The Beautiful Day), written by the conservative nationalist intellectual Leopoldo Lugones, was published in 1917, the year after the first commercially successful run of an Argentine feature-length film, *Nobleza gaucha*.[1] The poem is apposite for both its erasures and its origin in a far more restricted field of production. For its reader, who likely belonged to an elite, urban, highly cultured minority, the poem's antimodern conception of national space conspicuously erases any trace of modernity and the accompanying influx of immigrants, and in doing so naturalizes the privileged position in a hierarchy of being of the *terrateniente*, the landowning lyric subject of the poem:

> Tan jovial está el prado,
> Y el azul tan sereno,
> Que me he sentido bueno
> Con todo lo creado.
>
> El sol, desde su asomo,
> Derramó por mi estancia
> El oro y la fragancia
> Del polen del aromo.
>
> Sentimental, el asno,
> Rebuzna su morriña,

> Y ayer, como una niña,
> Floreció ya el durazno.
>
> So cheerful is the land,
> And the blue so serene,
> That I've felt fine with
> With all of creation.
>
> The sun, upon its rise,
> On my ranch spilled
> Gold and the fragrance
> Of the pollen of the myrrh tree.
>
> Sentimental, the ass,
> Brays his nostalgia,
> And yesterday, like a young girl,
> The peach tree already flowered.

The lyric subject is in prelapsarian harmony with a landscape he owns, and which in turn envelopes him with a sense of timeless, natural serenity through the stimulation of his sensorium. The blue he sees, the warmth of the sun he feels, the flowers of myrrh he smells, the braying ass he hears, and the peach he anticipates tasting all contribute to an affective order in which he is the privileged subject of aesthetic rapture. This timeless space was "created" (*creado*) by an entity of whom the *terrateniente* lyric subject is the favored son, but such solitude, such an insular perspective, to what is it responding? To insecurities regarding a national landscape conquered by coercion and violence only decades before, and at present undergoing a rapid and problematic modernization, primarily in the form of massive immigration? The only trace the poem contains of this modernity is its complete erasure from the landscape. So, the questions must be asked: What is the nature of this structuring absence? What was happening in the nation's rural spaces at the time Lugones was idealizing it for elite readers? Elina Tranchini offers an answer:

> Desde 1901 se sucedieron con una mayor o menor violencia, huelgas, movilizaciones y protestas de braceros, trilladores, estibadores, carreros, y otros trabajadores rurales. En la región pampeana los conflictos comenzaron en 1912 y se extendieron

durante toda la década de 1910 por las provincias de Buenos Aires, Santa Fe, Córdoba y La Pampa, incluyendo a chacareros, arrendatarios, pequeños proprietarios, que se oponían a las condiciones impuestas por terratenientes, intermediarios colonizadores, comerciantes y acopiadores. (1999, 126)

After 1901 there occurred, with varying degrees of violence, strikes, mobilizations, and protests by temporary farm workers, threshers, stevedores, cart drivers, and other rural workers. In the region of the Pampa the conflicts started in 1912 and extended throughout the 1910 decade in the provinces of Buenos Aires, Santa Fe, Córdoba and La Pampa, including farmers, tenants, small landowners, who were opposed to the conditions imposed by the large landowners, middlemen, traders, and brokers.

When contextualized by such conflict, Lugones's poem takes on a far different meaning, as yet another salvo in a cultural struggle to justify control over the national space in the face of a modernization project that brought demands, sometimes violent, from the dispossessed. His strategy was to portray space in ways that would favor the claims of elite sectors to national authenticity and cast out the immigrants as unredeemably alien.

But as the poem was being written and first read, the national culture was also undergoing rapid modernization as new media were fast expanding, with already a far wider reach than that of Lugones's lyric poetry. The most notable of these is the cinema, which by 1917 was settling into the feature film format with which it would find a mass popular audience. Friedrich Kittler's conception of the discourse network, as "the network of technologies and institutions that allow a given culture to select, store and process relevant data" (369), is useful to address the changes in the representation of the nation as data that might be included or omitted as the modern massification of culture accelerated. I would propose that a shift from a nineteenth- to a twentieth-century discourse network, analogous to those shifts elsewhere discussed by Kittler and many others, turns especially agonistic around the decade of the Centenary, during which the Sáenz Peña law establishes universal male suffrage, Hipólito Irigoyen is elected to the presidency, and progressive social reforms are passed. In opposition to such advances, a conservative historic revisionism led by Lugones comes into prominence. But paradoxically, while Lugones's representation of the national space might seem proper to a remnant, nineteenth-century discourse network that would soon cede to one more proper to the twentieth century, until almost 1960 the erasures that formed the cinema's conventional representation of rural space would be closer to those of the Lugonian image than might be expected. While often contested in the silent cinema, the *criollista* representation of rural space eventually becomes the default as the cinema is industrialized and finds a mass audience. But before turning to the cinema, a brief excursion into these apparently remnant representations and their erasures will help to further contextualize the arrival of the cinema.

A history of the canonical conceptions of Argentine national space could do worse than start with the image of fifteen cavalrymen on an otherwise empty plain that until recently appeared, along with the caption "La conquista del desierto" (The Conquest of the Desert), on the back of the Argentine hundred-peso note. The representation is in consonance with the imaginings of America as an empty desert and of Europe (and Buenos Aires as an extension of it) as plenitude that structured conceptions of space in the nation-defining texts of the mid-nineteenth century:

> ¿Qué nombre daréis, qué nombre merece un país compuesto de doscientas mil leguas de territorio y de una población de ochocientos mil habitantes? Un desierto. ¿Qué nombre daréis a la Constitución de ese país? La Constitución de un desierto. Pues bien, ese país es la República Argentina; y cualquiera que sea su Constitución no será otra cosa por muchos años que la Constitución de un desierto.
>
>   Pero ¿cuál es la constitución que mejor conviene al desierto? La que sirve para hacerlo desaparecer; la que sirve para hacer que el desierto deje de serlo en el menor tiempo posible, y se convierta en un país poblado . . .
>
>   Así, en América, gobernar es poblar.[2]

> What name would you give, what name does deserve, a country made up of two hundred thousand leagues of territory and a population of eight hundred thousand inhabitants? A desert. What name would you give to the Constitution of that country? The Constitution of a desert. Well then, that country is the Republic of Argentina, and whatever form its Constitution takes, for many years it will be nothing but the Constitution of a desert.
>
>   But which is the best Constitution for the desert? That which serves to make it disappear, that which serves to make

the desert stop being a desert in the shortest time possible, and to become a populated country . . .

So, in America, to govern is to populate.

This passage, from the writings in which Juan Bautista Alberdi laid out the foundations for the nation's Constitution, demonstrates the logic that justified Argentina's territorial expansion. Alberdi eliminates ethical complications by eliding the victims, thus presenting conquest not as a conflict between peoples, but as a simple movement into empty, abstracted space. The image on the banknote tells a similar story. It is a detail reproduced from an 1894 painting by Juan Manuel Blanes, *Ocupación militar del Río Negro bajo el mando del General Julio A. Roca, 1879* (*Military Occupation of the Rio Negro under the Command of General Julio A. Roca, 1879*). Commissioned by the National History Museum to celebrate the event in its immediate aftermath, the original painting allegorically depicts a heroic conquest of *barbarie* by military force, through the inclusion of indigenous figures and a white female captive. But the portion reproduced a century later on the note excludes these peripheral figures, and in doing so presents the conquest not in conflictually epic terms, but as a peaceful, even inevitable occupation of empty space.[3]

The terrain conquered is once again characterized by lack—*desertum*: an unpopulated place—and the land beneath the horses' hooves is a featureless, prenational void. There are no conquered, no evidence of culture or *civilización*, so in the all-encompassing terms of Argentina's foundational binary this could only be *barbarie*. This fictive emptiness is the basis for much of nineteenth-century discourse on the territory, despite the fact that rural space was indeed inhabited, as Fermín Rodríguez notes:

> El hecho de que bandas de jinetes nómadas, indios, gauchos solitarios, partidos de soldados, desertores, arrieros, caravanas de carretas, viajeros criollos y europeos, pulperos, estancieros y peones poblaran la llanura con sus idas y vueltas, no fue suficiente para romper el desierto teórico formado en el cruce de discursos científicos, políticos y económicos. (15)

> The fact that bands of nomadic horsemen, Indians, solitary gauchos, parties of soldiers, deserters, mule drivers, caravans of wagons, Creole and European travelers, storekeepers, ranchers,

and laborers populated the plains with their comings and goings, wasn't sufficient to break the theoretical desert formed in the crossings of scientific, political, and economic discourses.

Despite the real existence of such a variety of inhabitants, the mediating texts and images tended to represent rural space negatively, in terms of what it lacked. It was imagined as a landscape "sin árboles, sin cultivos, sin montañas, sin límites naturales, sin habitantes permanentes, sin viviendas, sin espíritu de progreso, sin vías de comunicación, sin instituciones, sin sentido de la autoridad, sin tradiciones, sin historia (without trees, without crops, without mountains, without natural limits, without a spirit of progress, without lines of communication, without institutions, without a sense of authority, without traditions, without history) (Rodríguez 16). This description of a geography of lack returns us to the image on the banknote, in which the alterations to Blanes's original are yet another example of this process of subtraction, but also to Lugones's poem, and upon comparing the three it becomes evident that while the objects of erasure vary over time—from *indios* to gauchos to, with the shift to a modern discourse network, immigrants, hunger, and social unrest—the act of erasure that opened a chasm between representation and reality remained constant.

This chasm between nineteenth-century national reality and discourses on the nation can be attributed to the fact that those who formulated the national project were primarily creole oligarchs who conceived of national identity in European terms, and for whom all things American were obstacles to their plans. But while this Europeanized national identity is dominant throughout the nineteenth century, at that century's end a shift was already underway toward a more Lugonian conception of national identity, one modeled after the decidedly non-European figure of the gaucho, in texts both visual and literary. Francisco Ayerza's photography of the 1890s and Lugones's literary texts and lectures contributed to the transfiguration of the gaucho into the representative of national identity sine qua non by the first decades of the twentieth century, in a rural-centered revision of national history that, paradoxically, again distanced representations from the reality on the land.[4] This time it was the history of links between landowners and the state that was, as Tranchini writes,

> diluída con ficciones, a través de la imagen de un mundo rural tan natural e inagotable como pródigo en virtudes y riquezas, y en el que el desprecio del inmigrante hacia el nativo convivió acostumbrado con el recelo del criollo hacia el extranjero. (108)

diluted with fictions, through the image of a rural world as natural and infinite as it was abundant in virtues and riches, and in which the contempt of the immigrant toward the native lived side by side with the distrust of the creole toward the foreigner.

The old conflicts, then, were forgotten and the new conflicts erased, in favor of a *costumbrista* pampa: "Las costumbres pastoriles de un campo sin conflictos, la pampa inmensa e insondable, el gaucho de a caballo . . . se fueron construyendo como mitos de la argentinidad . . ." (The pastoral customs of a countryside without conflicts, the immense and unfathomable Pampa, the gaucho on horseback . . . were constructed as myths of Argentinity . . .) (108). This newly invented tradition, which reached its apogee with the national Centenary of 1910, was a very elaborate and widespread response to anxieties surrounding the rapid modernization the country was undergoing, and the inequalities and resulting conflicts this process produced.

Ericka Beckman discusses the need for consensus among late nineteenth-century Latin American elites on the desirability of economic liberalization, and thus the role literary culture played in denying "the frequently dismal outcomes of capitalist modernization . . . which then as today have been marked by grave inequalities on the level of individual societies, as well as by poverty and subordination with respect to major centers of capital" (ix). Beckman refers to the "Export Age" of the nineteenth and early twentieth centuries, but the undesirable aspects of modernization are also conspicuous erasures of the classical cinema through the mid-twentieth century. This cinema is, of course, made and viewed in a period—from the 1930s to the 1950s—during which capitalist modernization is tempered by the Depression and its aftermath, when the Argentine state implemented more nationalistic and developmentalist economic policies, but the problems described by Beckman are of continued relevance under governments that needed to justify themselves as effectively solving them.

Perhaps the most productive way to conceive of these problems is in terms of uneven development, a term with various definitions, two of which are especially relevant to a discussion of representations of the national space. In his definitive book on the subject, Neil Smith discusses both. One is a simple uneven rate of development or modernization between spaces that would reflect somewhat negatively on the state and support a critique of neglect or incompetence. The other more directly refers to capitalism's effects on the land: "The pattern which results in the landscape is well known: development at one pole and underdevelopment at the other" (Smith 6). This stark expression of the relation between capital and labor is a necessary spatial division of labor that generates and maintains uneven development and a tendency toward the dual centralizations of capital and of the subjects of labor. Argentina has certainly not been an exception to this dynamic, but this type of uneven development has only very exceptionally been represented in its cinema, usually in the form of conflicts between labor and capital. While the Pampas of the early twentieth-century export economy was an unprecedented generator of wealth, it is clear that the *criollista* representations of it as a peaceful space where domesticated gauchos labored contentedly, which stood in metonymically for the nation's rural spaces, had very little to do with the reality on the land, since they elided those forms of existence that did not form part of a harmonious coexistence of rural laborer and landowner.

Following on Smith's discussion of the production of marginalized space, we can reconfigure the term "barbarism," so often used in the nineteenth-century Argentine tradition to describe that which had to be eliminated in order for the nation to become civilized, to instead conceive of a produced barbarism (or secondary barbarism) brought about by uneven development. The idea that the civilizing project might have produced spaces of *barbarie* is contested by *criollismo*, which represents rural poverty not as produced by modern Argentina, but rather as both preexisting it and as persisting within it, instead of as produced by capitalist modernization.

During the decades preceding the arrival of the cinema in the late 1890s, profound societal changes had been taking place that greatly altered the national culture's relationship to its rural spaces. The "conquest of the desert" had violently cleared the way for expansion into, and transformation of, those spaces that had been portrayed a few decades earlier as *barbarie* and *desierto*, and production and exchange expanded rapidly into them. The state functioned in assemblage with private capital to capture human and natural resources in those rural spaces where they had been until then subjected to more local power relations. As Jens Andermann writes, "(t)his mutually constitutive enhancement of state power and of capitalism depended on new forms of knowledge that registered, classified, and distributed human and natural resources in time and space" (2007, 1). Since obtaining knowledge of rural spaces was the first task necessary for their incorporation into the nation, the state-capital apparatus developed the visual tools—maps, photos, museums—to gather knowledge of the territory. Andermann calls this knowledge-gathering gaze the "optic of the state." Film, with few exceptions, had limited participation in this knowledge-gathering gaze aligned with the state, and in the mass-consumption form it would take on definitively in the 1930s, it performed quite the opposite function.[5] Far more in line with the erasures seen on the 100-peso note, the dominant cinematic gaze intentionally avoids gathering knowledge of marginal spaces, instead limiting its gaze to certain spaces and certain representations, foreclosing the possibility of documenting the national space.

But the uniquely modern, indexical nature of filmic representation, in which a profilmic reality is documented even in the process of creating fictions, alters the game of erasure. This quality unique to filmic mediation, a kind of friction exerted by the real on its representations, is of central importance, since its spectator tends to believe that what is seen on screen did exist in reality. This study asks how this friction of the real manifests itself in an Argentine cinema often under pressure, both state and commercial, to suppress its effects, especially when the reality causing the friction is that of spaces that contradict constructions of national identity and discourses of successful modernity. This contradiction between reality and representation is at first most pronounced in the case of rural space, and later in that of the edges of the urban, which in the last half-century have grown in extension and visibility as uneven modernization has driven internal immigration to populate urban margins. These spaces have gone from being excluded from the cinema, to being glimpsed, then documented, and finally serving as a not-infrequent setting for narrative fiction.

A productive way to conceive of these contested terrains of filmic mediation would be to consider what Judith Butler refers to as the field of representability. She writes that

> we cannot understand the field of representability simply by examining its explicit contents, since it is constituted fundamentally by what is cast out and maintained outside the frame within which representations appear. We can think of the frame, then, as active, as jettisoning and presenting, and as doing both at once, in silence, without a visible sign of its operation . . . (953)

In the specific case of Argentine cinema, the frame of representability has tended, with varying degrees of zeal, to actively jettison representations of certain spaces or to fictionalize them. When representations of these spaces have appeared in the cinema they have tended toward *costumbrismo*, and thus to erase the uneven modernization that has long characterized much of the nation's territory.

But the place of marginal spaces in Argentine cinema is anything but static. It varies from film to film, while forming wider patterns as various factors pressure the medium through time. By tracing these factors and their effects, this book finds that in the history of Argentine cinema there have been several periods of greater autonomy for filmmakers relative to state and economic power, during which the frame of representability becomes more porous. By autonomy I am not referring to aesthetic purity over the political à la art for art's sake, but rather an autonomy like that enjoyed by the modern writer or the *literato* described by Julio Ramos, one freed from the earlier *letrado* function of "writing as a rationalizing practice, authorized by the project of state consolidation" (53). This kind of autonomy does not bring with it an obligation to challenge national projects and associated discourses of national identity, and it will come as no surprise that some filmmakers of these periods chose to conform to these discourses. These periods of greater filmmaking autonomy are inevitably accompanied by shifts in viewership, as new cinemas contribute to the production of new viewers, with new expectations and desires and new ways of consuming sounds and images. These viewers in turn produce new ways of making film, as distinct cinematic gazes are formed at the intersection of ways of representing with ways of viewing. As these gazes both structure and are structured by representations of national space, the clearly enforced boundary between fiction and nonfiction film turns permeable, allowing the unacknowledged realities of the most contested sites of representation to enter into the cinema. The three periods of greater filmmaking autonomy are the 1910 decade, the period of roughly 1958 to 1974, and that of the late 1990s to the present.

Many, but by no means all films of the 1910s—the decade in which the feature-length format arrived in Argentina—renounce film's documentary charge, to instead narrate fictional stories, but when sound film appears around 1930 the near totality of both production and exhibition shifts to fiction. This negation of film's original scientific function, that of credibly documenting reality, prompts questions about its contribution to how rural space was imagined by its mass public. By the early twentieth century, in spite of the rapidly growing body of knowledge on rural space as it was integrated into the nation, the cinema persisted in a fictional conception that roughly corresponded to preexisting visual and literary discourses that depicted an idyllic rural space. Although the "mitología pacífica y armónica del gaucho" (peaceful and harmonious myth of the gaucho) (Montaldo 117) of *criollismo* tended to represent new immigrants to Argentina as illegitimate by way of contrast, this was the vision of rural space that, with a few important exceptions, the cinema embraced in its first several decades, even as it catered to a public composed largely of these recent immigrants and their children.

The role of the cinema of the 1910s as purveyor of conceptions of rural space is the subject of the first chapter of this book. During its first, silent decades, film production was cheaper and the camera more mobile than it would become with the invention of sound technology, so filmmaking was not yet as studio-bound as it would become with the dominance of the sound feature film of the studio system. Filmmakers of the 1910 decade enjoyed an authorial autonomy that would be lost with the industrialization of cinema and the heightening pressures from a state that increasingly recognized the power of cinema to influence the masses. The chapter closely examines three works by filmmakers who did not necessarily identify with the project of state consolidation and were therefore able to contest the conservative nationalism of the *Centenario* and the version of the rural universe it used to legitimize state violence against popular movements. Some do so through allegorical reconfigurations of national identity, portraying a gaucho in conflict with the state and national elites, and thus represent a conflictive rural space as produced in the modernizing process. Another, Alcides Greca's *El último malón*, uses the camera to document pernicious conditions produced by the modernizing project, portraying an unevenly modernized space—the *reducción*, or reservation—as a site of a violent struggle by an indigenous population impoverished and exploited for its labor.

The second chapter moves to the sound period, which began in the early 1930s, and the loss of filmmaking autonomy with the capture of production and exhibition by large studios and the recognition by the state of the cinema's power to influence the masses. Soon after 1930 and José Félix Uriburu's *golpe de estado* (military takeover), as the cinema was consolidated as a form of popular entertainment it increasingly restricted itself to the canonical conceptions of rural space. As a result, the image of a territory cleansed of traces of social conflict and its underlying causes and successfully integrated into a prosperous Argentina began to prevail in representations of national space by an industrial studio cinema that had to naturalize such conceptions of space in order to convincingly tell its stories. In its films, a reality effect produced by the cinema's inherent documentary charge functions in tandem with specific formal conventions that include the use of transitional ellipses (usually employing the train) that elide rural space and a cinematic version of the *cuadro de costumbres* that usually centers on cliched portrayals of gauchos or their rural heirs. These conventions result in the predominance of very partial but totalizing representations of the national space as prosperous, modernized towns or cities in which the story takes place, surrounded by a pastoralized rural universe. The study finds that during the period of the cinema studios—or, as it is often referred to, the classical cinema—even the few films that thematize the exploitation of the rural by urban or foreign interests remain invested in these kinds of canonical images of rural space, which went largely unexamined as the cinema eschewed the documentary possibilities of the filmic image.

The same chapter goes on to examine other aspects of the classical cinema, discussing how several narrative fiction films of the late 1930s participate in the generation of public consent for state-driven modernization projects (which included a road network, tourism, and petroleum extraction and distribution) by publicizing these projects and portraying a successfully interventionist state that undertakes them. The chapter then discusses masculinity, which the classical cinema often negotiates along an urban–rural trajectory, in which rural space typically corrects defective, urban masculinity. This section centers on *Con el diablo en el cuerpo* (1947), directed by the prolific Carlos Hugo Christensen, a road movie in which the mechanism of normalization is laid bare through a parody of conventional rural masculinities. The chapter closes with an examination of the first studio films to represent the *villa miseria* (shanty town)—a highly fraught space during the last years of the Perón presidency—which, at the classical cinema's demise, begin to open the field of representability and stimulate a spectatorial gaze that is more inquisitive about the nation and its lesser-known spaces.

Toward the late 1950s, certain filmmakers began to more directly address the cultural invisibility of certain spaces, formulating alternative representations of the *villa miseria* and questioning the canonical depictions of rural space. Chapter 3 begins with an account of how one of the earliest of these, Fernando Birri, documents marginal spatial practices in *Tire dié* and *Los inundados*. Among the various strategies employed by Birri, this chapter examines how he employs the train's movement through the landscape to take advantage of the capacity of film to document spaces and their inhabitants that are excluded by the classical cinema's conventions. Birri's films, then, help inaugurate a cinema that both responds to spectatorial curiosity and elicits a new gaze that inquires about the nation and questions the conventions through which it had been represented until then.

After Birri, many others turned the camera away from the train toward the rural, nonmodern or marginalized spaces that had gone willfully unrepresented in the previous decades. As a strategy of engaging with Argentine reality that responds to the national territory and the opportunities presented by the technology found there, this turn of the camera exemplifies how the cinema of the inquisitive gaze increasingly contested canonical representations of marginal space in the next two decades and expanded the field of representability.

The same chapter continues with an examination of the relatively independent feature films of the *Generación del 60*, centering on Lautaro Murúa's *Shunko* (1960) and Fernando Ayala's *Paula cautiva* (1963), which demonstrate a variety of strategies that call into question long-dominant representations of the national space, before it moves on to other modes, among them Gerardo Vallejo's militant film *El camino hacia la muerte del Viejo Reales* (1971) and the ethnographic films of Jorge Prelorán, whose innovative methodology is designed to explore the subjectivities of individuals from the most isolated places of the nation. Also discussed is Eva Landeck's *Gente en Buenos Aires* (1973), a narrative feature made during the brief cultural *apertura* (opening) that preceded the slide into dictatorship. Landeck made the film with a cooperative production model that allowed her a great degree of independence, and its incisive critique at the intersection of class and space contributed to its suffering industry and state pressures and the truncation of her career. The chapter ends with an account of how, after these filmmakers had brought marginal spaces into the cinema, certain commercial films responded to their presence and the spectatorial expectations they cultivated. The films examined—Armando Bó's Isabel Sarli vehicle *Carne* (1968) and the Palito Ortega–starring *Yo tengo fe* (Enrique Carreras 1974)—recuperate the settings and formal conventions of the cinema of the inquisitive gaze in order to depoliticize the representation of marginal spaces.

Chapter 4 closes the book by pursuing two lines of inquiry. First, it examines films that engage with a key feature of contemporary neoliberal space, the opposition between the *villa miseria* as locus of fear and the protected enclosure of the middle-class neighborhood and its most highly distilled form of the gated community (or *country*). Second, the chapter seeks out contemporary filmic strategies of revisiting the representation of rural space that engage with metropolitan conceptions of it. The chapter concentrates on the work of a very limited selection of contemporary filmmakers, most notably Lucrecia Martel, Lisandro Alonso, and Fernando Solanas. The films examined all engage with aspects of the neoliberal spatial configuration: the conception of the social margins in the national culture—particularly the widespread fear of less wealthy sectors and the spaces they inhabit—the resulting fear-driven concentration of wealth in the *country*, and the intensified dispossession inflicted on rural subjects. This final chapter traces up to the present the representation of rural spaces and of the urban margins, which, despite the changes in cinema's technology, viewers, and the nation itself, have remained a central concern of Argentine cinema for more than a century.

Chapter 1

National Modernization and the Production of Marginal Spaces in Early Feature Films

In the late nineteenth and early twentieth centuries Argentina's modernizing project produced both mass immigration from Europe and deep economic crisis. These two factors fueled popular movements that, with the progressive extension of voting rights, came to represent a serious threat to powerful interests and motivated frequent episodes of violent repression, which reached a climax after the 1910 national Centenary. Two events that took place in Buenos Aires frame the conflictive decade of the 1910s: the 1909 May Day Massacre of *Plaza Lorea*, in which police killed four protesting workers, and the *Semana Trágica* (Tragic Week) of January 1919, during which the violent suppression of a metal-worker strike and the subsequent attacks on the funeral of those killed led to a city-wide protests and reprisals that resulted in hundreds of deaths at the hands of police and paramilitary groups. But protests and repression were not limited to the capital city, as rural spaces were also the site of conflicts, often violent, that pit sharecroppers and small farmers against exploitative landowners and public authorities (Romero 37–38).

This ongoing conflict between labor and capital was only obliquely present in the national culture. The interests of the oligarchy were represented most famously by Leopoldo Lugones, a bearer of immense intellectual capital who had cultured a strong public presence as "organic intellectual of the Argentine oligarchy at the peak of its power" (Dabove 28). Lugones worked to reorient the cultural discourse away from urban themes, toward rural nostalgia, thus consolidating notions of national identity that excluded the immigrant sectors of the population. But his thematization of the rural elided a history of social conflict there as well, primarily through the construction of the myth of the domesticated gaucho, and as a result was able to depict the landowner—the gaucho's historical antagonist—as his successor in legitimacy. To this imagined lineage he opposed the new arrivals, completing the revision of national identity that served to legitimize state violence against the immigrants in the interest of elites.

The most important literary manifestation of Lugones's particular revisionism is *El payador*, a series of lectures delivered in 1913 in the exclusive Teatro Odeón and published in book form in 1916. Putting on display a wide-ranging erudition, he compared José Hernández's poem *El gaucho Martín Fierro* to the classical epics, thus proposing a place in the center of the high-culture canon for the previously marginalized gaucho, alongside the heroes of Homer and Virgil. Starting from this initial inversion of the Sarmientine binary in which the gaucho was a barbarian preferably exterminated from the national landscape, Lugones went on to argue that the eponymous protagonist of *Martín Fierro* (particularly he of the 1879 second part of the poem, *La vuelta de Martín Fierro*, in which the *gaucho malo* is tamed and integrated into the nation as a peon) represented the essence of Argentinity, and that the poem was an epic that bore the seeds of an "espíritu nacional" (national spirit). Lugones described the gaucho not as a resistant victim of the territorial expansion of the nation, but rather as a patriotic warrior who fought to bring territory into the nation during the wars of independence and the conquest of the indigenous. This idea would eventually form the basis of classics of the national cinema like *La guerra gaucha* (Lucas Demare, 1942) and *Pampa bárbara* (Demare and Hugo Fregonese, 1945).

Of course the gaucho was not a figure existing in the present for Lugones, but rather a means by which the Argentine nation was consolidated, and as such his passing into history is not to be lamented. But Lugones's revisionism suppresses the conflictive aspect of the historical gaucho, whose story as antagonist of the state-driven project of national territorial expansion had provided the material for much of the gauchesque literary genre. Lugones's strategy required the willful forgetting of the gaucho's frequent challenges to the state's monopoly on violence and his being outlawed as bandit throughout much of the nineteenth century, until his final integration into the nation as peon on the newly enlarged *estancias*. Such selective memory allowed Lugones to construct a nostalgic history that inverted the logic of exclusion implicit in Sarmiento's foundational binary of *civilización* and *barbarie*, which had led to the demonization of the gaucho and the official fomenting of European immigration to populate the continental void. The immigrant, then, becomes the internal other of Lugones's strain of *criollismo*, born of the writer's conflict with the new arrivals, as Montaldo writes:

> Son estos desarrapados que lo molestan los que generan—casi a la manera de una causa ausente—la nueva versión del mito gaucho . . . [Lugones] compone ese *pastiche* de héroe nacional en donde las tesis positivistas y la afirmación del mito latino y clásico confluyen para crear la imagen que espante como fantasma a aquellos que no podrán acercarse a él. Así el gaucho se convierte en guardián del pasado. (Montaldo 67–68)

> It is these people dressed in rags who bother him and who generate—almost as an absent cause—the new version of the gaucho myth . . . [Lugones] composes that pastiche of national hero in which positivist theory and the affirmation of classical myths come together to create the image that, like a ghost, scares those who cannot approach it. In this way the gaucho becomes the guardian of the past.

In Lugones's imagined national lineage, Argentina's historic territorial conflicts are subsumed into a single central conflict that bestows meaning on all sectors of the nation's inhabitants, and in which the immigrant is irredeemably other, "la plebe ultramarina que a semejanza de los mendigos ingratos, nos armaba escándalo en el zaguán" (the rabble from across the sea that, like ungrateful beggars, was making a racket in the entry hall) (*El payador* 15). Through this metaphoric representation of the nation as the private home of the *criollo*, Lugones's immigrants are troublemakers even before they enter a national space imagined not as a "desert"—a space wanting for inhabitants—but rather as a pastoral pampa already anachronistically but harmoniously occupied by the gaucho, which becomes the prime locus of the nationalist "recovery of the rural," as described by Diana Sorensen Goodrich:

> Pressed for a source of national identity with which to counter the sense of its loss caused by the immigrant mass, the hegemonic culture resorted to the recovery of the rural, turning it into a symbol of the nation rather than the epitome of barbarism as in *Facundo*. (147)

While the immigrant could serve as internal other in a modernizing present, the culture needed a historic barbarian to put in conflict with the gaucho and thus positively inflect the latter, retroactively. This figure was, conveniently, the most brutal character of *La vuelta de Martín Fierro*, the *indio*, who in an act of sublime infamy killed the infant son of the white *cautiva* and used his intestines to bind her hands. Both the indigenous "savage" and what is depicted as a postlapsarian urban crowd, then, are demonized in the revisionist culture in order to establish the gaucho-terrateniente lineage of national authenticity based on an imagined heroic ethos and a rural idyll, a totalizing metaphor that aligns the gaucho with the contemporary *criollo* elite to legitimize the violence used by the state to discipline the popular classes by suppressing political and labor movements. But not all of the national culture conformed to this *criollista* configuration of identity and the resulting representations of rural space. In the cinema of the 1910 decade, several examples of divergent representations can be found in the few still-existing films, a variety of oppositional strategies to be surpassed only in the 1960s.

This variety of representations would be lost with the increasing massification, commercialization, and homogeneity of film production as the decade of the 1920s advanced, and by the 1930s technological shifts and commercial concerns had fixed a set of conventions for the representation of rural space, as well as a careful avoidance of the urban margins, that would dominate until the 1960s.[1] These conventions, present even in the work of exceptional auteurs of social cinema such as Mario Soffici, are primarily two: the use of the train in travel sequences that elides rural space and the *costumbrista* representation of a rural spaces. A clear precursor of the latter is found in the gaucho photographs by Francisco Ayerza decades earlier. Ayerza was an early and influential member of the Sociedad Fotográfica Argentina de Aficionados (SFA de A, Society of Photography Aficionados of Argentina), an organization whose work played an important role in the configuration of the cinematic representation of the nation in the first decades of the twentieth century (Cuarterolo 2013, 115–117). Several of its members took up motion picture making, and two, Eduardo Martínez de la Pera and Ernesto Gunche, became the most important directors of early feature-length narrative films, including Argentine cinema's first blockbuster, *Nobleza gaucha*. Andrea Cuarterolo's examination of the archives containing the photos of the SFA de A reveals that its members avoided photographing the marginal spaces of Buenos Aires, and when they shot rural spaces they tended to create nostalgic idealizations in the form of carefully composed, mythic visions of gauchos that prefigured *criollista* revisionist readings of *Martín Fierro* (2013, 123–124). This type of representation of rural space would, with the classical cinema, become dominant, but in the 1910s filmmaking was still open to socially and ideologically diverse participants, which is reflected in the variety of representations of marginal spaces. Instead of maintaining the SPA de A's clear separation between modernization and rural space, these filmmakers engaged with the often traumatic effects of the former on the inhabitants of the latter and thus problematized received ways of representing the nation's marginal spaces.

Any account of the feature-length films of the 1910 decade is unavoidably incomplete due to the effects of time and neglect on their nitrate stock, which have reduced the approximately two hundred films made in Argentina before 1930 to a precious few.[2] To watch these remnant films is to see a cinema still finding its way, both formally and thematically, but enjoying an autonomy that would be lost with the gradual consolidation of the film industry into large studios by the mid-1930s and the increasing interest of the state in controlling the content of the new medium.[3] I will examine how certain films of the 1910s allegorically reconfigured discourses of national identity and authenticity in ways that did not conform to *criollista* imaginings of rural space. While they do not question the centrality of the gaucho in national identity, these films reconfigure the gaucho's alliances with populations present in modern Argentina. The inclusion or exclusion of certain sectors of the population in the national lineage is, then, based less on the portrayals of their representative characters—as moral, hardworking, and courageous or as cowardly, usurious, and corrupt—than on the alliances they form with the *a priori* authentic gaucho. These representations take on importance in debates on national identity when it is considered that the cinema was a mass culture medium in process of formation, and capable of reaching wide audiences, even semi-literate or non-Spanish-speaking ones. Such a public contrasts with the relatively small but economically powerful and highly cultured public of Lugones's poetry and conferences, to which it represents a burgeoning threat in the context of increasing labor activism and access to democratic processes.

By the mid-1910s the feature-length narrative film model was becoming the dominant mode of making and consuming film in Argentina. Although at present only six Argentine feature-length films made before 1920 are known to still exist, this limited sample shows the kind of variety of treatments of space, national identity, and social conflict that will not be seen again until the 1960s. The cinema's autonomy in the 1910s can be attributed to several factors. The silent mode of production was much cheaper than the sound cinema that would replace it in the 1930s, and filmmakers faced no competition yet from the coming vertically integrated industry that would monopolize film production and exhibition and effectively exclude independent producers from the medium for several decades. Nor did the state yet seem to fully recognize the power of the medium to influence the masses. It soon would, after 1930, when under Uriburu and the succeeding conservative governments national political figures would increasingly attempt to intervene in cinema production and distribution. By the 1930s, then, these and other factors would bring about a loss of the kind of authorial autonomy that had been enjoyed by earlier filmmakers. The first silent features (those of the 1910s) were also relatively autonomous vis à vis both economic power and the state when compared to the "republic of letters" of nineteenth-century lettered culture, which had been "assigned the authority to extend its domain over the contingency and anarchy of the represented world . . . to create a system in a society where representation meant the ordering of chaos, orality, nature and barbarism that was America" (Ramos 41). The industrial, studio-produced sound cinema that would by the 1930s displace the silents would come to fulfill a function somewhat analogous to that of the republic of letters, and as it lost its autonomy it would increasingly turn to *criollista* models to represent rural space.

My analysis of the 1910s takes as another point of departure Juan Pablo Dabove's 2007 book, *Nightmares of the Lettered City*, which discusses banditry in Latin American literature from Independence through the 1920s. The central theme of the book is rural violence, and as could be expected, the gaucho figures in many of the Argentine cases Dabove studies. He focuses on "the ways in which the European-minded, lettered, Creole, male, urban elite depicted, through literature, a form of non-state rural violence" (34), and how these representations functioned either "as a legitimating tool for the state monopoly of violence" (27) or as a challenge to the status of the state as "law-giver and ultimate source of legitimate violence" (31). As an example of the former, certain intellectuals had represented the outlaw *gaucho malo* as a "totalizing metaphor for the whole rural population" (7), thus legitimizing the violence inflicted on it in the struggle for control of resources. At other moments, the gaucho's portrayal as a powerless victim of unjust state violence served to question the trajectory the nation was taking on its path to modernity and the methods of coercion it employed. It is important to mention, in light of the analysis below of the film *El último malón*, that the object of Dabove's study is not specifically the gaucho, but rural violence, which in gauchesque literature also involves indigenous populations, usually as agents of the most extreme, barbaric violence. In the narrative poem *El gaucho Martín Fierro* the violence carried out by the *indio* motivates the *gaucho malo* to return to civilization, and Lugones employs the indigenous figure in a similar way, casting him as the barbarian in order to rehabilitate the comparatively less-barbaric figure of the gaucho. Since the new medium of the cinema became an arena for these same ideological maneuverings, in the films of the years immediately following the *Centenario* similar dynamics of inclusion and exclusion are often in play in reconfigurations of national identity that question the legitimization of state violence at the expense of rural or other non-elite populations. This questioning impulse reflects the autonomy enjoyed by film in the 1910 decade, to which I will now turn.

Filmmaking Autonomy in the 1910s

While the *Centenario*-era conservative revaluation of the gaucho was accomplished mostly through the high culture of exclusive lecture series and literary texts, by the 1930s the newer visual media, consumed on a more massive scale, would propagate a similar version of the gaucho, as Andrea Cuarterolo writes:

> La literatura fue sin duda el primer medio de divulgación de este discurso [lugoniano], pero la fotografía y el cine mudo fueron los medios más apropiados, por su poder visual, para llegar a las grandes masas, incluso de inmigrantes quienes no necesitaban conocer el idioma para comprender su mensaje. De hecho, fue el cine, símbolo de la modernidad, el que permitió que la vertiente nacionalista, ya en agonía hacia la época del Centenario, continuara sobreviviendo como discurso remanente . . . (2005, 29)

> Literature was without a doubt the first means of spreading of this [Lugonian] discourse, but because of their visual power photography and silent film were the most appropriate means of reaching the masses, even immigrants who did not need to know the language to understand the message. In fact, it was the cinema, symbol of modernity, which permitted the nationalist strand, already on the decline around the time of the Centenary, to continue surviving as a remnant discourse . . .

Cuarterolo is describing the *criollista* representations that reached a mass audience through the classical cinema of the 1930s and early 1940s, but earlier, nearer to its origins, this same conservative nationalism was contested in the cinema. This suggests that Argentine film production of that decade enjoyed an early window of autonomy that was lost as the cinema became industrialized starting in the 1920s, then subjected to more rigorous ideological pressure from the state during the *Década Infame* (Infamous Decade)—inaugurated in 1930 by Argentina's first military coup, in which José Félix Uriburu overthrew Hipólito Yrigoyen—through the Peronist period.[4] The field of film production during the silent period, then, appears far less monolithic and more accessible to independent filmmakers than it would become with the advent of the studio system and its classical cinema, which would remain the dominant mode of film production and consumption through the late 1950s.[5]

Although the earliest filmmakers were based, and the first cinemas located, in Buenos Aires, several of the known still-existing feature films made in the 1910 decade are set in rural spaces, possibly due in part to the immediate proximity of the *Centenario* and the national nostalgia for the premodern. Of the six features from that decade known to still exist, only one, *Hasta después de muerta* (Martínez de la Pera and Gunche, 1916), is wholly urban-themed, and the rest are set either completely or partially in rural areas. I will not discuss *Hasta después de muerta* or *Flor de durazno* (Francisco Defilippis Novoa, 1917), since neither directly engages with nationalist discourses on the rural or depicts politically significant violence. The four films relevant to this study then, are *Amalia* (1914), *Nobleza gaucha* (1915), *Juan sin ropa* (1919), and *El último malón* (1918). But first, a caveat is in order: in the copies available at the time of this writing *Amalia* lacks its ending, *Nobleza gaucha* is missing several brief sequences, *El último malón* is lacking some footage, and, at twenty-seven minutes and lacking intertitles, only when supplemented with a plot summary is a conclusive study possible of the available version of *Juan sin ropa*. These films present a diverse set of visions of the rural universe, in which the gaucho is either rendered a tamed *costumbrista* figure or the dynamic of inclusion and exclusion is reconfigured to ally him with Lugones's internal others and thus create a new national lineage, or alternatively, the logic of exclusion itself is critiqued and shown to be detrimental to the nation. With the exception of *El último malón*, which I will examine last, the films contain clear allegories presented in a formally conventional way.[6] My purpose in analyzing them is to suggest that the filmmakers own economic and political autonomy allowed them to question the revisionist representations of rural space that represent the newly arrived populations as dishonorable enemies of the gaucho and legitimize the state violence inflicted on them.

Three Gauchos

As mentioned above, early cinema's autonomy did not necessarily produce ideological dissonance with hegemonic discourses, as the first film I discuss will show. *Amalia*, made in 1914, is Argentina's first feature-length film, and rather than popular it is an example of an early use of the cinema destined for a restricted public. An adaptation of the "foundational fiction" written by José Mármol in 1855, the film was directed by Enrique García Velloso, "docente del Colegio Nacional de Buenos Aires y conferencista de temas históricos y literarios" (teacher at the National High School of Buenos Aires and lecturer on historic and literary themes) (Mafud 156). This *letrado*-director's high regard for tradition and disdain for popular culture is evident in the intertitles of his films. As Lucio Mafud writes of García Velloso's *Mariano Moreno y la Revolución de Mayo* (1915),

> el propio uso del lenguaje escrito en el filme responde a [su] afán instructivo. En un contexto donde la prensa denunciaba la deformación del idioma en los epígrafes de las películas mudas y sus perniciosas consecuencias sobre el espectador, un profesor de literatura como Velloso garantizaba que "los títulos que ilustran las notas gráficas han sido redactados con verdadera pulcritud." (156–157)

> the use itself of written language in the film responds to his efforts to educate. In a context in which the press denounced the deformation of the language in the intertitles of silent films and their pernicious consequences on the spectator, a professor of literature like Velloso guaranteed that "the intertitles have been impeccably composed."

Given such a resistance to popular uses of the language, it is perhaps unsurprising that members of the Buenos Aires aristocracy comprise the cast of *Amalia*. The choice to adapt a canonical national novel set in an already-distant past is a safe one, analogous to the French *film d'art*, which between 1908 and 1911 adapted prestigious literary texts in order to bring symbolic capital to the new medium.[7]

Originally screened at the exclusive Teatro Colón, the film comes across as an indulgence of the privileged class in the pleasure of seeing itself on film, more narcissistic attraction than art, and displays little notion of storytelling through images, since most of the work of narrating is done through verbose intertitles (which appear in an elevated linguistic register free of any specifically Argentine uses). The images are mostly either fixed-camera long-take *tableaux* or what look like Lumière-inspired *prises-de-vue*. The former show either static scenes such as dining and visiting, while the latter include more movement, such as a crowd exiting a church service, but equally as little plot information. Most of the long novel, then, is omitted, the plot condensed into certain key episodes.

The gaucho appears in *Amalia* only near the end of the film, in a folkloric interlude. Juan Manuel de Rosas's soldiers are seen in camp, dancing the *gato*, accompanied by pastoral verses on the intertitles.[8] This *divertissement* is disrupted by Rosas's arrival, and the plot advances again until its brusque ending due to the loss of the film's final sequences. The gaucho's appearance, as a figure belonging strictly to the past, provides a *costumbrista* attraction but little else, with the result that the film's depiction of rural space does not deviate in the least from canonical representations. While the source novel subscribes to a more nineteenth-century liberal than twentieth-century nationalist worldview, the film does not actively engage with Lugonian discourse, since it is set in a pre-mass-immigration era that shares few qualities with its own time, and steers clear of questions of modern (post-Rosas, that is) state violence. *Amalia* is nostalgic testimony to the aristocracy's liberal ideology and culture, in stark contrast to the next three films I will discuss, which are products of varied cultural producers and which employ images of rural space and its inhabitants to offer three very different versions of national identity and critiques of state violence.

The first internationally successful Argentine film was *Nobleza gaucha*. Despite the origins of its directors in the SFA de A, the film breaks in important ways with conventional representations of rural space. In her detailed analysis of photography and the film, Cuarterolo demonstrates convincingly that in *Nobleza gaucha* "los discursos positivista y nacionalista conviven y se superponen" (positivist and nationalist discourses coexist and overlap) (2013, 135), referring to the film's simultaneous exaltation of modernity and nostalgia for the rural. Cuarterolo traces the origin of *Nobleza gaucha*'s representation of the gaucho to Ayerza's *costumbrista* photos taken in the 1890s, which portray "una imagen pintoresca y dulcificada del campo argentino" (a picturesque, sweetened image of the Argentine countryside) (2013, 146). But despite its characterization of the gaucho as domesticated, I would argue that *Nobleza gaucha* goes beyond a mere nostalgic idealization of the gaucho, and that after activating this conventional image of the gaucho as a symbol of national authenticity the film allegorically configures his alliances in a way that shifts the spheres of legitimate and illegitimate violence. This configuration represents an alternative to Lugones's domestication of the gaucho in the interest of othering the immigrant as well as to the more resistant *gaucho-malo*-as-popular-hero model exemplified by the Martín Fierro of *La ida* and the protagonist of the *Juan Moreira* legend. Whereas Lugones used the gaucho "as a *dramatis persona* in letrado fables of self-legitimation and the legitimation of his class against the 'zoological tidal wave' (*aluvión zoológico*) of immigrants from Central Europe and the Mediterranean Basin" (Dabove 29), *Nobleza gaucha* depicts state repression in the interest of elites against a humble but courageous gaucho—whose importance as a model of national identity cannot be overstated here—as unjust and illegitimate. This is in alignment with the use of what Dabove calls the "gaucho as instrument of critique" to suggest that the oligarchy is the true bandit, against whom the violence carried out by the gaucho is therefore legitimate. Such a use of the gaucho by members of the SFA de A is notable, and could be attributed to commercial considerations, since the medium is targeted in large part at a popular public. A consideration of the intended audience might also help explain *Nobleza gaucha*'s portrayal of the Italian immigrant as the gaucho's ally, in contrast to gauchesque literature and theater, in which the Italian presence often heralds the arrival of a postlapsarian modernity and the immigrants themselves frequently display a morally reprehensible character, practicing dishonesty and even usurious exploitation of the gaucho.

Nobleza gaucha is set in two spaces, urban and rural, connected by a train journey. Here the switch in medium by De la Pera and Gunche from still photography to motion pictures, and the resulting need to narrate in time, invites the juxtaposition of the two incompatible discourses on spaces that in their photography had remained separate. This juxtaposition produces the ideological contradictions that the filmmakers resolve by reconfiguring the gaucho's alliances in a way that, I would argue, offers greater appeal to a popular spectatorship. The urban space, while celebrated visually for its modernity in the film, becomes a space of corruption, while the rural is an idealized space temporarily corrupted by the presence not of the immigrant, as might happen in a text by Lugones, but of a *terrateniente* whose primary residence is a mansion in the capital city. Formally the film is mostly limited to long and medium shots in the early continuity style of the time, with notable formal departures for attractions consisting of several interludes showing the modern sights of the city, two sequences containing traveling shots filmed from a train and an urban tramway, and *cuadro de costumbre* sequences that show staged rural gauchesque tasks. In the intertitles, verses appear from several gauchesque poems, most often those of *Martín Fierro*. Added after an initial box-office failure, these verses, rather than providing narrative information, merely serve to appropriate the symbolic capital of the poems, a commercial strategy often credited with giving the film a second box-office life after its initial failure (Di Núbila 17).

Nobleza gaucha opens with picturesque character exposition: "el gaucho Juan" is the hardworking hero of the pampa, while the villain, Don José Gran, is a wealthy Europeanized *estanciero* shown striking his gaucho peons with a whip as he patrols his lands, an unambiguous indictment of the use of violence by elites to enforce the exploitation of labor. This sets the film in line with the gaucho-as-popular-hero tradition, but soon the possibility of a more modern populist solidarity is raised: the gaucho protagonist pays a visit to his friend Gennaro, a recent Italian immigrant (an identity made explicit by his *cocoliche* speech reproduced phonetically on the intertitles), creating an alliance anathema to Lugones's Argentina as imagined in *El payador*, but more acceptable to the wider public undoubtedly cultivated by the film's producers.

After Juan saves a young woman from the back of a runaway horse and love blooms, the narrative gears only fully engage with an act of violence: the *terrateniente* kidnaps the woman, takes her to the city, and locks her up in his mansion. Juan, accompanied by Gennaro, follows in a train to the "maremagnum de la gran metrópoli" (maelstrom of the great metropolis), as the intertitle reads, where the two friends unknowingly lead the spectator on a spontaneous tour of the modern attractions of the capital—a streetcar ride, the *Congreso Nacional*, and other sights—before the intrepid gaucho rescues his love interest from the kidnapper's aristocratic palace. He does so in a way that sets himself up as a readily redeemable agent of legitimate popular violence, by subduing the landowner but sparing his life. Later, however, back on the pampa, unjust circumstances turn hero into outlaw, as is typical of gauchesque narratives, when he is pursued by lawmen doing the bidding of the vengeful *terrateniente*. He flees to the open countryside, but soon encounters the villain by chance, and as he pursues him on horseback the *estanciero* falls conveniently over a cliff to his death, a *deus-ex-machina* that allows the gaucho to leave his *facón* sheathed and spill no blood, assuring the audience he is no bloodthirsty *gaucho malo* and thus furthering the legitimacy of his challenge to authority. Freed from the control of the *terrateniente*, the rural space is restored to its premodern innocence, and gaucho and *prometida* will marry.

The death of José Gran presumably results in the cancellation of the mechanism of exclusion through which state violence is legitimized, the *bando*: the expulsion of certain individuals or groups from the state by a proclamation "meant for those who were not bandits, for those who did not (openly) support them, and for those who obtained a collective identity vis-à-vis that Other who was just (symbolically) 'thrown out'" (Dabove 8). In *Nobleza gaucha* the *bando* is never legitimate, due to the corrupt nature of the agents of the state, the illegitimacy of the landowner's actions, and the measured nature of Juan's violence. Thus, its cancellation and, as a consequence, that of the police persecution of the gaucho, restores the state's legitimacy (with the disappearance of its corrupting force), under which the gaucho, and his immigrant friend, can live within the law.

Whereas Lugones's intellectual labor had been carried out in the interest of the elites, working to reinforce the legitimacy of state violence against the new arrivals, *Nobleza gaucha* takes a contrary path by making the agent of corruption a representative of the elite class. When the gaucho carries out justice, he is immediately made a bandit in the eyes of an illegitimate state, under which the only legitimate violence possible is that of the outlaw. In this allegorical reconfiguration of authentic national identity and its alliances, the gaucho is central and on each flank are representatives of the factions that would be in political conflict for much of the twentieth century: the Italian immigrant of populism and the *terrateniente* of the oligarchy. Since the latter's power extends to both urban and rural space in the film, the criteria for national authenticity are shifted from the spatial—the Lugonian urban–rural opposition—to class, by allying the gaucho with the immigrant in popular opposition to the landowner. Where Lugones's goal was to legitimize the violence of the state in the interests of the elites against the newly numerous proletariat, *Nobleza gaucha*'s association of the recent immigrant with the authenticity conventionally afforded only to the traditional rural populace suggests that the state's violence can easily become corrupt, thus unjust and illegitimate.

Another film of the 1910 decade that reconfigures the gaucho's role in national identity is *Juan sin ropa*. Made in the wake of the *Semana Trágica*, it explores with graphic realism the theme of labor unrest and state violence, while simultaneously formulating a clear allegory of national identity by introducing a gaucho-like character into the urban world of strikes and battles between police and workers.[9] But here the gaucho is not a mere ally of the urban working class. He migrates to the city and joins the proletariat himself, in a revision of the national lineage that anticipates the appearance of a national-populist historical revision with the intellectual production of the Boedo group in the 1920s and FORJA (*Fuerza de Orientación Radical de la Joven Argentina*/Force of Radical Orientation of Young Argentina) in the 1930s.

The gaucho-proletarian character, Juan, is associated through the name of the film with the Juan sin ropa character of the many retellings of *Santos Vega*, the legend of the gaucho hero of the wars of Independence. At *Santos Vega*'s denouement, after national sovereignty has been secured, the diabolical Juan sin ropa arrives to challenge Santos Vega to a *payada* song duel. This challenger, who represents the onset of a modern Argentina in which the state's sovereignty over its territory spells the end of the gaucho's way of life, defeats Vega, who then passes into history.

The film *Juan sin ropa* shifts the signifier of modernity away from the mysterious supernatural character onto a gaucho protagonist who, unlike Santos Vega's passing into history, is able to successfully negotiate the transition from a traditional rural economy to the urban industrial economy. Authenticity, instead of passing from the popular to the elite—as Lugones would have it—remains with the popular classes. As the introductory title card reads, "el capital nuevo, el ideal moderno desnudo en su grandeza . . . viene a desvirtuar la falsa versión de la indolencia criolla" (new capital, the modern ideal, naked in its grandeur . . . distorts the false version of creole indolence). The original story's social Darwinism—shared by Lugones, who considers the gaucho unfit for a modern rationalized economy and thus destined to be replaced by the *criollo* elite—is neutralized as *Juan sin ropa*'s protagonist manages to refashion himself for success in the new capitalist economy. In my reading, this new lineage is less important as an attempt to redeem the already disappeared gaucho than as a transference of his symbolic capital (as authentically Argentine) to the recently disembarked proletariat.

The twenty-seven-minute fragmentary version of the film opens with an associative montage that first juxtaposes primitive men with city dwellers, then urban crowds with cows being led to slaughter, heavy-handedly suggesting the barbarity of a modern society in which the proletariat is subjected to violent exploitation by the powerful. For much of the rest of the film, a parallel montage similarly jumps back and forth to starkly contrast the world of the decadent boss with that of the resourceful new proletarian.

The film identifies Juan, a twentieth-century rural laborer, with the image of the gaucho through the inclusion of *costumbrista* footage of tasks similar to those depicted in *Nobleza gaucha*. His authenticity as a symbol of national identity established, Juan receives an offer to work in a meat-packing plant in the city—instead of the Vasena metalworks of the *Semana Trágica*, the strike will be at a *frigorífico*, the source of immense wealth for the beef-exporting elite—which he accepts, migrating to the city and starting work. We then see documentary slaughterhouse footage intercut with scenes of the idle lives of the plant's owners. The inclusion of this footage resignifies the earlier *costumbrista* sequences of rural labor, contrasting it with the kind of modern Taylorized labor that will remain unrepresentable in the future Argentine cinema until the crisis of the industrial cinema, in David José Kohon's 1958 short *Buenos Aires* and Humberto Ríos's 1960 short *Faena*, the latter famously quoted by Fernando Solanas and Octavio Getino in *La hora de los hornos* (1968). But this documentary mode of representation is only momentary in *Juan sin ropa*, and the film quickly returns to its narrative.

As the wealthy are shown leisurely enjoying their material comforts, the workers are suddenly laid off and their back pay is cut 20 percent. The union demands a takeover of the plant. With no other option, popular violence would seem called for, but Juan, on the barricades, advocates for negotiations. Management denies the workers' requests, and violence breaks out. The workers take over the plant, police arrive, and a very graphic battle ensues. The available footage ends soon after a love story subplot begins when Juan, fleeing the violence, is offered a ride in the carriage of the factory-owner's daughter. The rest of the film is mostly missing, but synopses recount that Juan returns to the countryside and through hard work eventually triumphs in the grain business, becomes a senator, reencounters the daughter, and marries her (Di Núbila 26). Without further footage it is difficult to draw more conclusions about the nature of Juan's successful economic and political trajectory, but it appears safe to say that it comes about in a morally unblemished way, through hard work rather than violence or corruption. Unlike the literary Santos Vega, this gaucho, his Argentine authenticity already established, has successfully managed the transition to modernity and even thrived, first as a proletarian, then a businessman, and finally a politician leading the nation into the future.

While in the wake of the *Semana Trágica* the immediate impact of *Juan sin ropa* lies in its graphically realist portrayal of the receiving end of the state's repressive violence, more striking in retrospect is its linking, through internal migration, of the proletariat with an oppositional use of the gaucho. They are one and the same individual, an amalgam of what are shown as the honorable and determined characters of both in the body of a single populist hero. Allegorically, this amalgam suggests an evolution in which the heir of the gaucho as authentic *modern* model of Argentine identity is not Lugones's *criollo* elite, but rather an upwardly mobile working class as driver of modernity, optimistically destined to bring progress to the nation if given the opportunity. The violent repression carried out against this class by the state is thus rendered illegitimate.

The portrayal of space in *Juan sin ropa* is also novel among the films of its time, although such an analysis is by necessity tentative, due to the loss of footage. While the film does employ a tamed version of the gaucho (which serves to establish a kind of moral exemplarity of hardworking honesty) the film quickly moves to an urban setting with the migration of its protagonist. This internal migration implies an uneven modernization between city and country, in which large-scale historical forces are at work in the destruction of the traditional rural economy as the nation modernizes. To say more, one would have to view the film in its entirety, which, given the laudable efforts currently being made by dedicated audiovisual preservationists in Argentina, is not outside the realm of possibility.

El último malón: Positivism, Early Ethnography and an Ethic for *Civilización*

Two representations of violence dramatize the contrasting portrayals of the indigenous in classical nineteenth-century Argentine culture and in the film *El último malón*. The first is that of the painting *La vuelta del malón* (*The Return from the Raid*) (1892), by Angel Della Valle, in which an indigenous group returns on horseback with its spoils from a raid on "civilization." The stolen items they brandish include a suitcase, a cross, and a white female captive. The painting subscribes to the dominant mode of representing the indigenous at the time, as powerful, intimidating, and violent while eliding the cause of their violence, or attributing it simply to their barbaric nature. The second representation is that of *El último malón*, filmed two decades later, which inquires about the social causes of the uprising it narrates. It portrays the indigenous violence as resulting from the dispossession of indigenous resources and the persistence of uneven modernization, suggesting that a faulty implementation of the nation's modernizing project resulted in the social exclusion of the indigenous population and their banishment to a space, the *reducción*, that remained impoverished even as nearby spaces modernized. The film formulates this critique of the primitive accumulation and structural violence that characterized Argentine modernity through an unusual combination of ethnographic documentary with a narrative reconstruction of a singular historic event, the "last uprising" of the Mocoví tribe. Alcides Greca's film further indicts the modernization project by resignifying the concept of barbarism: where the term might be generally applied to the *malón* and its violence, and by extension to the Mocoví, the film shows the uprising to be instead a result of the production and maintenance by the modern state of an isolated pocket of underdevelopment. The state practices of dispossession and *reducción* are suggested to be the cause of the Mocoví "regression" to barbarism that ends in the violence of the uprising.

Whereas *Nobleza gaucha* and *Juan sin ropa* were very much of their time, activating the existing image of the gaucho as representative of national identity in order to turn it against the nationalist discourse of the *Centenario* and critique the state's treatment of the peasantry and the proletariat, it could be argued that *El último malón* has affinities with a literary text that preceded the completion of the *Conquista del desierto*, Lucio V. Mansilla's 1870 *Una excursión a los indios ranqueles*, which examined the way in which a modernizing Argentina was integrating rural space and its population into the nation.[10] Mansilla's chronicle was written as he was leading a military expedition to sign treaties with the *caciques* who stood in the way of the nation's territorial expansion, but he introduced a critique of the violence with which this expansion was carried out. Similarly, rather than questioning the ideal of civilization and the need for the modernizing state to possess a monopoly on violence in order to bring it about, Greca points out the danger to the nation posed by the policies the state had implemented with this violence, specifically the dispossession and displacement of the Mocoví followed by their forced concentration in a *reducción* that guaranteed their impoverishment and economic exploitation.

In its documentary sequences, Greca's film displays its interest in the Mocoví plight, but at the same time its intertitles reveal an authorial faith in the concept of civilization that makes clear his positivist belief in modernization. Greca's position, and the film's seemingly anachronistic existence, can be explained by a post-conquest moment of crisis: although the national territory had been violently conquered some twenty-five years earlier, *la barbarie* belatedly bubbled up in 1904 with the violent uprising in the town of San Javier, province of Santa Fe. *El último malón*'s explicitly stated intent is to disseminate knowledge of this remainder of *barbarie*—the marginalized Mocoví people and their deplorable condition—left behind by the state, and it shows none of the reticence that would cause the near-totality of Argentine cinema of the next four decades to avert its gaze from the uglier realities of the nation. The opening intertitle informs us that "los indios . . . después de permanecer medio siglo en contacto con la civilización, se rebelaron contra el dominio de los blancos, poniendo en grave peligro la vida de los habitantes de aquella floreciente comarca" (The Indians . . . after being in contact with civilization for a half-century, rebelled against the control of the whites, putting the lives of the inhabitants of that flourishing region in grave danger).

The lamentation of the fact that the nation had allowed the Mocoví to "regress" to a "barbaric" state, even though *civilización* was in such close proximity for fifty years, allies Greca with the modernizing project while at the same time opening the way to question the practice of defining the nation through the exclusion of others as "barbaric." It must be noted that Greca's representation of the Mocovíes does not belong to the tradition of the noble savage. He argues that their current misery is not due to the ideal of Civilization, but rather to a specifically Argentine mismanagement of the civilizing project. Greca, that is, does not see civilization as an inherently corrupting force, but merely sees one historically specific instance of its faulty implementation—which produced the underdeveloped space of the Mocoví tribe—as pernicious. But his film lays out two separate and otherwise incompatible accounts of the cause of the uprising. Of these two accounts, one is generic in origin and the other sociological. The former follows the expectations of the melodrama genre and is contained in the film's narrative, while the latter is found in the documentary images and the information provided by intertitles.

Greca, a man of extensive credentials as journalist, poet, novelist, lawyer, socialist provincial and national *diputado* (representative), and university professor, employs his distinction to contest the essentializing circular logic of accounts of the uprising that might seek to unconditionally justify the violence that forced the Mocoví to the *reducción*. He appears in the film, elegantly dressed, addressing the public's lack of knowledge of this particular corner of the nation. First, he locates the site of the *malón*, San Javier, on a map, and then we see his hand writing about the film:

No será la poesía enfermiza del boulevard importada de París, ni el folletín policial ni el novelón por entregas. Será la historia de una raza americana, fuerte y heroica, que pobló de leyendas la selva chaqueña y el estero espejeado, de donde el chajá levanta su grito argento.

It will not be the sickly boulevard poetry imported from Paris, nor the police melodrama nor the serial novel. It will be the story of a strong and heroic American race that populated with legends the Chaco forest and the mirrored marshes where the *chajá* bird raises its silver cry.

Greca explicitly rejects the aestheticizing spiritualism of a Frenchified *modernismo*, as well as, implicitly, the long-running tradition that classifies the indigenous as barbarian. His romanticizing account that lays the ground for the melodramatic storyline is surprising in the context of a nation whose intellectual heritage almost unanimously cast the indigenous out of the national lineage. This is reiterated when the film abruptly shifts into a more critical mode with an intertitle that makes explicit Greca's view of how the Mocoví have been left behind by civilization: "A inmediaciones de este pueblo, donde los pionners [*sic*] de la civilización levantaron sus hogares y labraron su riqueza, una tribu de indios mocovíes arrastra su vida miserable" (In the vicinity of this town, where the pioneers of civilization raised their homes and carved out their fortune, a tribe of Mocovi Indians drags along their miserable existence).

By now it is evident that this section of the film will not be a Manichaean recounting of a battle between *civilización* and *barbarie*, but rather a document that denounces the nation's failure to include certain sectors of society in the modernizing project as equals, to instead maintain them as a reservoir of cheap labor. In support of this position, Greca employs the filmic medium's documentary charge to present background information that enables a more nuanced account of the state's role in the events. Unlike the other films discussed here, which privilege *costumbrismo* and attraction over a more documentary mode of filmic representation, *El último malón* takes full advantage of the latter to offer counter-knowledge that contradicts hegemonic national discourses on the indigenous.

Greca's particular strategy runs counter to what, due to the conventions that would soon characterize the cinema of the classical period, came to seem like a natural incompatibility between fiction and documentary.

He edits together, without transition or lapse in continuity, a melodramatic storyline, a narrative reconstruction of the Mocoví uprising and an *avant-la-lettre* ethnographic documentary. An image of a prosperous San Javier dissolves into the contrasting poverty of the Mocoví *reducción*, opening one of the very few examples of ethnographic documentary in all of cinema previous to the 1920s worldwide boom in documentary filmmaking. Some seven years before Robert Flaherty's *Nanook of the North* we see the Mocoví children, pets, material poverty, and customs of post-conquest life. The images and intertitles specifically address the issue of dispossession and the production and maintenance of an impoverished labor pool. With an intertitle that references late nineteenth-century primitive accumulation, the film shows the "antiguo señor de la comarca, desposeído de sus tierras" (the ancient lord of the region, dispossessed of his lands), fishing, hunting ostriches and crocodiles, then reduced to rounding up cattle for "los ricos ganaderos sanjavieranos" (the rich cattlemen of San Javier), before shifting into fictional reenactment and betraying its debt to then-current models of positivist sociology and social psychology.[11] Another intertitle informs us that the Mocoví's greatest enemy is alcohol, and that "los blancos le enseñaron a beber. Por eso le pegan y lo encarcelan" (the whites taught him to drink, for which they now beat and jail him). When several Mocoví are seen in a *tableau* set in a *pulpería*, or rural tavern, it is clear the intervention of the director in the mise-en-scène has increased and the film has shifted into a reenactment. As the drunken men stagger about the scene, policemen enter, beating and arresting them. The naturalism-inspired text explains how the Mocoví are victims not only of vice and misery but of exploitation at the hands of the nation that took their land and gave them alcohol in return.

Then the film again shifts mode, this time into melodrama. The intertitles explain that the old cacique, Bernardo López, collaborated with the Argentine state in selling out his people, while his illegitimate brother, Jesús Salvador, stayed faithful to a more traditional life. After Rosa Paiquí, mistress of Bernardo but secretly loved by Jesús Salvador, is introduced, the film again shifts mode, this time back to documentary. Various Mocoví men are interviewed describing the causes of the uprising—abuses by the whites—although this reasoning is presented in the intertitles as somewhat superstitious. Soon the film returns to a narrative mode, and in line with positivist discourse the Mocoví lose their rational autonomy when they begin to mass in preparation for the *malón*. The positivist fear of the irrational crowd dovetails tidily here with the specifically national fear of *la barbarie*. According to this exposition of motives, the psychological effects of the multitude on the individual function as a multiplier of the racial particularities inherent to the indigenous.[12]

This cross between positivism and a Sarmientine fear of barbarism bears its bitter fruit in the next section, "La regresión." After an intertitle diagnoses that "En el espíritu de los indios se ha operado una regresión hacia el salvajismo" (In the mind of the Indians a regression toward savagery has taken place), the Mocoví protagonists are replaced by white actors and the reenactment of the uprising begins. Following some intra-tribal dissension caused by the aforementioned love triangle, the Mocoví men revolt, stealing cattle, killing white settlers, and slaughtering and eating horses. The regression becomes symbolically complete when "el valiente gaucho Feliciano Luna, a quién los indios habían robado unos caballos, se decide ir a reclamarlos" (the valiant gaucho Feliciano Luna, from whom the Indians have stolen some horses, decides to go reclaim them). When the gaucho arrives to impose justice on the tribe by himself, the mass of "savages" sets upon him with spears and makes short work of this foremost representative of national identity, who is left agonizing on the grass. With this killing, the circle of Greca's critique of the modernizing project is closed: the Mocoví regression to barbarism had been caused by the fact that the modernizing nation had left the tribe marginalized and in poverty, but not until they regress to barbarism and kill the gaucho does the mismanagement of the nation reach its furthest symbolic consequences. The long-awaited pitched battle erupts on the dusty streets of San Javier, but the Mocoví archery being no match for the white man's rifles, the uprising is quickly put down and, melodramatic plot twists notwithstanding, the film soon ends.

In summary, Greca, a liberal intellectual from the provinces, employs the cinema to advocate for a racially inclusive ideal of *civilización*. He documents the marginalization of the Mocoví, then introduces the symbolically charged gaucho, but has the Mocoví kill him with an almost comic ease, suggesting the gravity of the danger to the nation posed by the marginalization (and the resulting regression to barbarism) of sectors of the national population and the production of impoverished spaces. Greca's willingness to represent nonstate violence in terms other than that of an essential and evil barbarism, and to instead show the factors that motivated it—primitive accumulation resulting in poverty and labor exploitation—suggests a call for the modification of the modernizing project and the lingering "neo-colonial pact" (Halperín-Donghi), under which the indigenous are segregated and reduced to being a source of cheap labor on *estancias*, as is documented early in the film.

Greca's critique forms a carefully articulated, if somewhat implicit, commentary on the consolidation of the state, which, as Dabove explains, depended on two conditions: first, its real monopoly on violence, and second, a social consensus on the legitimacy of this monopoly. It is clear that Greca supports in theory the state's monopoly on violence. In its disciplinary/pedagogical aspect, as an example of the "theater of the law" defined by Dabove as "a continuum of symbolic practices that encompassed both scaffold and poem" (24), the film does not criticize the state's expropriation of the means of coercion from the Mocoví that is seen in the violent suppression of the uprising. Although sympathetic to the Mocoví and their plight, the film does not go so far as to endorse the violence of the *malón*. Instead, fittingly for the positivist era, the uprising is seen as an undesirable symptom of a pernicious condition affecting what is ideally a healthy, unified body of the nation-state, a condition brought about by the dispossession and exclusion of the Mocoví and the resulting creation of the grossly underdeveloped space of the *reducción*.

The second condition necessary for the state's consolidation is the social consensus on the legitimacy of the aforementioned state monopoly on violence. This is where Greca's film is more critical, in its creation of a counternarrative to the many "narratives that would make the expropriation of violence by the state 'natural' and 'necessary'" (Dabove 26). Affirmed are the ancestral rights of the indigenous community to the local land and its resources—birds, crocodiles, and whatever else existed on the land of *barbarie*—that were appropriated by the whites, and documented is the Mocoví subjugation to the neocolonial pact, in the footage that shows them working on the *estancias* of San Javier cattlemen. The film's critique, then, resides in its opening room for debate on the legitimacy of specific instances of state and nonstate violence in the context of the same state's production of underdeveloped spaces.

Through the examination of the causes of the "final" episode of nonstate violence, the Mocoví are represented not as bandits to be excluded from the nation, but rather as potential citizens. The canonical claims about native propensity to violence are dismantled through a portrayal of the Mocoví as rational beings whose violence is a consequence of uneven development, or what could alternatively be seen as a lingering colonial relationship that had gone unacknowledged in the culture of the modernizing nation. It is here that Greca breaks with the tradition by which the state is consolidated by the exclusion of an other through the establishment of a clear distinction between bandit and citizen. He documents the social hierarchy of the Mocoví nation and their leader, portraying them as rational and capable of entering into a social contract and citizenship—when not driven to a mass "regression" to barbarism—thus as potential citizens of the Argentine nation, suggesting that Sarmiento was mistaken when he wrote in *Facundo* that in these rural spaces "la civilización es del todo irrealizable, la barbarie es normal" (civilization is completely unrealizable, barbarism is normal) (67). Where Sarmiento held that such differences were a natural result of local geographical particularities, Greca locates their cause in the racist exclusions built into Sarmiento's project. Sarmiento's conception of space had found objective expression in Argentine reality in the produced space of the *reducción*, a space in which an unredeemable *barbarie* could be safely contained in order to insulate *civilización* from its deleterious effects, and which in practice provided a reservoir of cheap labor in service of the export-oriented economic model. But the *reducción* appears in *El último malón* as the produced barbarism that is also known as underdevelopment.

It could be argued that Greca's film anticipates militant film by showing just violence as a consequence of a relationship between colonized and colonizer, even while Greca himself, trapped in humanist universalism, may have been blind to such a conclusion. The Mocoví's violence is clearly incited by the forced relocation that moved them out of the living knowledge upon which their survival depended, but Greca instead explains the violence in terms of, first, a faulty civilizing project, and second, the melodramatic plot mechanism of the fraternal conflict between Bernardo López and Jesús Salvador. It could be said, then, that Greca's use of the camera to document, rather than narrate, gives his film an autonomy relative to its maker that is unique in Argentine cinema until the appearance in the late 1950s of those filmmakers who, with a faith in the medium's capacity to provide a transparent window onto the social, turned their cameras toward the nation's marginal spaces.

Although the literary texts of the *Centenario* have been widely studied, little scholarly attention has been focused on these earliest Argentine feature-length films in a way that responds to the particular cultural dynamics of the 1910 decade, during which the nation was intensely debating questions of identity after having undergone an abrupt modernization. With luck, other films will be rediscovered and the study of the decade will be expanded, but the few films studied here already display a surprising variety of representations of figures of authenticity in national identity that call into question the legitimacy of state violence carried out at the expense of the nation's internal others, both immigrant and indigenous. *Nobleza gaucha* and *Juan sin ropa* provide glimpses of the kind of populist alliances that would eventually bring Juan Perón to power, while the seemingly belated *El último malón* is also a precursor of the increased focus in the 1960s on marginalized populations. My analysis of these films suggests that during the 1910s filmmakers possessed an autonomy relative to economic and political power that allowed them to counter hegemonic discourses on identity and national space to a degree that would not be seen in Argentine cinema for several decades. These films provide a glimpse, albeit necessarily partial, of a unique moment in which the cinema's ability to critically engage with national reality was relatively unencumbered by the political and economic concerns that would soon lead to the dominance, on Argentine screens from the 1930s through the 1950s, of more conventional representations of the social and spatial margins.

Chapter 2

The Classical Cinema and the Perpetuation of a National Fantasy

The decades-long dominance of film production in Argentina by large studios was in many ways analogous to that of other classical cinemas. Its productions took on the conventional form of the ninety-minute film, illusionistic continuity editing, up-to-date production values, and the use of a star system, all part of what was above all other considerations a commercial enterprise (Bordwell, Staiger, and Thompson 3). But an account of these conventions misses the adaptations of the Argentine classical cinema to the particularities of the national culture and public that resulted in further, locally specific conventions for representing marginal space. One important factor that contributed to these conventions was the class component of the cinemagoing public. As Matthew Karush argues, "The Argentine movie audience was divided roughly along class lines: while Argentines of all social classes saw Hollywood films, the audience for domestic movies was composed primarily of the lower and middle classes" (82).

The target audience of locally made films, then, did not generally include the wealthier sectors, since the cinema formed "a cultural field marked by a hierarchy of taste. At the top of this hierarchy were the major new Hollywood films, shown for a high price at fancy downtown theaters. At the other end of the spectrum were Argentine films, shown at barrio theaters at prices accessible to nearly all" (83).[1] According to Karush, this popular audience configuration ensured that cinematic expressions of national identity in Argentine films were by necessity in sympathy with the popular classes: "As in the rest of Latin America, elites had embraced European products and cultural practices throughout the nineteenth century;

Argentine 'high culture' offered little that was distinctive. The only cultural practices that could be packaged as authentically Argentine were those of the poor" (10). As a result, the portrayals of class relations in the classical Argentine cinema generally expressed a sympathy for the humble and a disdain, if not animosity, toward the economically powerful. But, I would argue, even as this cinema served positive images of a popular audience to itself, it propagated representations of the national space that were strictly conservative, even Lugonian.

Karush's thesis allows us to consider how the cinema's target audience might have contributed to the classical cinema's representation of marginal spaces. Identification with characters of the popular classes appealed to popular, mostly urban, viewers and for commercial reasons the industry had to be careful to avoid alienating or inflicting unpleasant surprises on them. It was thus in the industry's economic interest to repeat the dominant *costumbrista* conceptions of rural spaces and their role in the national self-image. In addition to production models that made it more economic to film in studios than on location, I would argue that concern for maintaining these idealizations in the face of the danger posed by film's documentary charge—to disregard the pervasive uneven modernization that characterized many rural spaces, that is—also conditioned cinematic representations.

The popular classes were generally portrayed in the classical cinema as hardworking, honest, docile subjects, at times exploited by corrupt businessmen, *caudillos*, or simple bullies who generally got their comeuppance in the end, often with the help of a state portrayed as benevolent. Those popular classes are seldom seen, in the classical cinema, as victims of systemic economic exploitation, a negligent state or an unjust social order, and thus, with very few exceptions, are not violent resisters of state coercion.

Such cinematic representations are very much in line with those propagated elsewhere by the conservative nationalist state of the 1930s. In the public schools, for instance, the image of the gaucho as model of national identity became the official position: "A partir de las disposiciones ministeriales, los textos escolares y las revistas de educación, se configuraría una representación del gaucho como 'modelo,' no sólo de patriotismo, sino también de buen comportamiento y moralidad" (through ministerial regulations, school textbooks, and educational magazines, an image was formed of the gaucho as "model," not only of patriotism, but also of good behavior and morality) (Poggi, Pacciani, and Casas 14). This image of the model gaucho propagated in school textbooks of the 1930s, consistent with those of Ayerza's domesticated gaucho of the 1890s, is exemplified in an article entitled "El gaucho," published in the second-grade textbook:

La prosa iba acompañada por dos ilustraciones en las que se mostraban actividades que se consideraban habituales en la cotidianidad de los gauchos, como cuidar su caballo y tomar mate. En el texto se destacaban otras supuestas aptitudes como: "Con frecuencia, el gaucho contaba hazañas de otros tiempos, en las que siempre abundaban los actos de valor y nobleza." (Poggi, Pacciani, and Casas 14)

The prose was accompanied by two illustrations that showed activities considered habitual in the daily life of the gaucho, like caring for his horse or drinking yerba mate. In the written text other supposed aptitudes stood out, such as, "The gaucho often told of deeds of past times, in which acts of valor and nobility abounded."

This pastoral gaucho, whose less-predictable adventures afield are safely banished to the preterit, is akin to those rural subjects who appear in many films of the classical period.

Literary sources of these conventional representations of rural space are in no short supply. As discussed in the introduction, in the decades following the national Centennial of 1910, efforts to define a national literary tradition proceeded on several fronts. In addition to Lugones's conferences and books, institutions were founded and tomes were written in the interest of cohering a population of vastly diverse origins into a national collective subjectivity. The Cátedra de Literatura Argentina of the University of Buenos Aires' Facultad de Filosofía y Letras was founded in 1912, the Instituto de Literatura Argentina in 1922, and Ricardo Rojas's *Historia de la Literatura Argentina* was published in four volumes between 1917 and 1922. These are the most canonical aspects of a wider ideological project. Predictably, the images produced by this project often center on the gaucho, with traits selected out from nineteenth-century imagery that are deemed compatible with the modernizing Argentina of the twentieth century. The most important elision is that of the historic conflict between the state and the gaucho.

This *costumbrista* imagery becomes dominant in the cinema during the classical period, which began in the mid-1930s. The studios produced many historic films in which the gaucho is repackaged as a patriotic fighter for national independence from Spain or against the savage Indian, an ideological transformation that reaches its peak with the wildly successful classics *La guerra gaucha* (Lucas Demare, 1942) and *Pampa bárbara* (Demare and Hugo Fregonese, 1945). Of this genre of film, Andermann writes that "the rural other was . . . folklorized and prehistoricized as irredeemably 'other' and thus as bound to succumb sooner or later to the forces of progress and a civilization whose agents . . . had already claimed moral victory" (2014, 56). These films feature proto-patriotic gauchos who struggle to found or defend the same centralized power that historically had rounded him up to labor or fight. This institutional appropriation of the gaucho by the cinema follows the lead of Rojas, who, in the words of Graciela Montaldo,

> construye un entramado cultural en el que se establecen los lugares que los integrantes de la comunidad ocupan en él; proclamar que la tradición gauchesca y rural está en la base de la argentinidad, es una forma de establecer las diferencias al tiempo que inaugurar una comunidad; a fin de cuentas es decir que hay una historia—que esa historia es pasado—y que el presente y el futuro tienen que reconocer ese lugar de identificación. (77)

> constructs a cultural framework in which are established the places occupied by the members of the community; to proclaim that the rural gaucho tradition is the base of Argentinity is a way to establish differences as well as inaugurate a community; in the end it is to say that there is a history—that that history is in the past—and that the present and the future must recognize that space of identification.

In Rojas's configuration of this newly inaugurated community, as in that depicted by Lugones, the transfiguration of the gaucho and the marginalization of the immigrant are complementary moments of a single movement. Present and future immigrants to Argentina are shown their place as newcomers distanced in time and space from the inaccessible authenticity of the gaucho, who takes his new place as the "roca primordial" (primordial rock) (Rojas) of national identity. This profiling of the gaucho as distant bedrock of the national identity as opposed to being the historical victim of the modernizing project had in large part taken place through representations in the popular medium of the *folletín*, in which, according to Montaldo, "lo rural y gaucho ha perdido su riesgo estético-político para acomodar parte de sus antiguas motivaciones a los requerimientos del público urbano y semiurbano; podrá haber un poco de injusticia pero es más bien el melodrama, el conflicto sentimental el que se va imponiendo" (the rural and gaucho theme has lost its aesthetic-political risk in order to accommodate part of its old motivations to the requirements of an urban and semi-urban public; there can be a little injustice, but it's rather the melodrama, the sentimental conflict that dominates) (89–90). Montaldo's description of the *folletín* as averse to political and aesthetic risk due to consumer desires could apply equally well to many of the stories told by the classical cinema. Now that the national territory had been conquered and the gaucho has ceased to exist in his premodern form, an unthreatening gaucho turned his concerns to forming a family and populating the desert, as Alberdi had recommended a century earlier.

Montaldo is one of many critics who discuss the role of literary texts in this revision of the national tradition, but far fewer have discussed how the cinema would increasingly perpetuate the same project. After the relative autonomy in the 1910s of a marginal, somewhat artisanal movie-making practice, by the 1930s a commercial, politically docile industry was reproducing canonical images of national identity, in consonance, with few exceptions, with those of Lugones and Rojas. As such, classical cinematic images of rural space tend overwhelmingly to ignore the uneven modernization and the resulting social conflicts that characterized early twentieth-century Argentina and had been portrayed in several films made in the 1910s. Between Argentina's desired self-image and its reality was the distance that separated the fantasy of civilization from the reality of uneven modernization, a distance that, predictably, given the commercial concerns of the classical cinema of the 1930s, led to fairly homogeneous portrayals of national space.

The cinema's reluctance to show images of the nation's rural places and people to the mostly urban film consumer had several other catalysts: Mass immigration combined with democratic reforms had led to the *golpe* of 1930, after which state pressure on cultural production increased. This was paralleled by the decline of artisanal film production—a practice made more difficult by the advent of sound cinema, which was far more costly than silent—and the above-mentioned increasing dominance of industrial studio production, a shift that altered not only the medium itself but the content of its images and the expectations of its public. Industrialization led to the formation of filmic genres that both formed and catered to the desires and expectations of the audience. These genres tended toward urban themes, such as the tango, and as Karush points out, sympathetically portrayed the popular classes.[2] This does not mean that few films were set in rural spaces. Many were, but instead of questioning the literary models and conventional representations of rural space, by the 1930s it appears that it had become more expedient to allow the nation's rural spaces to continue to be imagined as they had been than to document them or portray the uneven modernization under which they remained subject to urban economic power.

In the face of continued rural protest and the consolidation of labor-based movements, during the period between 1930 and the Perón presidencies "se conforma una alianza entre los sectores más concentrados de la burguesía, las Fuerzas Armadas y la Iglesia Católica que promueve la restauración del orden político anterior a la Ley Saenz Peña" (an alliance is formed between the more concentrated sectors of the bourgeoisie, the Armed Forces, and the Catholic Church that promotes the restauration of the political order previous to the Saenz Peña Law) (Kelly Hopfenblatt and Trombetta 251). The Ley Saenz Peña had been enacted in 1912 to widen participation in the democratic process, deepening the threat that led the conservative power alliance to look to entrench its favored notions of Argentinity. So it comes as little surprise that from the 1930s on, with the commercial cinema industry having come to dominate production and distribution, rural space was almost exclusively represented in the cinema in ways that were readily assimilable into existing schemes of imagining the nation.[3]

But what kind of danger would filmic documentation present? As an indexical medium, film's images rigorously document profilmic reality by capturing "the physical imprint of what they record with photo-mechanical precision thanks to the passage of light energy through lenses and onto a photographic emulsion" (Nichols 84).[4] As a registration of everything that comes before the camera, the motion-picture image possesses a credibility as document that is eloquently described by Siegfried Kracauer:

> Film brings the whole material world into play; reaching beyond theater and painting, it for the first time sets that which exists into motion. It does not aim upward, toward intention, but pushes toward the bottom, to gather and carry along even the dregs. It is interested in the refuse, in what is just there. (qtd. in Hansen, "Introduction" vii)

A possible cause of power's consternation at filmic representation of national spaces appears here: while the camera is unable to provide objective truth, since it is subject to manipulation through selection and editing, thanks to its rigorous capture of everything in its visual field it both resists the intentions of the filmmaker and carries a documentary charge in the eyes of its viewer. Thus it is at the same time a relatively unruly and credible medium, one by its nature more likely to problematize prescriptive representations.

In the case of Argentine rural space, for example, it can credibly show an existing landscape to be distinct from an imagined *desierto* or negate claims of a successfully modernized space. The aura of objectivity raises the image's epistemological status at the same time that film gathers the "dregs" and "refuse" in its image, allowing it to capture the people and places failed by the modernizing project. Filmic registration of marginal spaces could thus be perceived as running the risk of providing ideological support for forms of politics that challenged the interests of those in power, and it could be argued that this risk is reflected in a heightened reluctance by the industrial cinema to show images of rural spaces and the urban margins to the mostly urban film consumer.

But if a conservative alliance of bourgeoisie, military, and church did exert power over the cinema, how did it do so? While direct state censorship was slow in appearing, there certainly was pressure from anxious but powerful sectors toward film producers and exhibitors. In 1936 Carlos Alberto Pessano was appointed director of the Instituto de Cinematografía Argentino (Argentine Institute of Cinematography), the still-weak organ of government control over the medium. In the preceding years the sound film had arrived in Argentina in fits and starts, becoming more or less functional in the 1933 feature films *Tango!* (Luis Moglia Barth) and *Los tres berretines* (Equipo Lumitón). These films are dependent on comic dialogue, like the popular theater of the time from which they borrow themes and actors, and they consolidated what would become a dominant genre of the early sound cinema in Argentina, one often set in the popular space of the milonga, where the tango is played and danced. But in that same year, Pessano, recognizing the cinema's importance, disapprovingly editorialized in the journal *Cinegraf* that

> La Argentina debe hacerse conocer y el cinematógrafo es quien ha de lograrlo para ella más eficaz y rapidamente que otro medio. Pero el cinematógrafo, en cualesquiera ineptas manos, puede desfigurar una realidad . . . ¿[Argentina] ha de tolerar impunemente como hasta ahora que se la presente de la más inexacta y antipática de las formas, que es la que bordea el ridículo? (qtd. in Kelly Hopfenblatt and Trombetta 254)

> Argentina should make itself known and the cinematograph can accomplish this for her more effectively and faster than any other medium. But the cinematograph, in just any inept hands, can

disfigure a reality . . . Should [Argentina] tolerate with impunity as it has until now that it be presented in the most inaccurate and unpleasant of ways, which borders on ridicule?

The films that Pessano saw as offensive to the national honor were those that depicted the urban proletarian and immigrant-populated milieux, like *Tango!* and *Los tres berretines*. He and other conservative critics found the unflattering portrayals of Argentinity in these films sufficiently offensive to justify calls for heavier state intervention. Pessano in 1936:

> Los comerciantes no tienen el menor intento de practicar un patriotismo sin tangos . . . lo único que periódicamente se muestra en otros países . . . es el cine argentino de "cabaret life" . . . Es con él como la Argentina contribuye a formar una idea del argentino. Todo lo cual es tan imposible y grave como para que el gobierno impida la exportación de películas hasta que ellas sean dignas de exportarse y no nos avergüencen como ahora. (qtd. in Kelly Hopfenblatt and Trombetta 255–256)

> The commercial producers don't have the least intention to practice patriotism without tangos . . . the only thing that is regularly shown in other countries . . . is the Argentine cinema of cabaret life . . . with which Argentina contributes to forming an idea of itself. This is so intolerable and serious that the government should impede the exportation of films until they are worthy of export and do not make us ashamed, as they do now.

Here Pessano advocates for an increased role of the state in maintaining the national image abroad, with a direct call for intervention in favor of other genres that might portray more traditional lifestyles. The next year, Decree 98.998 was passed, requiring that the government review prior to release any films that portray "total or partially" matters of national history, state institutions, or national defense. This open-ended definition basically gave the state the ability to intervene in nearly every film, but, according to Kelly Hopfenblatt and Trombetta, in practice explicit state control was mostly limited to approval of the exportation of films.

There are, however, numerous cases of state agents going beyond this mandate and directly interfering in the circulation of films they personally deemed unacceptable. According to Peña, the government of the Province of

Buenos Aires threatened to prohibit Manuel Romero's *El cañonero de Giles* (1937), an action its producer, Lumitón, countered by agreeing to make a film that portrayed the provincial police in a positive light. That film turned out to be *Fuera de la ley* (1937), a crime drama that glorifies the police, and which is widely considered the classic early film of the *policial* genre (Di Núbila 164; Peña 2012, 56). In a case involving another film by Romero, the Comisión Nacional de Cultura (National Commission of Culture), headed by Matías Sánchez Sorondo, ordered the police to cordon off a theater to prevent spectators from entering to see *Tres argentinos en París* (*Three Argentines in Paris*, 1938). Sánchez Sorondo's objections were that the film, "por su argumento, por sus personajes y por el desarrollo de su trama, atenta contra el decoro y el buen nombre del país y constituye una expresión netamente antiargentina" (because of its story line, because of its characters, and because of the development of its plot, threatens decorum and the good name of the country and constitutes a truly anti-Argentine expression) (Peña, *Cien años* 57). This time Lumitón responded by changing the name of the film to *Tres anclados en París* (*Three Anchored in Paris*) and adding the disclaimer that its characters did not represent Argentina. The film was allowed to screen and became a popular success, likely aided by the publicity generated by the episode.

By the early 1940s the efforts of Pessano, Sánchez Sorondo, and others to use the force of law to coerce the production of positive depictions of Argentina had lost relevance (Kelly Hopfenblatt and Trombetta 258), but this did not mean that state intervention in Argentina was over. In fact, it would become far more institutionalized near the end of the decade by Peronism, albeit with very different objectives:

> Mientras que en la gestión de Matías Sánchez Sorondo la construcción de la argentinidad estaba determinada por los presupuestos de una mirada elitista que depositaba en las clases bajas todos aquellos valores no dignos de ser mostrados al resto del mundo, en el período peronista dicha valoración se invirtió. Aquellos valores que la oligarquía criticó, adjudicándolos desdeñosamente al ámbito popular, fueron reformulados positivamente durante el peronismo. (Kelly Hopfenblatt and Trombetta 259)

> While during the administration of Matías Sánchez Sorondo the construction of Argentinity was determined by the presuppositions of an elitist viewpoint that deposited in the lower classes all

those values unworthy of being shown to the rest of the world, in the Peronist period said valuation was inverted. Those values that the oligarchy criticized, attributing them disdainfully to the popular sphere, were reformulated positively during Peronism.

Under the Perón governments, which lasted from 1946 to 1955, the conservative fantasy of Argentina ceded to the exaltation of other national fantasies. First was that of the *pueblo peronista*, the source of the movement's legitimacy and electoral support, and later, the purported success of the Peronist state at righting social wrongs to create what it called a *Nueva Argentina*. Under Perón, control over producers of images became more direct. Aside from a copious production of propaganda films, concrete actions were taken by the state during this period at the behest of the Undersecretary for Information and Press, Raúl Alejandro Apold, who required in many cases the addition of a disclaimer or framing sequences to ensure that a film would not be understood as a critique of the Peronist present. Such direct censorship was intensified after 1950, resulting in the prohibition of certain films and an increasing level of modifications imposed on others. But far more consequential state actions were the imposition of tariffs on foreign films, the requirement that exhibitors screen a certain quantity of locally produced films, the punitive use of ratings, and the selective protection of the local industry through subsidies given to films that conformed to the models approved by Peronist functionaries (Kriger 27–108; Kelly Hopfenblatt and Trombetta 261–265). Filmmakers, then, were made aware of the possible consequences of falling afoul of state power both in the 1930s and the Peronist period by denigrating the nation, and in both cases the problems had to do with the representation of marginal spaces. In the 1930s the danger was that of representing those morally questionable characters who supposedly inhabited marginal urban spaces, and under Perón care had to be taken to not denigrate the *pueblo* or contradict the notion that Peronism had eliminated the kind of social inequalities that in reality persisted in both urban and rural spaces. But although it is clear that from the 1930s through the mid-1950s the state responded to an increasing awareness of the power of the cinema to influence public opinion, Kriger warns her reader not to think of the relationship as one of simple authoritarian control by the state. In response to canonical interpretations by Di Núbila and others who considered Peronism to be an efficiently authoritarian regulator that ruined a successful film industry through excessive intervention, Kriger is careful to point out the limitations of conceiving of such a unidirectional exercise of power, and recommends that one think of

> las consecuencias de la intervención del estado en el ámbito cinematográfico como el resultado de negociaciones que implicaron acuerdos, resistencias y sometimientos. Lo producido a partir de allí no puede ser un material homogéneo, sino un conjunto de textos fílmicos con múltiples expresiones estéticas y culturales que satisfacen, en alguna medida, las apetencias de todos los sectores. (Kriger 18–19)

> the consequences of state intervention in the area of cinema as the result of negotiations that implied agreements, resistences and subjugations. What is produced from such a situation cannot be homogeneous, but rather an ensemble of filmic texts with multiple aesthetic and cultural expressions that satisfy, in some way, the appetites of all social sectors.

Kriger acknowledges that state intervention greatly increased under Peronism, but points out that there was still ample room for producers to work as long as care was taken with images of the *pueblo peronista* and the *Nueva Argentina*. Given that the popular classes often inhabited marginal spaces, it is clear that the depiction of these was potentially problematic for both film producers and exhibitors, and generated pressures to self-censor. While it is impossible to pinpoint the exact reasons for specific decisions made by film producers and directors, it is clear that the industrial cinema that dominated film production from the 1930s through the mid-1950s did not have the kind of autonomy from capital and the state enjoyed by the filmmakers of the 1910s, and instead tended toward safe, reassuring portrayals of the nation. In the process it developed a unique filmic language that, as it conformed to the economic demands of classical film production, minimized the chance of contradicting comfortable conceptions of the national territory.

Formal Conventions and Rural Space

Argentine classical films were closely scripted, featured national star-system actors, and their representations of rural space tended toward a *costumbrismo* based on existing visual and literary models, an aesthetic that effectively prevented filmic documentation of the territory and its inhabitants and relegated the landscape to the status of mere backdrop in a figure-ground dynamic. This representational paradigm is conspicuous in films made from the mid-1930s through the exhaustion of the studio system in the mid-1950s, although exceptional films such as Mario Soffici's "social-folkloric" films of the late 1930s and Leónidas Barletta's *Los afincaos* (1941) do portray the rural interior and its inhabitants as caught in webs of power relations and economic exploitation that results from uneven modernization and the absence of the state.[5] But even in these exceptions, despite their themes, little effort is made to document rural spaces and peoples.

An additional element of this conventional strategy employed in the depiction of rural space is the use of the train in transitions. In Argentina the train was both symbol and instrument of modernity, the machine that pushed back the frontier between *civilización* and *barbarie*. From the perspective of those in "barbarie," it represented the coming threat of civilization, and as such was feared by the cacique Mariano Rosas in Lucio V. Mansilla's 1870 literary chronicle *Una excursión a los indios ranqueles*. By the opening decade of the twentieth century, in an Argentina eager to define itself as modern, filmmakers participated in the "culto a la máquina" (cult of the machine) by integrating the train into formal strategies, specifically by bringing the camera on board to film tracking shots that exploited the attraction of novel experiences for their viewers (Cuarterolo 2013, 129).[6]

In *Nobleza gaucha* the moving train was employed as a platform from which to film shots in which the spectator can glimpse the rural landscape and the urban margins through a window. This practice likely springs less from a will to document rural space than from the imperative, typical of early cinema, to provide the attraction of novel visual experiences that result from the combination of cinematic and transport technologies. But while the views from moving trains and tramways seen in *Nobleza gaucha* may have been a novel attraction in the 1910s, they were much less so two decades later, and would disappear as the Argentine cinema entered its classical period in the 1930s and developed the formal conventions it employed to represent rural space, in which the train was used as an element of continuity editing syntax, in transitions that moved characters and narrative focus from one diegetic space to another.[7] Sean Cubitt refers to a similar use of the automobile in U.S. cinema when he writes of "Hollywood's assimilation of the car as magic carpet of volition, whisking protagonists instantly from scene to scene under the invisible cloak of editing . . ." (25). While in the classical Argentine cinema it is the train, not the car, that is used in this way, in Argentine reality the train carried out an additional, very different function, that of transporting the national territory's goods to its port city. On film, this latter function is usually elided and the former, that of Cubitt's "magic carpet," is assimilated into the cinema's formal conventions. In terms of visibility, it is important to note that this means that the industrial script-based cinema turned the camera away from the landscape, toward the train instead, thus negating any possibility of documenting any indication of the complex webs of social and economic interactions that existed on the national territory. In the process, the train, instead of being portrayed as a mover of goods away from the interior to the port of Buenos Aires, is almost exclusively represented as a mover of people.[8]

On the rare occasions that the land is shown in the classical cinema, the shot tends to conform to the conventions of *costumbrismo*. The opening sequence of *Nobleza gaucha* had provided a precursor, showing gauchos carrying out a series of ranch tasks that domesticates both them and rural space. Opening this film considered to be Argentine cinema's first blockbuster are images centered on the gauchos and their tasks, a carefully selective portrayal of the rural world that helps set the conventions that will prevail over the next decades as the cinema remains invested in an idea of a rural space free of poverty and social conflict.

The use of the train in transitions and the cinematic *cuadro de costumbres* are complementary strategies that serve to elide real rural space as they contribute to the construction of a cinematic space that stands in for the Argentine nation. Following Michel de Certeau's account of spatial practices, these strategies could be said to form a cinematic poetics of asyndeton and synecdoche. The restriction of the train to transitions that omit the journey through space functions analogously to asyndeton, the poetic suppression of linking words. When applied to representations of space, in a function much like that described by de Certeau, asyndeton "selects and fragments the space traversed; it skips over links and whole parts that it omits . . . It practices the ellipsis of conjunctive *loci*" (101). In the case of the Argentine cinema, the ellipsis between the fade-out of an image of a train leaving one place and the fade-in of it arriving at another links relatively modernized diegetic places while eliding the rural space in between and eliminating the risk of calling into question conventional images of the national space. Complementary to this asyndeton is the synecdoche by which the *cuadro de costumbres* stands in for the totality of the rural national space. Synecdoche "expands a spatial element in order to make it play the role of a 'more' (a totality) and take its place" (de Certeau 101). This combination of asyndeton and synecdoche reduces diegetic space to relatively modern islands on which the story is played out—where characters are born, live, marry, and die—and in-between pastoral spaces in which hardworking, obedient gauchos go about their tasks. The resulting exclusions allow for the formulation of what Lusnich calls a "visión ideologizada del paisaje" (ideologized vision of the landscape) (156) that conforms to the imperatives of the powers of each moment:

> El pasado se lee e interpreta en función del presente, especialmente en relación con los programas y los discursos políticos que signaron la década de 1930 (la sucesión de gobiernos militares) y el período de desarrollo de los dos gobiernos peronistas. El retorno del mito del gaucho, la promoción de figuras militares y del discurso castrense, la imposición del Estado como instancia reguladora de los procesos históricos y sociales . . . explican la creación de ficciones potentes tanto como la posición que adopta la institución cinematográfica frente al Estado y la realidad política. (2007, 198)

> The past is read and interpreted according to the present, especially in relation to the programs and political discourses that marked the decade of 1930 (the series of military governments) and the period of development of the two Perón governments. The return of the myth of the gaucho, the promotion of military figures and of militarist discourse, the imposition of the state as governing authority of historic and social processes . . . explains both the creation of powerful fictions and the position adopted by the cinematic institution toward the state and political reality.

The periods mentioned by Lusnich neatly contain the classical cinema, and the close links between cinema and power, or to consider it differently, the relative lack of autonomy on the part of the former relative to the latter, tends to produce representations of rural space whose very banality betrays anxieties regarding the nation's uneven modernization.

Among the occasional films that thematized the conditions brought about by uneven development in rural areas, the most notable were those directed by Soffici, along with Leónidas Barletta's sole film, *Los afincaos* (1941). The latter is unique in Argentine cinema, both as a production of the pioneering independent theater company, the Teatro del Pueblo, and for the vision it presents of rural space and its inhabitants. Barletta, one of the Boedo group of socially committed writers, founded the independent Teatro del Pueblo in 1930 with the objective of reflecting reality and thus contributing to the greater ideal of progress through the raising of the consciousness of a popular public, an ethos clearly reflected in the very didactic *Los afincaos*. The aesthetic of the resulting film is one of exaggerated ugliness that renders the rural universe an insular, bestial place, inhospitable to any modernizing impulse in the absence of the state. According to Peña, the film was prohibited for viewers under the age of sixteen, but whether this was due to the film's extreme realism or to an attempt to suppress its social critique is not clear (75–76).

The film is set in a rural province, to which a young school teacher, the allegorically named Aurora, arrives. She is eager to educate the local children, but finds her mission impeded by the influence of the local caudillo, Don Rufino, the de facto owner of the land and master of its inhabitants. Interested in having a young woman around for reasons that soon become clear, he has sent away the previous teacher because of her age. When Aurora arrives, he makes clear his desire to sexually possess her, and her resistance results in the school being closed. When she goes to the police, the local sheriff's passivity underlines the thesis of the film: the state's absence in rural areas results in the proliferation of exploitative power relations on the local level. The sheriff's lack of power is total, as he says, referring to the caudillos, "Yo no puedo hacer nada. Aquí el comisario, la ley, el gobernador y todos los poderes juntos, son ellos, solitos ellos, ¿me entiende?" (I can't do anything, Here the police chief, the law, the governor and all the powers together, are them, just them, do you understand me?). Faced with the inevitability of submitting to the *caudillo*, Aurora kills herself. The film appears to have been shot entirely in a studio, but crudely, somewhat like a filmed play, and even in such an exceptional film, despite its apparent goal of demonstrating the falsity of the dominant pastoral image of rural space, there is no documentation of real space or its inhabitants. Of course in the case of Barletta's radically independent film this is understandable, since the cinema is used here to narrate a fiction that thematizes rural power relations, not to document them, and decades would pass before filmmakers would begin to opt for the latter strategy.

The Cinema and National Modernization Projects of the 1930s

The economic crisis that followed the stock market crash of 1929 led to disenchantment with export-oriented economics across the continent and the eventual beginning of what is often called the Age of Development.

In Argentina, the resulting shifts in economic policies meant an increase in state action to stimulate industrialization on the national scale. I will discuss how three films participate in the construction of public consent for these actions by positively portraying an interventionist state as undertaking modernization projects or by publicizing these same projects, in what Paul A. Schroeder Rodríguez refers to as a turn toward corporatism that is reflected in Argentina's cinema "through a variety of genres that shared the representations of corporatist resolutions to narrative conflicts as new foundational fictions for a united nation ruled by justice and love" (92).

Despite the 1930s opening with a military coup (that of José Félix Uriburu) and being characterized by a relatively authoritarian state, it is likely that consent for the projects was important, since the scale of the reconfiguration of the movement of commodities and humans throughout the nation's territory would have required major, often traumatic, disruptions to ways of living and working. It would seem that, faced with such a challenge, the state considered the mass medium of the cinema to be potentially useful for its capacity to imagine positive outcomes for the national development projects. The deployment of a corporatist logic on the part of film producers that align themselves with a campaign to modernize the nation's territory suggests that by the 1930s Argentine cinema had lost much of its autonomy from economic and political power. Schroeder Rodríguez expands on the economic and power dynamic that brought about the loss of autonomy in his description of the "corporatist discourse of modernity" of the classical studio period:

> Throughout this period, and in response to the prohibitive costs associated with industrial modes of production, many private studios sought support from corporatist states, who saw this as an opportunity for them to control representation by countering Hollywood's stereotypes with positive representations of their own. (5)

The lack of distance described here between state and film industry after the early 1930s contrasts starkly with the autonomy enjoyed by the makers of films like *El último malón* and *Juan sin ropa* two decades earlier. The films of the 1930s I examine all represent, and positively inflect, state-driven modernization projects. These projects to develop the rural interior of the country were undertaken by an increasingly interventionist state in order to integrate more territory into the national economy, in a dramatic shift that can be attributed to the combination of successful social revolutions elsewhere, the widely recognized exhaustion of the agro-exportation economic model, and the worldwide crisis after the 1929 crash (Ballent and Gorelik 2001).[9] The most ambitious aspects of this project were designed to develop cheaper means of transportation in order to draw more of the national space into the economy as means of production. Key to the achievement of this goal were the building of a roadway network that would compete with the British-owned railways and the increased exploration, extraction, and distribution of the petroleum that lay under the national territory. Secondary aspects included the development of tourism and the dedication of national parks.

There had been long-running conflicts between rural agricultural producers and the British-owned railway companies over the exorbitant shipping costs maintained by the latter's monopoly on rail transport, and the roads were conceived of as a way to break this monopoly and lower freight costs in order to spur economic production in areas that were too far from the existing railway network to be commercially viable under the existing transport regime. The roadway expansion was conceived, then, as part of a comprehensive economic plan of substituting national production for imports, and supporting industries were also developed. Petroleum extraction and distribution (through the state-owned hydrocarbons company Yacimientos Petrolíferos Fiscales, or YPF), which included the strategic placement of service stations, is the most notable of these, but other aspects of the project were the construction of public grain elevators, the manufacture of automobiles and tires, the development of automobile tourism, and the establishment of national parks. As these projects were being undertaken by the state, the national cinema produced several films that thematized various elements of them. I will examine how road construction, tourism, and petroleum extraction and distribution appear in three films of the period, Manuel Romero's *La rubia del camino* (1938), Arturo S. Mom's *Petroleo* (1940), and Soffici's *Kilómetro 111* (1938). A deeper examination of the concrete links between the films' producers and the state is beyond the present possibilities of this project and will have to remain an open question for the moment.[10]

Petróleo, as its title implies, thematizes hydrocarbons production, an area of heightened conflict between the Argentine state and foreign, mostly United States, interests since the 1920s. In 1907, the first Argentine petroleum discovery took place near the southern town of Comodoro Rivadavia, and from that moment debates raged around energy policy and how best to use natural resources for national economic development. After the initial oil discovery, the sides in the conflict were quickly defined. The interests of the central government based in Buenos Aires were pitted against those of provincial power and private landowners allied with foreign oil companies, most notably Standard Oil. This alignment caused the central government to take a nationalist stance when it came to oil, and the provinces a more liberal one. In 1922, YPF was formed, and in part due to laws that lessened the provinces' power, it was soon able to compete successfully with foreign companies operating in Argentina. Later in the decade, however, a conflict between province of Salta and the national government broke out. The provincial powers had aligned themselves with Standard, the U.S. company vehemently opposed by nationalists, and given it large extraction concessions. YPF had designs on the same fields, however, and by the late 1920s the conflict ended up in the Supreme Court, which after the 1930 coup decided in favor of Standard. Ballent and Gorelik write that "en la literatura de la época del golpe del 6 de septiembre fue bautizado como 'golpe petrolero.' De hecho, notorios representantes de la Standard Oil . . . formaron parte del gabinete de Uriburu y esa empresa consolidó su poder en Salta" (in the literature of the time the coup of September 6 was baptized the "petroleum coup." In fact, notorious representatives of Standard Oil . . . formed part of Uriburu's cabinet and the company consolidated its power in Salta) (161). While the political and economic machinations around oil in the early 1930s are too complex to further elaborate here, briefly, despite the role of Standard in national politics, its state-owned competitor expanded rapidly. In response to the court decision favoring Standard, the central government proposed legislation defending YPF, which in 1935 was passed into law by Congress: "There would be no further concessions although joint ventures were to be permitted between private investors and YPF on a 50-50 basis; otherwise the companies were to be confined to their existing holdings" (Philip 179). YPF's importance as a nationalist symbol of the territorial modernization project is reflected in its publicity campaign of the time, which featured the phrase "YPF hace caminos, YPF hace patria" (YPF makes roads, YPF is patriotism). Petroleum distribution and roads expanded hand in hand, with 180 YPF service stations built between 1938 and 1943 (Ballent and Gorelik 163), thus making possible both automobile tourism and roadway freight transport.

Petróleo was the first film produced by Estudios San Miguel—whose owner, Miguel Machinandiarena, funded film production with casino largesse from the touristic development of Mar del Plata—and was scripted by two writers, Arturo Cancela and Pilar de Lusarreta, whose political orientation is made clear by the fact that, according to Héctor Kohen, they both had signed a manifesto in support of the Nationalists at the outbreak of the Spanish Civil War (14). Sympathy with Fascism is evident in the film, which, as part of its emphatic call for a defense of national sovereignty in petroleum production, clearly denounces the U.S. oil industry's rapaciousness and indulges in the kind of cartoonish antisemitism that has long marked conservative Argentine nationalism. The anti-U.S. and anti-Semitic sentiments were exacerbated during the war by Argentina's refusal to renounce its neutrality and join in an anti-Axis alliance, and the film opens with a text that exemplifies this strident nationalism: "La defensa del suelo patrio contra el capital sin patria" (The defense of the soil of the fatherland against capital without a fatherland). This enemy is characterized cartoonishly by a group of men in suits, with foreign accents, filmed in canted compositions to presumably express their sinister nature. They utter—each speaking a single clause in turn—a justification in first-person plural of neocolonial rapaciousness:

> El petróleo es dominio, en la guerra y en la paz. Necesitamos controlar el petróleo virgen de América. Para especular en la guerra, para especular en la paz. Para imponer la guerra y la paz, el petróleo de México, el petróleo de Venezuela, el petróleo de Perú, el petróleo de Bolivia, el petróleo de Comodoro Rivadavia.
>
> Petroleum is control, in war and in peace. We need to control the virgin petroleum of America. To speculate on war, to speculate on peace. To impose war and peace, the petroleum of Mexico, the petroleum of Venezuela, the petroleum of Peru, the petroleum of Bolivia, the petroleum of Comodoro Rivadavia.

These maleficent speculators are soon opposed by a hero, Bustamante, a patriotic landowner who has discovered oil on his property near Comodoro Rivadavia. After he refuses buyout offers from foreign investors, saboteurs materialize and bomb his well, and he is blinded in the incident. A romantic subplot is quickly added when Bustamante's beautiful daughter, Ana María, is driving through Salta province and hits a man, Ibarra, who happens to be both handsome and a petroleum engineer. To briefly summarize what follows, Ana María and Ibarra move to Comodoro Rivadavia and are working to keep the oil in Argentine hands, when a foreign owner of the "Oil American Company" with the familiar name of "Mr. Morgan" is introduced.

He ascribes to a sort of Monroe Doctrine of hydrocarbons, declaring that "Los informes son claros: hay un mar de petróleo bajo esa tierra, nuestro petróleo. Todo el petróleo de América tiene que ser nuestro, caiga quien caiga" (The reports are clear: there is a sea of petroleum under that land, our petroleum. All the petroleum of America must be ours, whoever must fall). Morgan quickly finds the vulnerable point of the national body, Bustamante's foreman, with the racially inequivocal name of Berkovich, whom he bribes to sabotage his employer's operation. This eventually sets up a symbolically loaded fight between a loyal gaucho with his *facón* and the treacherous Jew, who pulls a gun and shoots the gaucho. But after several more plot twists the oil ends up staying in Argentine hands and the film ends with a gaucho chasing Berkovich across the starkly picturesque Patagonian landscape, through a herd of seals on a beach, and the traitor eventually falls over a cliff to his death. With the Semitic contaminant eliminated, the nation will presumably be able to better defend its oil from predatory foreign capital. While it is one of several films to thematize the national development efforts, *Petróleo* appears to be a unique, ideologically isolated film, and I am not aware of other examples of such blunt conservative nationalism to have been produced in the Argentine classical cinema.

La rubia del camino is a film far more typical of its time, an example of the screwball comedy genre in which a man and a woman overcome difficulties to form a couple. The film's canonical status is confirmed by Di Núbila's claim that it is the first "sophisticated comedy" of the Argentine cinema (190). In Manuel Romero's Lumitón-produced film, the amorous union crosses class lines to contrast the down-to-earth character of the popular classes with the superficial cosmopolitanism of the wealthy. Romero was a prodigious director of popular films and, as discussed above, the target of many conservative attempts in the 1930s to suppress his works due to their perceived denigration of the nation.

Karush addresses the film's intersection of class and space when he writes that "reproducing the country versus city binarism that had played such a central role in domestic cinema since *Nobleza gaucha*, *La rubia del camino* associates Buenos Aires with a modernizing elite caught up in slavish imitation of Europe" (171). The film, considered the first Argentine road movie, stages a voyage across the interior of the country that prompts the overcoming of the class differences that separate the couple. As might be expected, the film's populism results in a *costumbrista* representation of rural space and little documentation of it, as rural popular authenticity is set against a class that has abandoned its roots to live in an artificial urban space. This dynamic is seen often in the classical cinema, and will be transformed from parody to militancy by the late 1960s.

As for the plot, a brief synopsis will suffice: the wealthy snob Betty is vacationing in the luxury Hotel Llao Llao, in Nahuel Huapi national park, when her wealthy fiancé cheats on her. She leaves alone by car for Buenos Aires, but on the way she runs out of gas and a handsome, down-to-earth freight trucker happens by, from which point the encounter between the "hateful rich and noble poor" (Karush 171) is as predictable as the pampa landscape across which they drive. As Karush writes, "the emergence of Betty's femininity, her nurturing, maternal instinct, allows her to overcome her shallow arrogance and embrace the music and food of the Argentine masses; gender trumps class, enabling Betty to join the national community" (172). Under the trucker's influence Betty questions her class prejudices and the two eventually end up in love, with, importantly, the woman converted to the man's working-class way of life, not the other way around. The story is boiler-plate generic, and the importance for this study is instead the film's thematization of two elements of the public works projects: tourism and road freight.

The significance of the media campaign behind the projects to develop a tourism industry is addressed by Ballent and Gorelik:

> el turismo dentro del país había sido impulsado como recreación masiva por periódicos modernizadores de los hábitos sociales como *Crítica*, que destinaba corresponsales en las zonas pintorescas del país. Se otorgaba al turismo una función 'civilizadora' de doble vía, vinculada al conocimiento del país: 'desprovincializar' a los habitantes del interior, para borrar los rastros de 'odioso regionalismo,' y 'argentinizar' a los porteños, que 'conocen en sus mínimos detalles el París elegante' pero 'ignoran paladinamente cómo se vive en el interior de su propia tierra.' (164)

> tourism within the country had been promoted as mass recreation by periodicals that set out to modernize social habits, like *Crítica*, which sent correspondents to picturesque zones of the country. A dual "civilizing" function was attributed to tourism, linked to knowledge of the country: to "deprovincialize" the inhabitants of the interior, in order to erase the traces of "hateful regionalism," and to "Argentinize" the inhabitants of Buenos Aires, who "know

the most minimal details of elegant Paris" but heroically ignore how one lives in the interior of their own land.

The imagery of *La rubia del camino* suggests that as well as newspapers, the rapidly massifying medium of the cinema was employed to publicize tourism. Behind the opening credits is a series of panoramic shots of the majestic alpine landscapes of the Nahuel Huapi area, the last of which stops and holds on the Hotel Llao Llao, an important attraction represented in a quasi-publicity mode in the film. As the area was being developed as a site for elite tourism as distinct from mass tourist developments like Mar del Plata, the Llao Llao was constructed in 1930 as an icon of this area marketed as an "Argentine Switzerland," and the stunning alpine landscape shown in the film is indeed visually comparable to its European competitor.[11] Nahuel Huapi was one of Argentina's first national parks, and in 1934 was integrated into the recently created Dirección General de Parques Nacionales (General Directoriat of National Parks) as a kind of crown jewel of the push to foment tourism to compete with Europe, a carefully targeted form of import substitution described by Ballent and Gorelik:

> [E]n la década del treinta tuvo lugar una acción decidida por parte del Estado, basada en el objetivo de integrar la industria del ocio y el turismo en la tarea de puesta en régimen y explotación del territorio nacional. En tal sentido, el impulso brindado al Nahuel Huapi superó notablemente los esfuerzos destinados al Iguazú, ya que se juzgaba que el potencial económico del Sur era mayor que el de la selva tropical, y que permitiera competir con el turismo desarrollado en Europa. (168–169)

> During the 1930s the state took action determinedly, based on the objective of integrating the leisure and tourism industry into the task of incorporating and exploiting the national territory. To this end, the impulse provided to Nahuel Huapi notably surpassed the efforts expended for Iguazú, since it was judged that the economic potential of the South was greater than that of the tropical jungle, and would allow it to compete with already existing tourism in Europe.

In *La rubia del camino*, the creation of a national tourism market for wealthier Argentines who might otherwise opt for Europe is reflected in the choice of Betty's aristocratic family to vacation nationally, instead of transatlantically. But these elites are only one pole of a class opposition that fuels the romantic conflict to be resolved, and on the other side of the opposition emerges another aspect of the modernization project, freight transport, that brings obvious class implications as an occupation of working-class drivers.[12]

The film's take on class relations is far from neutral, for reasons Karush makes clear. As he states, in an Argentine cinema that was primarily intended for a popular and national audience, the sympathetic characters tended to be those of the working class, while the rich come off as spoiled, unproductive, and dismissive of those less wealthy. Betty is no exception, stating at one point, "Yo soy rica. No tengo por qué luchar, ni trabajar, ni sufrir" (I'm rich. I have no reason to struggle, nor work, nor suffer). She is played by Paulina Singerman, in her first film role, as a *niña bien* marked as an inauthentic Argentine in several ways. In addition to being blond, she prefers "Betty" to her given name Isabel, proclaims proudly to have been educated in France, and, perhaps most symbolically damaging to her Argentinity, turns up her nose at *yerba mate*. Her lack of empathy with those of other social classes is made clear in her dismissal of her maid's request for free time to get to know the area, which could be understood as an ironic critique of the state's tiered tourism marketing: "No olvide que la hemos traído a Nahuel Huapi como criada, y no en calidad de turista" (Don't forget that we've brought you to Nahuel Huapi as a maid, not as a tourist). Such an opinion could be seen as a challenge for an *arriviste* middle class eager to appropriate the status symbols with which Betty's social class distinguishes itself.

In line with Karush's thesis, the class tensions are eventually resolved through Betty's abandonment of her own social sector in order to form a couple with her new working-class mate (played by Fernando Borel). This resolution happens as a result of the journey to Buenos Aires, during which the characters stop at several points for encounters that provide displays of a rural working-class solidarity that eventually prompt Betty to renounce her own social origins. Besides this use of the rural voyage to question class privilege, not much is explored with regards to economic relations between the classes and the nation's real spatial relations, as the film limits itself to broad characterizations of its protagonists. As for the rural space crossed on the fictional road trip, very little was filmed, as Di Núbila comments:

> Pese a parecer una *road movie*, La rubia . . . tuvo muy pocos exteriores directos: algunos en Bariloche y alrededores, y otros de sospechoso *look* bonaerense. En las tomas de frente con Paulina

> y Borel en el camión no hay referencia de paisaje, y en las de costado los fondos fueron proyectados. En cambio abundan las escenas de interiores en Bariloche, casas del camino y Buenos Aires. La astucia de Romero fue barajarlas, repartirlas y jugarlas tan rápido en escenas cortas que al público le pareció estar viendo un viaje auténtico. (194)

> Despite appearing to be a road movie, *La rubia* . . . used very few direct exteriors: some in Bariloche and environs, and others with a suspicious look of Buenos Aires. In the frontal shots with Paulina and Borel in the truck the landscape is not seen, and the shots in profile the backdrops were projected. By contrast, scenes of interiors in Bariloche, houses on the road and Buenos Aires are abundant. Romero's shrewdness was to shuffle them, deal them and play them so fast in short sequences that to the viewers it seemed like they were watching a real voyage.

While this lack of filmic registration of rural space should come as no surprise in a studio product such as this, the filming of the Nahuel Huapi area, not at all conventional, is an innovation in publicity that massifies the images of the national park and the Llao Llao, reflecting the corporatist logic of commercial film production in the late 1930s.

Another film to engage with the national modernization projects is Mario Soffici's *Kilómetro 111* (1938), which provides, of the three films examined here, by far the most politically progressive analysis of the nation's faulty modernization, into which it integrates a direct endorsement by its sympathetic protagonist of the projects of the 1930s. The film is notable for its exceptional portrayal of the train as primarily a mover of goods, which allows it to join in the widespread condemnations of what was then commonly called "British neocolonialism." The political dynamic around the theme of transport opposed the idea of road to railway freight, and

> como resultado, el camino aparecía enfrentado a todo aquello que, en la economía y el territorio argentinos, representaba el trazado ferroviario, sinónimo de los males del país, especialmente de la crisis de la producción rural y del crecimiento descompasado de las diferentes regiones argentinas. (Ballent and Gorelik 157)

> as a result, the road appeared in conflict with all that which was, in the Argentine economy and territory, represented by the rail-

way layout, synonym of the country's ills, especially the crisis in rural production and the uneven growth of its different regions.

Road construction came to be considered by nationalists of all stripes an affirmation of a sort of authentic Argentinity that had been oppressed by the railway, which had been constructed by British interests. According to Ballent and Gorelik this interpretation was subscribed to by "un amplísimo espectro político, que reunía desde la izquierda hasta los sectores nacionalistas, y que presentaba al camino como un símbolo de la voluntad de desarrollo económico nacional" (a very wide political spectrum, which spanned from the left to the nationalist sectors, and which presented the road as a symbol of the will to national economic development) (157). The description of the anti-British alliance provides the means for understanding how a filmmaker like Soffici could find interests in common with the conservative nationalism of *Petróleo* under the umbrella of economic nationalism, even as each thematized different aspects of national economic development. Both find themselves operating under the corporatist logic of a nationalist assemblage united only in its opposition to foreign capital.

In 1933, just as the road-building project was getting underway, in *Radiografía de la pampa* Ezequiel Martínez Estrada formulated his well-known condemnation of British economic dominance:

> El trust de los transportes a vapor . . . imposibilita la existencia de caminos de tierra o de asfalto. . . . La ruinosa competencia que en Norteamérica, Inglaterra y Francia hacen al tren los camiones y ómnibus, aquí nunca existirá, porque el camino es nuestro y la vía de otros. Para tener treinta y ocho mil kilómetros de vía férrea hemos tenido que renunciar a centenares de millares de kilómetros de pavimento. Debieron ser, los caminos, doce veces más extensos que las vías, y lo son apenas poco más de la mitad de ellas. Sin carreteras, el auto es un dragón a nafta que se atasca en el barro, como un artefacto diabólico que el caballo del sulky ya contempla sin miedo al pasar. (67)

> The steam transportation cartel . . . makes impossible the existence of dirt or asphalt roads. . . . The ruinous competition that trucks and buses are giving the railroads in North America, England and France will never exist here because the roads are ours but the rails lines belong to others. In order to have thirty-eight thousand kilometers of iron ways, we have had to renounce

hundreds of thousands of kilometers of paved roads. The extent of roads ought to be twelve times greater that than of the rail trackage, but it is scarcely more than half of it. Without highways an auto is a gas-driven dragon that sticks in the mud, like a diabolic artifact that the horse, pulling a sulky, contemplates without fear when he passes. (Nouzeilles and Montaldo 259–260)

Martínez Estrada's concerns were already widespread. By October of 1932, in order to lower the freight costs for agricultural products and make Argentine exports more competitive, the Ley de Vialidad (Transport Law), which authorized the road-building projects and set up the institutions needed to carry it out, had been passed (Ballent 13). In the middle of a serious economic crisis and with predictions of drastic reductions in cost, the project was undertaken quickly, and on October 5, 1935, the landmark at the center of the new roadway network, dubbed Kilómetro 0, was inaugurated at Buenos Aires' Plaza del Congreso.[13] The fact that the railways also radiated out from the capital makes clear the relevance of the setting of Soffici's film, in which the train is depicted as the monopoly mover of goods from the interior to the port city, thus as a key element in the subjugation of rural space to urban capital as the disadvantaged pole of persistent uneven modernization.

The film directly links foreign capital to the exploitation of a tightly knit community of struggling settlers who are depicted as modern-day gauchos and representatives of the *pueblo*. Completing the thesis is the designation of the state as a potentially redemptive force, by way of the under-construction roadway network. The political affiliations of the film are made clear by taking into account the identities of the film's writers. Its screenplay was co-written by Enrique Amorim, Carlos Oliveri, and Sixto Pondal Ríos, all associated with either the Boedo group of writers or FORJA, both of which contributed to the populist historic revision that would inspire the eventual nationalization of the railway system.

The film's protagonist, Don Ceferino (played by the comic star Pepe Arias), is the stationmaster at Kilómetro 111, an outpost that serves to link grain production with markets in Buenos Aires. The local grain farmers are hardworking, noble, but long-suffering settlers (or *colonos*) depicted as twentieth-century gauchos. After a successful harvest they struggle to get their product to market, impeded by a corrupt broker (or *acopiador*) who speaks with a foreign accent and enjoys a monopoly on the local grain market. A subplot extends the critique of neocolonialism to the cultural realm, specifically the dominance of Hollywood cinema. Ceferino's niece, the young Yolanda (Delia Garcés), is infatuated with Hollywood stars (a photo of Cary Grant hangs next to her bed), and instead of marrying the young settler Nicanor, she sneaks away (by train) to Buenos Aires to attend acting school, where she hopes to eventually triumph in the cinema.

The film is not at all averse to the possibility of social progress, despite the centrality of a modern version of the gaucho, who it instead employs in a social critique by showing the symbol of Argentinity as victim of structural economic injustice. There is no condemnation of modernity or technology—the settlers are able to get information on grain price fluctuations thanks to the radio, the road creates competition and ends the broker's monopoly—and no demonization of the immigrant. Instead the condemnation is of exploitation of the workers by the monopolizing *acopiador* and the corporate administration of the railroad in the interest of foreign capital. Thus the importance for this study of *Kilómetro 111* lies in the film's treatment of the train as a realist theme to be explored for its social and political implications—the need to modernize the territory—instead of as a mere syntactical element or symbol, as is the norm in the classical cinema.

In the film's key sequence, after Ceferino breaks company rules to advance the gauchos a line of credit so they can ship their grain to market and bypass the broker, his subterfuge is detected in an audit and he is summoned by the railway's board of directors. In front of a large map of the nation, he gives a speech in his own defense that encapsulates the film's imperative to move away from corporate capitalism's abstract conception of rural space: "El campo no es como aparece en los mapas, lisito, ni los ferrocarriles son rayas, ni las estaciones son puntos. Allí hay miseria, hay granizo, hay sequía y acopiadores. Uds. en mi lugar habrían hecho lo mismo" (The country isn't like it looks on the map, smooth, nor are the railways stripes, nor are the stations points. There's misery there, hail, drought, and brokers. In my place you'd have done the same).[14] But his simple eloquence is insufficient to overcome the gulf between the two ways of understanding space, because the executives are permitted to act only in the interest of the corporation's capital accumulation. While Ceferino has firsthand experience of the land and its local economies, the executives can only consider symbolic representation—lines, points, and numbers—of the movement of goods through a void, in an abstract conception of space. But since the corporate directors are obligated to accord a far greater epistemological status to the abstract representation than to the oral account of its inhabitant, Ceferino's speech does not move them to question capital's spatial abstractions. Through the obligatory dismissal of the perspective of those who inhabit and move through rural space, the corporate executives continue to conceive of the train solely in its function that facilitates capital accumulation through exploitation of the resources existing on the land, including the labor of its inhabitants. Since such logic disregards any possible grounds for solidarity, Ceferino is fired.

But here, as in many of his films, Soffici presages the coming rise in political importance of popular movements. Upon hearing the news of Ceferino's dismissal, the angered gaucho-*colonos* violently attack the station at Kilómetro 111 *en masse*, reconfiguring the often-domesticated symbol of Argentinity into an agent of popular power when pushed to desperation by economic exploitation. But social justice, and thus order, is eventually restored by the state through the road-building project. Earlier in the film Ceferino had complained bitterly about roads supplanting the railway, saying that "son un retroceso a la civilización" (they're a step backward for civilization), but now he has come over to a nationalistically correct position on the side of the automobile, as owner-operator of a service station sporting the iconic YPF sign that the *colonos* buy for him with their earnings.[15] The new roadway network is, then, represented as a step toward an economically just progress. This denouement activates the ethic of the *gauchada* that stresses the eventual benefits of solidarity in the face of inevitable exploitation at the hands of the economically powerful. Importantly, this gaucho-inspired ethic is not a call for a nostalgic return to the past, but an opening toward a progressive future that depends on the willingness of the state to challenge foreign capital in the interest of the *pueblo*.

The spatial configuration in *Kilómetro 111* is far more complex and engaged with reality than that of most films of its time. As discussed earlier in this chapter, in most classical Argentine films rural space is represented as homogeneous. But the particularities of space take on great significance in *Kilómetro 111*. It is important that this fertile pampa and train station lay at a distance from the city that would be easily traveled by automotive freight transport. This presents the colono-gauchos—unlike the typical *cuadro de costumbres* gaucho who inhabits a timeless, idealized pampa—as facing specific problems brought about by uneven modernity for which specific solutions can be addressed.

In the film, Buenos Aires is a "central place"—roughly following the terms of Walter Christaller's hierarchy of "central places" discussed by Franco Moretti—where important activities are exclusively located. These are sites of cultural production, corporate management, and markets for agricultural and cultural goods, all of which are absent in the lower-rank towns like Kilómetro 111. Two characters travel on the train to Buenos Aires. Yolanda goes there to find stardom in the film industry, while Ceferino goes to face the judgment of the railway board of directors (and to retrieve Yolanda). But even more important is the role of the train as carrier of freight: the wheat needs to get to market in Buenos Aires to be of value. The importance of this spatial hierarchy in the film cannot be overstated, since it provides the tension that generates all of the plot strands and contains the film's incisive spatial analysis. The distance between Kilómetro 111 and Buenos Aires, which would be easily overcome by road travel, is made greater in terms of relative space (as experienced by its inhabitants) by the railway monopoly and thus determines all of the possible tragic outcomes: the wheat harvest will be lost if not delivered to market, which will result in the death of the son of one of the *colonos* (he is sick and needs to undergo a modern medical procedure in Buenos Aires); if Yolanda continues to be seduced by the idea of film stardom she will surely end up a fallen woman in the capital city, leaving Ceferino in disgrace and Nicanor's projected family unrealized. *Kilómetro 111* tells, then, what Ian Duncan would call a "provincial" story, in which the local is defined by what it is lacking relative to the capital city, or "core area" (Moretti 1999, 15). One hundred eleven kilometers is the distance the grain needs to travel to market, Ceferino and Yolanda need to travel to the capital, and from which decisions are made that affect the destiny of the outpost of Kilómetro 111 and, ultimately, the distance between two poles of Argentine uneven modernity.

As Ceferino says when the governor's train rushes through the town without stopping, it is a "pueblo miserable, no lo conocen ni los maquinistas" (miserable town, even the train conductors don't know it). There is no discernable circular distribution of spaces that due to an importance of local economic forces would structure what Duncan calls a "village narrative" or a "regional novel," in which "the region is a place in itself . . . the source of its own terms of meaning and identity . . . while the province is defined by its difference from [the capital]" (qtd. in Moretti 2007, 52). The fact that this is a "province," not a "village" or "region," marks it as a disadvantaged pole of uneven modernization. In the 111-kilometer trajectory an internal border is crossed, one that is omnipresent in a classical Argentine cinema that steadfastly refuses to explore its implications. In the classical cinema, a voyage between Buenos Aires and rural space is always a trip back in time from the "core area" (Moretti 1999, 15) to an earlier stage of history, but this stage is almost invariably presented through a *costumbrismo*—as an idyllic space inhabited by domesticated gauchos—that nullifies any potential critique. *Kilómetro 111*, by contrast, shows how this internal border between modernity and underdevelopment exists in the interest of capital. The settlers live at the pole that is maintained as a source of cheap labor and agricultural production due to lack of access to modern technology. The son of the settler Don Pedro cannot get the operation he needs, and the only functioning transport technology is not only already premodern but is operated as a monopoly. In the film, the maintenance of this internal border allows those with access to technology and power to exploit rural space and labor. The roads, however, promise to erase this border and allow for a more even development, and the state is portrayed as the possible agent of such an economically just modernization, the sole force capable of countering capital's self-interested maintenance of marginal space as such.

At the meeting of the corporate board of the railway company, the director had complained that the state was not building roads perpendicular to their tracks, which might connect isolated spaces with their own railway stations and increase corporate profits (as today's neoliberal state might engineer a roadway network), but instead plotted the roads parallel to the railways in order to break their monopoly. Thus, by defending the *pueblo* from international capital, the state becomes the hero and the conditions are set for Ceferino's shift in allegiances. Where he had cursed the roadbuilders—"¡Sigan haciendo caminos, enemigos de la civilización!" (Keep making roads, enemies of civilization!)—after his switch in allegiance he declares that "¡El camino es la civilización! ¡El camino es el progreso!" (The road is civilization! The road is progress!). While it is one of the few classical films to thematize the exploitation of the rural poor and the redemptive capacity of the state, *Kilómetro 111* is also important for this study and for Argentine cinema history for its raising of certain questions regarding differing conceptions of space and the problem of representing these not only to a corporate board but also to an urban cinema audience. How to represent both the lived experiences of rural space and the international mechanisms of economic exploitation? This is a question that will not be fully taken up by the cinema until two decades later, by films that reject *Kilómetro 111*'s classical narrative form that, despite its progressive message, employs static, postcard-like compositions of landscapes that effectively neutralize film's capacity to document rural space. *Kilómetro 111* is, however, exceptional in its critical examination of both space and economics in the context of an industrial cinema that zealously avoided such troubled intersections.

National Spaces and Masculinities

The spatial conventions of the classical cinema intersected with other conventions, such as those of gender. An important cultural site of normalization, the classical Argentine cinema often negotiated masculinity along a rural–urban trajectory, by employing rural masculinity as a model of correction and rural space as a proving ground to normalize defective, urban masculinity. But the complex history of masculinity in the national culture needs to be taken into account in order to understand its manifestations in the cinema. In late nineteenth- and early twentieth-century Argentine culture, portrayals of masculinity tended to follow two prevalent models. The first is a somewhat remnant, nineteenth-century model described by Ignacio Sánchez Prado and Ana Peluffo as a "modelo civilizado de la masculinidad . . . basado en privilegios de clase que remitían a la posibilidad de hacer buen uso de los refinamientos de la cultura y de la moda" (civilized model of masculinity . . . based on class privileges that referred to the possibility of making good use of the refinements of culture and fashion) (12). The upper-class, sophisticated male is often positively valorized in literary texts of the nineteenth century, but with the nationalist return to the rural such an aristocratizing, European-modeled masculinity became less appealing and a frequent foil for new models of masculinity. The same authors describe the imperatives presented by such emergent models: "No ser como las mujeres, no ser infantil o no ser como los homosexuales son algunas de las consignas identitarias de una forma de masculinidad viril que se afianza en el imaginario sexo-genérico latinoamericano a principios del siglo XX" (To not be like women, not be infantile or not be like homosexuals are some of the identitary imperatives of a form of virile masculinity that was consolidated in the Latin American sex-gender imaginary at the beginning of the twentieth century) (13). In Argentina this model, which most often took the form of the emphatic masculinity of the gaucho, extended far beyond literary texts into mass culture and even advertising, as Elina Tranchini explains:

> Las imágenes de gauchos barbudos e inofensivos Moreiras son comunes en los anuncios y propagandas comerciales de las dos primeras décadas del Siglo XX, y parecen haber servido para aumentar las ventas de todo tipo de productos, incluidos los diarios y revistas, exaltando el gaucho, su fortaleza, destrezas y atributos, e invocando a los habitantes de la ciudad a imitar la

sencillez, la grandeza, y el espíritu de libertad del gaucho pampeano . . . (2000, 116)

The images of bearded gauchos and inoffensive Moreiras are common in the advertisements of the first two decades of the twentieth century, and they seem to have served to raise the sales of all types of products, including newspapers and magazines, by exalting the gaucho, his strength, skills, and attributes, and appealing to the inhabitants of the city to imitate the simplicity, the nobility, and the spirit of freedom of the gaucho of the Pampa.

As discussed in chapter 1, the proliferation of this gaucho model in the culture of the early twentieth century forms part of the backlash against the arrival of millions of immigrants from Europe. The resulting model of masculinity, its spread fueled by an incipient national consumerism, was in sharp contrast to the qualities of the urban consumers, as Carolina Rocha describes:

The association of national identity with the masculinities of rural men resulted in the perception that men residing in the cities—as well as the recently arrived immigrants—were not manly, a fact that quickly became a paradox as immigration and urbanization were both processes related to the country's modernization. As Argentina became a more diverse society, it was perceived as more feminine and modern by those who equated Argentineness with rural manhood. (5)

In the cinema the rural model of masculinity tended to be privileged over the urban, which was often used to caricature upper- or middle-class urban males as effeminate, economically and sexually unproductive, or otherwise insufficiently virile. This critique of urban masculinity marked it as distinct from that of the urban proletariat, which, given the cinema's commercial concerns, is unsurprising, since the bulk of the local audience was popular and urban (Karush).

Since the gaucho–upper-class opposition corresponded to rural and urban spaces, when the cinema thematized masculinity it often did so by telling stories that underlined conflicts between masculinities (as well as femininities) as a result of travel along an urban–rural trajectory, such as in *La rubia del camino*. These often relied on the new possibility of road travel to compress time and allow for contact between tradition and modernity. The prevailing convention is that this contact confirms the rural model and corrects the urban male, but not all films followed these conventions uncritically. Carlos Hugo Christensen's *Con el diablo en el cuerpo* (1947) lays bare this mechanism of normalization as it parodies traditional masculinities.

In the film, the urban male is portrayed as what Vito Russo, in *The Celluloid Closet*, calls a "sissy"—frivolous and asexual, that is (31)—and positioned as insufficient vis-à-vis rural masculinity, but these traditional models are undermined through comically hyperbolic displays of their attributes, at the same time that the urban model of masculinity is shown as more resourceful and better adapted to a modern Argentina. Also a road movie, *Con el diablo en el cuerpo* contrasts with *La rubia del camino* in that the couple is of the same social class—both wealthy, that is. This lack of popular presence within the couple allows the conflictive encounter brought about by travel to shift away from social class, to differentiated masculinities. As a result, *Con el diablo en el cuerpo* exemplifies how the Argentine industry was able to adapt Hollywood genres and their anticipatory models of spectatorship to local cultural specificities. The conventions are those of the screwball comedy genre, which prompts spectatorial desire for two heterosexual protagonists to form a couple, but in addition to such borrowings, in *Con el diablo en el cuerpo* a clear tension is evident between convention—both of gender and genre—and auteurist subversion. The agency of this subversion need not be attributed to any one figure, be it Carlos Hugo Christensen as director, César Tiempo as scriptwriter, or anyone else, since I am less concerned with identifying the agent than with examining how the conventions of genre are adapted to call into question those of masculinity proper to both Argentine culture and cinema more generally.

The conventional screwball comedy plot is driven by two characters, one male, the other female, who share an immediately evident sexual chemistry but are not in a romantic relationship when the film begins. The male, though marked as heterosexual, is often depicted as insufficiently masculine due to distraction or a lack of sexual interest in the heroine. In the classic example, Cary Grant's studious paleontologist in *Bringing Up Baby* (1938) is reconstructing a dinosaur skeleton, but has "lost his bone"—in non-metaphoric terms, the last bone needed to complete the skeleton—and is thus too distracted to respond to the romantic prompts of Katharine Hepburn's character. The genre dictates that the couple eventually form, and by the end of the film the Grant character has been normalized and marriage ensues. *Con el diablo en el cuerpo* follows these conventions, but inserts into them the cultural particularities of Argentina and adds a queer subtext for those prepared to understand it.

The seventeen-year-old *ingenua* is Valentina (Susana Freyre) and the male protagonist (Juan Carlos Thorry) is Severo Echeverri, a name that lays down a challenge to the masculinity of its bearer, who does not rise to it as the film opens. He is a single man, apparently uninterested in sexual activity of any kind. Under Perón, homosexuality officially did not exist, and though Severo's sexuality is left implicit he has many attributes of Hollywood's sissy as described by Russo. He exhibits a fussy concern for hygiene, flights into hysteria when confronted with female sexuality, and nervous tics that reveal an underlying emotional instability.

When asked by his godfather, Jupiter Uriondo, when he plans to get married, Severo responds, "No me casaré nunca, el matrimonio es antihigiénico" (I will never marry, matrimony is unhygienic). His character exposition includes several other details that reveal a lack of heterosexual inclination, such as in an early sequence when the attractive, apparently virginal Dorotea winks seductively at him and he reacts with visible panic, failing to respond to the prompt. In another detail, he responds to an insinuation by Valentina that he has had past affairs by declaring "Se equivoca señora, soy vegetariano" (You're mistaken, ma'am, I'm a vegetarian). But Jupiter, his granddaughter Valentina, and a small community of conspicuously single men conspire to normalize Severo so that he will marry Valentina. They invent a ruse—that Valentina and her new husband, Carlos, are set to honeymoon in the provinces, but she missed her flight and Severo must drive her there—in order to trick him into taking her on an improvised road trip. The resulting voyage provides the premise for encounters with models of hyperbolic rural masculinity that engage Severo in tests of skill that respond to what Sánchez Prado and Peluffo (after Elisabeth Badinter) describe as "la obsesión constante del sujeto masculino viril por hacer visible su fortaleza por medio de complicadas pruebas, sacrificios y competencias . . ." (the constant obsession of the virile masculine subject with making his strength visible through complicated challenges, sacrifices, and competitions . . .) (8). These encounters eventually succeed in normalizing Severo and bringing him together with Valentina, but the film does not play this process completely straight, providing a subtext that parodies these models of masculinity and the mechanism of normalization itself.

Severo's lack of heterosexual initiative is, it could be said, out of the closet when in the company of fellow non-normative family members and friends that make up the community that, evidently at the behest of Valentina, will conspire to set up his marriage with her. All are relatives of Valentina. Jupiter is her grandfather, the unnamed painter is her cousin, and Carlos is her brother. With the intent of mediating desire on the part of Severo for Valentina, they set up a fictional heterosexual triangle in which Carlos plays the role of her husband. While the male conspirators are all related, on the level of subtext they form a community united in non-normativity, all corresponding to Russo's description of the sissy. In addition to an evident lack of romantic relationships with women, they are represented as doing little or nothing that could be understood as socially productive, in the sense of contributing to economic progress or "populating the desert," as Alberdi called for a century earlier. Jupiter is the first conspirator we meet. Despite references to him as Valentina's grandfather, no evidence of a wife or children is seen or mentioned. When we first see him he is alone in his luxurious apartment, blowing bubbles with a child's toy and clearly exuberant at the resulting spectacle. His artist grandson is the next conspirator, and the one most explicitly characterized as a sissy, through both mannerisms and mise-en-scène. When we first see him, he admiringly refers to his own painting as "surrealismo puro," but when we see the painting it seems clearly meant by the filmmakers to be a parody of avant-garde art. Later, in an instance of queering by mise-en-scène, he is placed in profile in a close-up facing a strategically placed model airplane that only the least capable of understanding would fail to see as a phallic metaphor. The remaining male conspirator, Carlos, is presented as Valentina's fiancé, though we later find out that he is really her brother and a constant companion of her painter cousin. Through these depictions, what could be called a queer community is formed in which the principal attributes of hegemonic masculinity—economic production and sexual reproduction (national imperatives proclaimed by Alberdi and Sarmiento)—are conspicuously absent.

Valentina, we eventually find out, is the final participant in the conspiracy that will only be revealed at the end of the film, though in hindsight its machinations are fairly obvious: In the opening sequence, while Severo is visiting Jupiter's apartment, Valentina receives a phone call from her new husband. She exaggerates her affection, kissing him through the phone and calling him pet names, and informs Severo that she is scheduled to fly to La Falda (province of Córdoba) that same day to honeymoon. But when she misses her flight, the conspirators recruit Severo to drive her there, setting the two on a road trip that puts them in contact with the exaggerated models of rural masculinity that will eventually normalize Severo and result in their marriage.

The exemplary rural *machos* will be two, a gaucho and a "turco," Ireneo Pedernera and Ahmed Berajá, respectively, both primitively masculine and hyper-reproductive to the point of parody. They will appear after the introduction of the nonreproductive urban males, which establishes an intrinsic urban masculine norm and with it an urban perspective from which the exaggerated heteronormativity of the rural males will be defamiliarized, marked as hyperbolically displaying the attributes of supposed normalcy.

After the initial sequence that takes place in Buenos Aires, where apparently all males are both economically and sexually unproductive, the protagonists set out on the road trip. They soon suffer two flat tires, and as a result encounter the film's first exemplar of hyperbolic masculinity, the gaucho Ireneo Pedernera.[16] Ireneo offers Severo and Valentina a ride in his jalopy and invites them to his ranch, near a town where a *fiesta criolla* (creole festival) is in progress. As part of the festivities Severo is obligated to undergo a series of gendered challenges. Some of these are sexually suggestive, such as climbing the *palo enjabonado* (a ritual in which, in order to obtain homosocial approval, a man straddles an oiled erect pole, grips it with his arms and legs, and attempts to shimmy his way to the top), or eating a massive piece of meat (following on Severo's sexually loaded claim to vegetarianism). Other challenges are more explicitly heterosexual: Severo and Valentina are made to sleep in a bed that is a locus of sublime reproductivity, in which Ireneo claims he sexually initiated his wife (the intimidatingly named Robustiana) and in which their fourteen children were conceived and born. Coming as they do after the establishment of the perspective of the initial urban community of unproductive males, these hyperbolic representations of the rituals and attributes of normative masculinity appear as parody, and all the while that Severo is undergoing these challenges, Thorry—Argentina's foremost romantic-comedic lead and a talented physical comedian—plays up his discomfort through the kind of facial and bodily tics that Russo identifies with the cinematic sissy.

The discourse with which Ireneo Pedernera introduces Severo and Valentina to the bed they will sleep in (Valentina has told him they are on their honeymoon) engages with rural masculinity's exemplarity as compliant with the reproductive imperative that fueled the national modernizing project: "Aquí pasamos la noche de bodas con la patrona. ¿Te acordás, muchacha? Aquí nacieron nuestros catorce hijos" (Right here we spent our wedding night, the boss and I. Remember, girl? Right here our fourteen children were born). Then to Severo with a nudge: ¿A ver cómo se porta, mi doctor? Recuerde lo que dijo Sarmiento: 'La Argentina no será grande hasta que tenga cien millones de habitantes'!" (Let's see how you behave, sir. Remember what Sarmiento said: Argentina won't be great until it has a hundred million inhabitants!). Reference to such imperatives appears to triangulate desire in Severo, and he soon begins to betray an attraction to Valentina, which intensifies during the next stage of the road trip. But the next stop offers new complications in the form of other women who will both intensify Severo's heterosexual desire and redirect it.

This final site of challenges for Severo comes after yet another automobile incident, this time a roll-over accident near their destination of La Falda, the name of which has begun to take on a metaphoric function as Severo's new virility blooms. He and Valentina are given a ride by an enthusiastically heterosexual young man, Alí, who brings them to his father's country mansion. The father is Ahmed Moisés Berajá, and his exotic identity as a Moslem allows for the introduction of orientalized models of hyperbolic masculinity and femininity, both of which pose further challenges to Severo. Berajá is introduced sitting in the living room of his rural mansion, smoking a water pipe and shooting targets with a pistol. Then his ten daughters enter. Contrary to Western stereotypes, they are hypersexualized and very modern young women, but these qualities seem to go unnoticed by their father. All are attractive, scantily dressed, and dance athletically to American swing music. In contrast to the earlier stop, here it is assumed that Valentina is Severo's daughter, which allows for further plot complications and opportunities for humor. As Alí pursues Valentina, showering her with compliments and eventually asking her to marry him, the attention that Ahmed's abundant daughters lavish on Severo soon completes his normalization. As he declares his lust for Angora, the principal figure among the daughters, any remaining doubts about his masculinity are dispelled. But since such a coupling would be contrary to screwball comedy genre conventions, the jealous Valentina convinces Ahmed that Severo is really the lusty demon Asmodeo, which forces Severo and Valentina to flee the armed and suddenly murderous *paterfamilias*. With Angora left behind, a final encumbrance to the resolution of genre convention remains: Valentina's *flamante* husband and their impending honeymoon.

But we soon find out that Valentina's purported marriage was merely part of the conspiracy, and when the now resolutely heterosexual Severo marries her in the final sequence, we see the screwball comedy fulfill its generic expectations even as the subtext involving the queer community becomes more explicit. The non-normative, sympathetic males that have helped Valentina in her quest to seduce Severo are the only guests at the wedding, and the only female present is the bride. This would seem to establish clearly that none of the males present have significant others, unless they form couples among themselves, which, given the context, is the most readily assumed conclusion. The sexuality of Valentina's brother Carlos is now defined negatively, as *not* Valentina's husband, and his closeness to her cousin leaves implicit, but just barely so, a non-normative sexual relationship.

Despite heterosexual generic demands, the film's critique extends to the very imperative of heterosexual marriage. In a slightly earlier sequence, in which Severo and Valentina have just committed to marriage, a subtle commentary is visible. Severo, worried that they are now fugitives (he is not yet in on the ruse), is seen on a train hiding behind a newspaper he and Valentina pretend to read. As the camera tracks forward to show Severo present their tickets to the conductor, a cartoon printed in the newspaper becomes visible: In a domestic scene, a woman throws a bottle that hits a man in the back of the head. But another detail is key: the man in the cartoon is hidden behind a newspaper, as Severo is hidden at that moment. Does this mise-en-abîme further subvert the conventional heterosexual domesticity of the happy ending of the screwball comedy?

Such subtexts may be intended for a limited sector of the public, one prepared to understand them, and by the end of the film Severo's is a docile, productive body, one well suited for national priorities as a heterosexual and future family man. But it could be argued that in its ironization of rural normative masculinities and its sympathetic representation of the non-normative conspirators, *Con el diablo en el cuerpo* formulates, and to a degree legitimizes, an alternative model of urban queer masculinity. While it is certainly relevant that the non-normative community is depicted positively, it is of equal importance that in the film the antagonistic opposition between queer and heterosexual masculinities is neutralized, since in the film the ingenuity of the former is needed in order for the latter to be reproductive. While the community of conspirators is clearly not a procreative one, it plays a necessary role in the formation of the central couple and its procreative future. This contribution subverts the model of masculinity that relies on an opposition in which rural masculinity is the positively inflected, productive and reproductive pole, and urban masculinity is negatively inflected as economically and sexually unproductive. The national master imperative of procreation, even as it remains intact, is parodied through hyperbole in the exemplars of rural masculinity. This parodied rural masculinity is answered with an urban masculinity shown not only sympathetically, but as sophisticated and resourceful, capable of the kind of ingenuity and subterfuge needed to realize the conspiracy that leads to the marriage and, importantly in the content of this genre film, the gratification of spectatorial desires.

An examination of the historical context of the film further situates its significance in the context of the national culture. Rural folklore had played a prominent role since the Centenary, and had been made official state policy under Perón. According to Oscar Chamosa, the five-year plan of 1947 (the year of the film's release) recommended "action to preserve oral poetry, dances, and music from the countryside and the design of programs to educate all citizens about the criollo traditions through school lessons, festivals, and radio broadcasts" (114). As a result of these policies, "a generation of Argentines grew up learning that the culture of the rural criollo from the interior constituted the authentic manifestation of Argentine nationality" (114). Within such a context, the parody of gauchesque culture—a central element of official Peronist cultural policy—seen in *Con el diablo en el cuerpo* takes on a more immediate critical resonance.

While a definitive account of the film's reception seems to not exist, the few references to it point to a possibly problematic encounter with state power under Perón. Despite being directed by Christensen, one of the foremost directors of the time, and featuring the star power of Thorry and Freyre, the film goes unmentioned even in comprehensive national film histories that detail the work of Christensen, such as those of Maranghello and Peña.[17] Kelly Hopfenblatt and Trombetta note that the film suffered direct censorship under Perón, as two lines of dialog spoken by Thorry were ordered cut (260), and the film received the commercially limiting qualifications of "No apta para menores de catorce años" (Not apt for children under fourteen years of age) and "Inconveniente para menores de dieciocho años" (Inappropriate for minors under eighteen years of age) (Manrupe and Portela 126). While this evidence is merely anecdotal, it could point to state censorship arising from its takes on masculinity and folklore, and certainly creates intrigue around the film's absence from cinema historiography.

The Urban Margins and the End of the Classical Cinema: From *Arrabal* to *Villa*

With the overthrow of Perón in 1955 and the sudden suspension of state subsidies to the industry by the self-named "Revolución Libertadora," the classical cinema studios entered into a crisis that only one would survive with its production facilities intact (Peña 130).[18] With this crisis the conventional representation of the margins of the capital city as *arrabal* broke down. The classical cinema's tango-film genre setting, a neighborhood that existed purely as nostalgic fiction, began to cede to representations of the margins of the city as *villa miseria*, acknowledging the existence of a space that had been ignored by the studio cinema despite its existence in reality since the 1930s.[19] That decade had seen the beginning of a wave of migration internal to Argentina, and many of the newcomers, unable to afford housing in the city, set up precarious *ranchos* on its margins. These spaces coexisted with a classical cinema that did not acknowledge them or, on rare occasions, distorted them through a *costumbrista* lens, as seen in Luis César Amadori and Soffici's 1936 *Puerto Nuevo*. The reasons behind this omission are no mystery, given commercial interests and the history of state pressure to not depict Argentina in an unflattering light, but toward the mid-1950s radical changes to the political situation caused the *villa* to begin to appear on film in more critically charged ways.

These portrayals of the urban margin are no longer inflected by nostalgia, and transform it instead into a space from which its fictional inhabitants try to escape at all costs. Instead of a cause for lament, as was the lost *arrabal* of tango lyrics and films, its eradication became a national imperative. But despite such intentions, these spaces were destined to take on an increasingly visible role in Argentine social reality and in mass culture's representations of it. Instead of fading into nostalgia in the face of an inexorable progress, the *villa* was to grow in territorial extension, population, cultural visibility, and reputation to become a ready source of fear for the residents of today's city. Its name changed through time, from *barrio gris* to *villa de emergencia* to, eventually, *villa miseria* (the latter coined by Bernardo Verbitsky in his 1957 novel *Villa Miseria también es América*) around the time that the cinema began to acknowledge its existence, with León Klimovsky's *Suburbio* (1951), Soffici's *Barrio gris* (1954), and Lucas Demare's *Detrás de un largo muro* (1958).

Gonzalo Aguilar calls the *villa* films of the 1950s a "ciclo de la visión moderna sobre las villas que tiene como horizonte imaginario su erradicación definitiva y su reemplazo por edificios confortables y limpias" (cycle of a modern view of the *villas* that envisions their definitive eradication and replacement with comfortable and clean buildings) (2013, *La representación*). But while the underlying imperative present in all of these films is that of the improvement or eradication of the *villa*, each reflects the political particularities of its time, in denunciations of cynical populist uses of the *villa* by politicians as well as of the kind of state negligence that will continue to be a concern through the 1960s and beyond.

The period of the breakdown of the classical and the appearance of the new cinemas in the mid- to late 1950s can also be seen, then, as a gradual transition in which films set in the *villa miseria* contribute to the cultivation of a new spectatorial gaze that inquires about the national reality. Seen in this way, the shift in spatial representation from the nostalgia-inflected *arrabal* to the politicized exploration of the margins is of central importance, since it represents a shift away from the cinema as the classical escapist dream machine toward being a window onto the national reality. Although mostly in keeping with the melodramatic tone and conventional mise-en-scène of the studio cinema, these *villa*-set narrative films already blur the boundaries between fiction and documentation by filming at times on location and using some nonprofessional actors. These relatively new strategies in the context of 1950s Argentina—though they were regularly practiced in the 1910s—are in step with the wider influence that Italian neorealism was having at the time. In criticism on Argentine cinema, they are strategies almost exclusively identified with the later Nuevo Cine, despite their earlier appearance in these semi-industrial productions.

The first was Klimovsky's *Suburbio*, released while Perón was in power, in 1951. In part shot on location in the marginal neighborhood of Avellaneda, as Kriger points out, the story is marked as taking place before the Peronist period (by a glimpse of a newspaper headline). The film is much more classic melodrama than realist social critique, and its political vision is conservative, combining calls for charity and individual responsibility with pessimism about the capacity and willingness of the state to bring about social progress. Its protagonist is an upper-class woman doctor, Amalia, who in an earlier, more frivolous stage of her life had struck and killed a local child while speeding in her car. Motivated by guilt, she has since dedicated herself to working humbly in order to improve the conditions of the *suburbio*. As such, she is now redeemed in the eyes of the viewer and possesses the moral authority to verbalize the film's message, which she does by subjecting two young delinquents to a discourse on hard work and individual responsibility: "Los dos son flojos porque no tienen el coraje de luchar para salir del barro trabajando y siendo decente" (You two are lazy because you don't have the courage to struggle to get out of the mud by working and being decent). As a doctor, Amalia is the representative of a science still capable of regarding modernization with optimism, but she is forced to carry out the struggle by herself, since no help is forthcoming from the state until a plague breaks out in the rat-infested neighborhood and threatens the nearby middle-class sectors. When the state belatedly makes itself present, the *villa* is quarantined and fumigated. Left unresolved is whether or not the metaphoric "barro" (mud) of the *suburbio* will prove stronger than the state's efforts to bring about progress, but it is clearly suggested that only a threat to middle-class space can prompt the state to act.

A central theme is whether or not science, personified by Amalia, is capable of saving the *suburbio*. In a climactic scene, Laura, a young local woman, is stricken with disease, and as Amalia tries to cure her and spread the warning, a carnival scene surrounds her with music and dancing in a grotesque key. In this highly expressionist sequence, the spectator is prompted to identify with Amalia's perspective, from which the irrational forces subsume, thus inextricably associate, disease and the popular classes. The challenge posed to science and progress is so serious that eventually Amalia herself dies of the plague. This pessimistic climax inevitably leads to questions about censorship under the Peronist state, since despite the brief indication of the story taking place in the past, this is certainly no laudatory depiction of Argentina or of the state. Clara Kriger gives an account of a more optimistic, but lost, ending that had been added to please the Peronist censors, in which the state has successfully transformed the area into a model workers' neighborhood. According to Kriger, this ending was destroyed soon after Perón's overthrow by the Revolución Libertadora, which was clearly not interested in the celebration of any such projects that might have benefitted neighborhoods populated by Peronism's base of support.

The next film of the *villa miseria* cycle is Soffici's *Barrio gris*, also filmed and screened under Peronism, in 1954, and required to include frame sequences that show a present of "casas blancas, humildes pero honradas y modernas, y . . . parques de juegos llenos de niños" (white houses, humble but honorable and modern, and . . . playgrounds full of children) (España 48). But between these framing sequences, the film's setting is a neighborhood stricken with infrastructure problems, flooding, and a dangerous criminal element. Despite these conditions, and although the members of the film's protagonic family all dream of moving to a middle-class quarter, their present neighborhood appears very different from the *villa miseria* documented later in the decade, and the film does not appear to be shot on location. But despite what appears to be studio filmmaking, Soffici and fellow scriptwriter Joaquín Gomes Bas did not write the script with actors in mind, as was the usual practice in the classical cinema, but chose actors later and ended up using nonprofessionals for some of the roles, according to Paula Halperin, who also reports that in the Argentine media *Barrio gris* was associated with neorealism and considered to be an open challenge to the industry's established production model (131). But a shift in production model is only partially evident upon watching the film, which treats the neighborhood with some of the nostalgia seen earlier in tango films and lyrics and employs a storyline more proper to the cinematic *arrabal* than to the *villa*, in which a young delinquent protagonist finds true love with the innocent girl next door. Nor has the visual representation of the *villa* in *Barrio gris* broken away from the classical model, as the false poverty bears a closer resemblance to the *costumbrismo* of *Puerto Nuevo* than the location shooting of Lucas Demare's *Detrás de un largo muro*, which would be released only four years later. In terms of spatial representation in the classical cinema more generally, *Barrio gris* could be considered a transitional film, a timid step away from remnant practices of representing marginal space.

Demare's *Detrás de un largo muro* (1958) was made and screened in what Pamela C. Gionco (following Claudio España) describes as an interregnum: "Entre 1956 y 1959 hay un interregno, un lapso de tiempo donde conviven el texto clásico en crisis y las emergencias del texto moderno" (Between 1956 and 1959 there is an interregnum, a period in which the classical text in crisis and the emergence of the modern text coexist) (269). We have already seen how this crisis might be traced beyond the period delimited by Gionco, to the *villa*-set films made earlier in the 1950s, but this transition is intensified between 1956 and 1959, driven by what she describes as the

> imperiosa necesidad, por parte de los directores y de los guionistas, de representar el pasado inmediato, o bien el tiempo presente, plasmando su particular interpretación de los acontecimientos contemporáneos, marcando una posición ideológica ante el conflicto político. (Gionco 270)

> pressing need, on the part of directors and scriptwriters, to represent the immediate past, or the present time, giving expression to their particular interpretation of contemporary events, staking out an ideological position regarding the political conflict.

The political conflict referred to is that of the last several years of Peronism and its overthrow, which is in fact a double crisis, industrial and political, that both dried up finding and released producers and directors from the conditions imposed by the studio system and state subsidies. Many of the studio directors were opposed to Perón, an animosity that produced an imperative to engage critically with national reality that is seen clearly in the film made by Demare, who Gionco describes as a radicalized anti-Peronist, in reference to his vehemence and willingness to criticize the Peronist project. This position is manifested in the novel representation of space in *Detrás de un largo muro*, a treatment that makes it the film of the cycle that most incisively addresses the problem of visibility and the shifting field of representability. The title describes the barrier between the film's *villa de emergencia* (as it is referred to in the film) and the highway that passes alongside, a wall constructed as part of Perón's *mise-en-scène* of successful national modernity in order to make poverty invisible to the eyes of passing motorists.

A brief synopsis should make the political intentions of the film clear: a young woman, Rosita, played by Susana Campos, and her father live on a farm near a small town on the pampa, from which most of the population has migrated to Buenos Aires. Rosita's knowledge of the city is heavily mediated by what she hears on the radio and reads in letters from a friend who moved to the capital, which makes her, like Yolanda in *Kilómetro 111*, long for the attractions of the city. When a truck driver, Andrés, breaks down near their farm, he and Rosita fall in love, but he soon has to leave to complete a delivery, promising to return for her as soon as he can. Before that can happen, her bankrupt father is forced to sell the farm, and they move to the capital. She is initially pleased to do so, but when they arrive at the *villa de emergencia*, the ironically named Villa Jardín, she is shocked by the conditions in which they are forced to live. During a horrifying stay they get mixed up unknowingly with a band of auto thieves, one of whom murders her father. Eventually Andrés finds her, and the film ends with Rosita boarding a bus to meet him in the provincial town of Pergamino, in a somewhat happy ending.

But the film's storyline is less important than its treatment of space. The strident tone of Demare's anti-Peronism was evident two years earlier in his propaganda film *Después del silencio*—in which Peronist thugs persecute and torture those in opposition—and *Detrás de un largo muro* is a clear repudiation of Peronism's encouraging of internal immigration to the capital. This repudiation is seen in the film's depiction of media portrayals that lead to Rosita's fantasies of Buenos Aires, the state's attempts to hide, rather than eliminate, the squalor of the *villa*, and the political use of the *villa* in photo opportunities of highly publicized but never-undertaken improvement projects. At one point a sharply dressed politician and his entourage make a brief visit, during which he pronounces a discourse: "... y en lugar de estos infectos pantanos, pronto veremos levantarse aquí viviendas dignas y confortables. ¡Y ahora, señores, la foto!" (... in place of these infectious marshes, soon we will witness the building of decent and comfortable dwellings. And now, sirs, the photo!). Needless to say, in Demare's film ground is never broken for the new houses.

The vehemence of the film's anti-Peronism leads it to an antimodern spatial opposition that surpasses credibility at moments, an unconvincing diegesis in which rural *costumbrismo* coexists with urban realism. Near the end of the film, all of the migrants from Rosita's town have decided to return from the city, and Rosita herself has abandoned Buenos Aires for the town of Pergamino to live with Andrés. In this amalgam of the old *costumbrista* notion of rural space with a vehemently realist critique of Peronism's internal immigration policies, the interior is inhabited by good-natured innocents who are driven to the city by a faulty economy in combination with an absent state, then driven back from a *villa* represented in an almost neorealist mode.

Wide panoramic location shots of the *villa* are seen, a fact notable in a film by this classical director who had previously participated in the cinema's avoidance of documenting marginal space. Such decisions are due to the film's will to repudiate Peronism's discourse of a *Nueva Argentina* in which poverty had been eradicated, a repudiation that Rosita, her eyes opening to social reality, puts into words:

> Cada vez que venimos al centro Villa Jardín me parece más horrible. Me cuesta más volver a los ranchos de lata ... al mal olor de los pantanos. Yo soñaba con Buenos Aires, ahora la odio. Es muy linda por afuera, muchas luces, mucho lujo, y detrás ... esos barrios malditos. Es como una mujer hermosa que tuviera un cáncer.

> Each time we come downtown Villa Jardín seems more horrible. It's more difficult to return to the tin shacks ... to the stench of the marshes. I used to dream of Buenos Aires, now I hate it. It's very beautiful from outside, so many lights, so much luxury, and behind ... those wretched neighborhoods. It's like a beautiful woman who has cancer.

In this passage is seen one pole of the old rural–urban opposition of the revisionism of Lugones and others, in which urban space is barbarized as the rural is pastoralized. In terms of space, the film's gaze is both inquisitive and politically predetermined, an attempt to open the spectator's eyes to nearby misery and nail shut the coffin of a recently deposed Peronism, which nonetheless would rise again and again, qua vampire or redeemer, depending on one's perspective. But in the process Demare managed to produce a metaphor for the previous three decades of the national culture's treatment of the urban margins at the same time that he contributed to the demolition of this same "largo muro."

These three films of the 1950s *villa miseria* cycle are striking in that they possess qualities associated with both studio classicism and Nuevo Cine innovation and realism. But it makes less sense to see them as belonging to either mode—classical or modern—than as individual responses to the beginning of the end of the established industrial mode of production, a demise that opened up room for more autonomous and ideologically varied work. Seen in this way, these films can be considered a hinge that, intentionally or not, opened the door for the next generation.[20] The breakdown of the line between fiction and nonfiction is evident in their location shooting and use of nonprofessional actors, but most important is their shift in attitude toward the national space, their will to thematize and document marginal spaces and marginalized people that had been ignored by the industrial cinema, and by doing so spur the spectator to inquire about what lies behind the metaphoric "largo muro" that had framed the national culture's field of representability. The continuation of these transformations will be the subject of the following chapter, but first a brief detour to another film of Demare will be necessary, this time one set in a rural space.

Despite these efforts to problematize the *villa*, the remnant classical conventions of spatial representation persisted beyond the demise of the studios. This is seen clearly in another film directed by Demare, *Zafra* (1959), which, while notable for its clearly delivered indictment of uneven modernization, exploitation of indigenous labor, local corruption, and repressive state violence, stubbornly insists on conventional representations of its rural settings and on its almost comical use of white actors in indigenous roles. Although the credits proclaim the appearance of "auténticos trabajadores de la zafra jujeña" (authentic workers from the Jujuy sugar harvest), these are relegated to laboring as extras, while Graciela Borges stars as the indigenous blanket seller Damiana, *prometida* of Alfredo Alcón's Teodoro, both in unconvincing brownface.

The story exposes a mechanism by which a ruthless sugar plantation owner, in connivance with a corrupt state, uses debt servitude to obligate the inhabitants of the *altiplano* to migrate to his lowland plantation to labor on the cane harvest. As the film puts in the landowner's mouth without subtlety: "La Puna es nuestro criadero de peones baratos" (The Puna is our farm of cheap laborers). As edifying as it may be to denounce such structural violence, the casting is indicative of the limitations presented by the classical cinema's remnant conventions, which by the late 1950s were coexisting with the emergent forms that will be discussed in the next chapter. The nonspeaking roles that populate the abundant location shots employ indigenous nonprofessionals, while the parts that require dialog employ white actors in brownface betrayed by notably metropolitan accents. This repetition of Alcides Greca's casting strategy in the narrative section of *El último malón* forty years earlier produces what must have been a very different effect after neorealism's successful use of nonprofessionals in starring roles. While Borges, sporting long braids and a bowler hat, does her best to act like a submissive Indian, avoiding men's eyes by looking at her feet and maintaining a forced smile, she is far from convincing in the role. In general, the indigenous characters are infantilized, portrayed as naïve victims of transparent machinations of the greedy whiter characters. The film seems a product of conflicting goals: an indictment of the continuation through the Peronist period of uneven modernization and the economic exploitation of the subaltern classes, along with a remnant, costly production model that requires the attraction of star actors. Alcón was already an established leading man in commercial cinema, Borges had appeared in Fernando Ayala's *El jefe* the year before, and the long-famous Atahualpa Yupanqui is cast as a singing and guitar-playing doctor doing his best to contain a tuberculosis outbreak among the cane cutters.

The film performs cultural sensitivity, but in the end its conventional production employs the indigenous in the same paternalistic, neocolonized way that the plantation owner does, as subordinated bodies and faces never to be given a voice. Despite its location shooting, the film combines a mostly conventional mode of representing rural space with remnant strategies to appeal to the demands of a wide public—charismatic star actors, received ideas about the indigenous, denunciation of rural caudillos in the sugar-producing internal-other provinces of Argentina. The film resurrects strategies and storylines used by Greca and Soffici decades earlier, but in a present in which new sectors of the Argentina cinema were already developing modes of film production and viewing that more effectively employed the documentary possibilities of the medium to satisfy a greater curiosity about the national space. This new, inquisitive mode, discussed in the following chapter, will produce some of the most enduring examinations of marginal space in the history of the national cinema.

Chapter 3

An Inquisitive Gaze on the Nation

The opening three shots of the "El País" ("The Country") chapter of *La hora de los hornos* (Fernando Solanas and Octavio Getino, 1968) employ a zoom lens to make visible, then invisible, the human inhabitants of what had been represented as *desierto* in the literary texts of the nineteenth century. Each shot begins as a wide landscape carefully composed around a person and their livestock. In the first, a human figure and several animals walk in the distance along a road crossing a wide plain as mountains loom in the background. This framing is held static for several seconds, then a rapid zoom-out reframes another composition, this one a far longer shot, in which walker and animals are no longer visible and the already wide plain is revealed to be exponentially wider. Two similar shots follow: a shepherd on a ridge disappears into a wide sloping hillside, then another shepherd on a road is made invisible against an immense mountainous landscape. This use of scale produces a perceptual effect similar to that which Kant described as the mathematical sublime, rendering for the viewer a space of a magnitude and diversity far beyond that which can be comprehended. The documentary confirmation that such enormous spaces are inhabited triggers a stark epistemological shift regarding the national space, as the easily understood totalization of *costumbrismo* gives way to sublime unknowability, and the knowing gaze cedes to an inquisitive gaze that thirsts for knowledge.

Coming eight minutes into the four-hour film, these three shots show the viewer that what might appear to be a desert from a distance is only so if seen through civilized eyes and camera. If seen through any other gaze, from any other perspective, the nation, no longer knowable, prompts a questioning, inquisitive gaze. A viewing experience such as that of the sequence described generates an imperative of curiosity, a call to an inquisitive mode of spectatorship left unsatisfied and uncomfortable by the conventionalisms, erasures, and *costumbrismos* with which the classical cinema had in the previous decades left its audience satisfied and comforted. An inquisitive spectator might instead wonder what (and who) lies beyond the frame, behind the camera, or invisible against the landscape. Such a spectator makes possible the remarkable expansion of the field of representability in the Argentine cinema that took place from the late 1950s until the frame was slammed shut in the mid-1970s by the Peronist right wing and the military dictatorship.

This brief sequence from *La hora de los hornos* is emblematic of the *Cine Liberación* project's often-stated intention to use the cinema to form new spectators who would be political subjects capable of participating in the transformation of the national space, but such an intention is by no means limited to the work of Solanas and Getino, or even *Cine Liberación*.[1] The story of the inquisitive gaze begins earlier, even before Fernando Birri explored the urban margins, David José Kohon brought the camera on a train to explore those previously elided spaces, and Lautaro Murúa demonstrated how, for reasons of race, economics, or gender, some inhabit the margins even when they are in the city center. An inquisitive gaze is felt awakening in the *villa*-set films of the late-Peronist period, and its effects will extend beyond the socially committed cinema, into the commercial cinema made in implicit support of the dictatorships and even beyond, as we will see later in this chapter. But its most intensely transformative works are those of the New Cinema of the 1960s, which Ana M. López characterizes in terms of its intentions

> a desire to change the social function of the cinema, to transform [it] into an instrument of change and of consciousness-raising . . . a social practice that revels in the diversity and multiplicity of its efforts to create an "other" cinema with "other" social effects as a prerequisite of its principle goal to reveal and analyze the "reality," the underdevelopment and national characteristics, that decades of dependency have concealed. (1997, 139)

The imperative to produce social effects that resulted in new, inquisitive, politically charged gazes will be traced in this chapter.

A curiosity about people and places never seen before in Argentine cinema implies a consciousness of the erasures established and jealously policed by the canonical discourses on the national space, as well as a profound desire to overcome them. But of course the inquisitive gaze does not refer only to the side of film production, but also its reception. Whereas the classical cinema, so dependent on the conventions of genre and on normalizing state subsidies, catered to the spectator's expectations as if they were fixed, even preferring that they remain so in its own economic interest, the new cinemas bet on change, on altering the way the spectator looked at the image. It goes without saying that a change in the social function of cinema requires a change in its spectator, the creation of a new spectator who would consume in a more active way the images and sounds that represent the nation.

Even though the new cinemas usually remained less visible and with relatively limited distribution relative to the commercial cinema, I would argue that the creation of a new spectator—one not content to merely look for information that might forward the narrative or confirm his or her knowledge about the nation—is clearly reflected in their form, and that this new, inquisitive spectator produced in turn a counter-response both thematic and formal by the more commercial cinema, a response that has gone unexamined and which, due to the limited scope of this book, I will only begin to explore. But first I will examine the films that contributed to the formation of the inquisitive gaze.

In my account of the cinema of the inquisitive gaze I am deliberately avoiding the use of the term "counter-cinema," because this type of conceptualization implies a rigid political position that might exclude the work of certain filmmakers, such as Jorge Preloran and Eva Landeck, and which would be unable to account for the eventual appropriation and redirection—in a kind of reactionary *détournement*—of inquisitive formal practices by a more commercial cinema that is clearly not oppositional. While the genesis of an inquisitive gaze cannot be traced unequivocally, it will be worth examining the Argentine cultural field of the period in which it began to take on importance. The inquisitive gaze appears to spring from a productive tension in the culture of the late 1950s and early '60s between cultural modernization, in the form of aesthetic experiment and increased political commitment, and periods of authoritarian repression, in the form of military coups that make the frame of representability explicit and drive spectators and cultural producers into a questioning mode.

According to Paula Félix-Didier, by the 1950s Argentine cinema was widely seen as increasingly distanced from national realities, trapped in a spiral into irrelevance:

Desde la década del 40, los estudios se asentaban sobre una forma de relato y convenciones de puesta en escena que, con el paso del tiempo, no fueron cuestionados y quedaron vacías de sentido. Ya sea por la comodidad que a partir de 1948 les brindó la intervención económica del Estado, o por simple inepcia, una mayoría de productores y realizadores se limitaron a prolongar un modo de hacer cine que ya estaba agotándose en todas partes del mundo. (2003, Introducción 12)

Since the 1940s, the studios settled into a form of story and a conventional mise-en-scène that through time were not questioned and ended up being meaningless. For reasons of convenience, since after 1948 the state intervened economically, or out of simple ineptitude, the majority of the producers and directors limited themselves to prolonging a mode of making films that was already spent elsewhere in the world.

Although not specifically mentioned by Félix-Didier here, the set of relatively static conventions the classical cinema used to represent the national space had been emptied of meaning. The *costumbrista* mise-en-scène of rural space and the willful ignorance of what was happening on the urban margins not only further eroded the cinema's political relevance, but alienated those sectors of the public who may have wondered what the national space was really like. As Félix-Didier writes, the young filmmakers responded with a new conception of cinema: "La nueva generación concibió al cine como un medio de conocimiento de la sociedad argentina y como un espacio de reflexión acerca de la argentinidad y no como un soporte pasivo para la transmisión de valores nacionales residentes en algún lugar abstracto" (The new generation conceived of the cinema as a means of providing knowledge of Argentine society and as a space of reflection on Argentinity, and not as a passive medium for the transmission of national values that resided in some abstract place) (2003, Introducción 20). With the industry locked in a still-profitable but critically inert logic that resulted from an assemblage that implicated established filmmakers, producers, distributors, and the state, certain dissatisfied sectors of the public looked for escape in the form of the *cineclub*, which showed primarily foreign films and cultivated a small but intensely cinephilic public. This in turn fed publications on cinema, and by the 1950s prompted the formation of film schools both private and public.[2] These often took advantage of new technologies, especially the 16-millimeter camera, which, by lowering costs relative to the industry-standard 35-millimeter, facilitated a flow of more autonomous productions.

These factors coincided with society-shattering political events, most notably the ousting of Perón in 1955. The number of commercial feature films released plunged from forty-three in 1955 to thirty-six the following year and to a mere fifteen in 1957, and this crisis led to protests by the cinema sector that resulted in the passing of the *Ley de cine* (Cinema Law) in 1957. In addition to abolishing censorship for a time, the *Ley de cine* established the Instituto Nacional de Cine (National Cinema Institute), designated to foment film production, mostly through subsidies to finished films.³ It would select fifteen films per year to subsidize, in an ascending order that would correspond to the amount of the subsidy to be granted. Predictably, the INC's selection process was soon corrupted, causing the larger subsidies to go to powerful producers and often ignoring superior independent films. The productions of Argentina Sono Film were especially favored (Félix-Didier 2003, Introducción 13–20) in this state-industry alliance that sowed the seeds of the problems that would eventually be faced by the independent filmmakers known as the *Generación del 60*.⁴

But a brief window of opportunity was opened that produced some of the most innovative treatments of marginal spaces in the history of the Argentine cinema. If we consider this transition to be gradual and include in it the *villa*-set studio films discussed in the previous chapter, it becomes difficult to identify a foundational moment of the New Cinema. Although many have argued for Fernando Birri's *Tire dié* (1956–1960) as constituting just this kind of moment, I would argue that the inquisitive gaze had been developing but is able to first fully manifest itself in Birri's film, due to the relative autonomy of its production in the absence of commercial, governmental, or spectatorial demands. Of course a lack of exigencies has always been bound to a lack of available screens, and the reduced circulation of Birri's work shows that it was no exception to this rule. But nonetheless the autonomy Birri enjoyed allowed him to fully express the new filmic gaze that will be the subject of this chapter.

This second period of relative autonomy in Argentine cinema produced a great variety of films and production models, and the filmmakers' greater autonomy vis à vis the state and the studios is, predictably, reflected in its treatment of rural and other marginal spaces in ways that had not been possible in the industry. The strategies varied widely, from Birri's faith in cinematic transparency at the Escuela Documental (Documentary School) of Santa Fe, which was radically responsive to the particularities of rural space and its inhabitants, to the more avant-garde emphasis on montage associations between the city's center and its margins in David José Kohon's short *Buenos Aires* (1958). But the common factor was an interest in the social margins that until then had only been glimpsed in the cinema, an interest that Pablo Piedras describes:

> Actores sociales olvidados o apenas esbozados por las producciones de la época clásica, se presentan por primera vez en la imagen cinematográfica . . . junto a ellas, zonas y espacios del interior del país obtienen una representación realista y austera que elude el costumbrismo y el pintoreesquismo al cual el cine clásico los había relegado. (2010, 14–15)

> Social actors who were forgotten or barely hinted at in the productions of the classical period are shown for the first time in the cinematographic image . . . together with them, zones and spaces of the interior of the country are represented in a realist and austere way that eludes *costumbrismo* and the picturesque to which the classic cinema had relegated them.

The makers of these films shared a faith in cinema's transparency, its potential to credibly serve as a window onto the social. Instead of staging *cuadros de costumbres*, they carried the camera, often the cheaper and lighter 16-millimeter, to marginal places and peoples to bring back images of uneven modernization, institutionalized violence, and, increasingly toward the end of the 1960s, imperatives for action in the name of the *pueblo*. The voiceover in Gerardo Vallejo's *El camino hacia la muerte del Viejo Reales* (1971) summarizes these intentions: "Intentamos aproximarnos al conocimiento de nuestra propia realidad, y lo hicimos a partir del contacto directo y vivo con su principal protagonista, que es nuestro pueblo" (We tried to approach the knowledge of our own reality, and we did so through a direct and live contact with its principal protagonist, which is our *pueblo*). The search for knowledge of places and peoples that had been excluded from the national culture—often, as in the case of Vallejo's film, in the sugar-producing province of Tucumán—is the imperative that would motivate the explosion of creative solutions examined in this chapter.

In what follows it will become evident that although the filmmakers of the 1960s and '70s took a variety of political positions—from Peronist (Solanas and Getino) to Trotskyist (Raymundo Gleyzer) to Prelorán's gestures toward neutrality—they had in common a gaze that was new to the mid-century Argentine cinema and which prompted a blurring of the distinction between fiction and nonfiction and an expansion of the field of representability. The attentiveness of this gaze to the social, its inquisitiveness, is especially evident in its privileging of marginal spaces. Unlike the classical cinema, Kohon, Birri, and those who came after had no qualms about putting on display the fact that the reality of the interior and the margins of the city could not be adequately represented through conventions and that the relationship between center and margin was characterized by uneven modernization and structural violence.

Whereas the classical Argentine cinema tended to employ prescriptive representations of identity, the examples I will discuss instead search for formal strategies that serve to inquire about what is out there on the margins but is not integrated into the national identity. The relatively autonomous film productions I describe in this chapter never supplanted the hegemonic model—since a postclassical commercial model continued to dominate national film production, although at times not very robustly—but they did lead to changes in it as a response to the inquisitive gaze. Before discussing this response, I will examine how certain films of the period participated in the creation of this inquisitive gaze.

The Birth of Cinephilia and the Short Film

Shortly before the overthrow of Perón in 1955 two university film programs were created that would soon take on great importance. These were the Escuela Documental de Santa Fe, at the Universidad Nacional del Litoral, and the Escuela de Cine at the Universidad de la Plata. They facilitated a renewal of Argentine cinema and of ways of representing marginal space, in part because they served as a pipeline for the flow of foreign ideas and films, but also because the institutional academic setting allowed its productions a degree of autonomy. Several faculty members had studied at the Institut des Hautes Études Cinématographiques in Paris or at Rome's Centro Sperimentale, bringing back, among other things, the intentions and techniques of neorealism.[5] The names associated with the two local university programs would be essential to this renewal not only in Argentina, but throughout Latin America: in addition to Kohon and Birri, the list includes Simón Feldman, Rodolfo Kuhn, Nicolás Sarquís, Gerardo Vallejo, and many others.

As in most university-based film programs, short noncommercial films were the principal product. While most of these are difficult to view today, a reduced selection is in circulation, and I will examine several of them. These late-1950s shorts brought to the fore certain features that in the classical cinema had been relegated to a limited, formulaic function, often doing so to interrogate the canonical conceptions of the nation's marginal spaces. The most notable of these formal features is the use of the train, as seen in *Buenos Aires* (David José Kohon, 1958), *Contracampo* (Rodolfo Kuhn and Manuel Antín, 1958), and *Tire dié* (1956–1960), a collective project of the Escuela Documental de Santa Fe, directed by Birri.

Buenos Aires is a twelve-minute experimental short that, as Laura Podalsky writes, "subverts the mythic association of the city with civilization and progress by forcing the spectator to look at Buenos Aires from a different perspective" (2004, 92), offering "a new vision of the city through new formal techniques" (2004, 94). Innovative form, then, is key to the creation of a questioning perspective on the city. Most immediately notable is the use of montage to bring together margin and center, which results in illuminating contrasts, but the film also uses the train in a novel way, to which I will return. I would argue that the "different perspective" pointed out by Podalsky is articulated around the notion of uneven development, through the use of a counterpoint between the modern industrial sectors of the city and the nearby *villa miseria* in which its workers live. Such a perspective interrogates the city center–*villa miseria* binary by showing the frontier between the spaces to be porous to the workers' movement (but not to that of the commodities they produce) and demonstrating that this porousness is necessary for the functioning of the city's modern economy, as a response to capital's "imperative that larger and larger numbers of workers are spatially concentrated in close proximity to the workplace," as Neil Smith writes (116).

The film opens with a montage of the cityscape, with vertical pans emphasizing its upward growth above the flat landscape. The camera holds on a print advertisement for a luxurious bourgeois apartment, which a sudden backward camera movement shows to be posted on the wall of a tarpaper shack in a *villa*. This example of counterpoint montage within the shot is one of the first times a non-*costumbrista* depiction of the capital city's margins (and the dark skin of its inhabitants) enters Argentine film culture. It is followed by a tenuous narration in which those who awaken in the shacks on the urban margins move in to the city center to work in the modern economy, as the factory worker of the urban industrial base and the letter carrier necessary for the system's efficiency. The production of modern urban space is made possible by these workers, but it only allows them in for the purpose of work, banishing them by night to the *villa*. In *Buenos Aires*, then, the opposition that classical Argentine culture had considered two mutually exclusive poles becomes two necessary parts of a single assemblage in which the contiguity of unevenly modernized spaces and the mobility of the inhabitants of the *villa* are due to capital's need for a source of cheap labor. Conceived of in this way, the condition of the margins is not at all accidental. Its poverty and high unemployment are produced, and integral to capital accumulation as a reservoir of highly flexible labor. The film highlights the culture's denial of the fact that it is dependent on, and even produces, those spaces it had labeled *villa de emergencia*. The traditional Sarmientine conception of modernity as emanating from the center toward the periphery, and the notion that marginal spaces owe to urban space whatever modern traits they might have, is demonstrated to be false.

After shots of a man whitewashing over campaign graffiti with the names of Arturo Frondizi and Ricardo Balbín—who were soon to represent yet another failed hope for developmentalism—the film closes with tracking shots filmed from a train as it passes through a *villa* on the outskirts of the capital. The shots from the train are neither transitions nor part of a montage sequence, but rather extended takes that document the social margins. This use of the train is novel in the context of a national cinema so averse to depictions of spaces that did not conform to hegemonic discourses on the nation, but as was seen in Demare's *Detrás de un largo muro*, the issue of marginal urban space was a pressing one, since Peronism had long portrayed itself as having bettered the lives of the popular classes through state-directed housing initiatives and other projects. The demise of the Peronist state and the lifting of its strong hand in the cinema opened up the possibility of critical documentation that might contradict this long-standing justification of the movement.

Kohon's *Buenos Aires* was not the only film to engage critically with existing conceptions of national space and the human experience of negotiating a reality characterized by uneven development. *Contracampo* (1958) is a self-consciously modern narrative short directed by Rodolfo Kuhn and Manuel Antín, with a soundtrack consisting of "música concreta" (concrete music) by Tirso de Olazabal and photography employing inventive angles and double exposures. The most striking shots turn abstract due to inventive techniques that combine moving vehicles with the camera, which is attached to the turning wheel of a horse-drawn cart, then a rollercoaster, and taken on board a train. But its self-conscious film-school modernism aside, the film engages with both traditional representation and the modern Argentine experience, specifically that of internal migration. While such migration had become very common under Perón, its stories had seldom been told from the point of view of the migrant, whose urban experience was often less than ideal.

The film's narration begins with its protagonist, recently arrived in the capital, seen in his precarious urban existence, fishing unsuccessfully for food on Buenos Aires' riverside coast before returning to a *conventillo* (tenement) crowded with new arrivals. As he is shown deep in thought, an internal flashback returns us to the country and he is seen setting out on his journey to the city. The film represents the voyage not with the conventional image of the train, but with images shot from the train, a subjective shot from the point of view of the migrant protagonist. Once he arrives to the city, he is unable to find work, since he has none of the skills that are in demand (signs are seen for employment opportunities for a carpenter and a machinist), and he eventually returns to the country, at which point the film engages with the conventional images of rural Argentinity. The protagonist reprises the role of the literary Santos Vega, a nineteenth-century symbol of Argentinity who meets modernity and is vanquished. He encounters Juan Sin Ropa, the diabolic symbol of national modernity, who challenges him to a *payada* singing duel. But the protagonist claims he has forgotten how to sing due to the disappointment of his failed attempt to migrate, stating that "me habían hablado tanto de aquello" (they had told me so much about it). He tries to play the guitar, but a string breaks, and he instead falls over and dies. Unlike the filmic heroes of the more optimistic *Juan sin ropa* (1919) and *Santos Vega vuelve* (Leopoldo Torres Ríos, 1947), *Contracampo* is an antimodern return to the original fatalism of the literary model of Santos Vega, here transformed into a criticism of the internal migrations of the mid-century so strongly associated with Peronism.

The most well-known short film of the period is *Tire dié* (1956–1960). It was made as a collaborative project of the Escuela Documental de Santa Fe, and directed by Birri. The production of it and *Los inundados* (1961) was designed, according to Birri, to allow for local contingencies to enter into the films, an objective reflected perhaps most clearly in their innovative means of treating space. By virtue of their questioning of canonical discourses on national reality, these two films are located by critics at the origins of the Latin American New Cinemas of the 1960s and '70s, but it is important to note the specific context in which Birri's first films were made.⁶ The students at the Escuela Documental de Santa Fe collaborated in the making of the films, and the school's marginal position relative to the Buenos Aires–based national film industry made possible—or necessary—the many innovations seen in them.

The opening sequence of the short *Tire dié* contextualizes its subject through images of the city of Santa Fe filmed from an airplane, a "totalizing eye" (de Certeau) perspective that transforms the city from a lived space into the geometrical, striated urban space synonymous with a successful process of modernization. In this opening sequence, all appears to follow the script of modernity. Such success is confirmed by a disembodied male, thus authoritative voiceover that locates the city with exactitude, then lists statistics and facts, the objective attributes that qualify it as modern:

> 31 grados de latitud sur y 70 de longitud oeste. Ubicada en la confluencia de los ríos Paraná y Salado, en el feraz litoral argentino. Fundada por Juan de Garay en el año 1573, bajo el imperativo "hay que abrir puertas a la tierra." 200,000 habitantes hasta hoy, 1958, con 5133 nacimientos el año pasado. Importante centro agrícola-ganadero, con un puerto con 3,200 metros de muelles de piedra, con capacidad para 40 buques de ultramar a la vez, 26 guinches de 1,500 a 25,000 kilogramos, graneros y galpones para 250,000 toneladas de grano . . .

> 31 degrees South latitude and 70 West longitude. Located at the confluence of the Paraná and Salado rivers, in the fertile Argentine river region. Founded by Juan de Garay in 1573 under the imperative "We must open doors to the interior." 200,000 inhabitants today, in 1958, with 5133 births last year. An important agricultural-livestock center, with a port with 3,200 meters of stone piers, capacity for 40 ocean liners at once, 26 cranes of 1,500 to 25,000 kilograms, granaries and warehouses for 250,000 tons of grain . . .

But as the voiceover continues to list the statistics—". . . 50 joyerías, 200 peinadores de señoras, 6 museos . . ." (50 jewelry stores, 200 women's hair stylists, 6 museums . . .)—that further attest to the success of the modernizing project, the airplane flies lower and lower, leaving behind the abstract grid of streets, the civilization just confirmed in statistical terms and, most shockingly for its viewer, the comforting erasures that produced the reassuring

Argentine cinematic experience of the preceding half-century. The plane passes over the *bajo* (floodplain) at an altitude low enough to distinguish a *villa miseria* of improvised *ranchos* and the people and animals that inhabit them, a reduction of distance that brings about a transition from the realm of the ideal to that of the factual. This transition destroys the certainty of the former through the reemergence of that which had been excluded as the theoretical basis for the modernizing project.

The subsequent section of the film consists of interviews with local people who survive by selling vegetables, hunting birds, collecting rags, making jewelry out of plastic refuse, and other improvised activities. Here the switch in epistemological mode is completed. The quest to reveal a truth about Argentine society leads Birri to leave behind the institutional inventory of the modern city in favor of an analysis of "everyday practices . . . the microbe-like . . . organization" (de Certeau 96) of the economy of the margins. The inhabitants of this space display the singular practices they have created to scrape out a survival in the interstices and on the decay of the modern. These practices are of course invisible to a totalizing eye whose projects—nation, civilization, modernity—eradicate them in theory at the same time that they produce them in the reality of their margins.

A final sequence shows the *tire dié*, a recurrent event in which the children of the families that live in the *bajo* run alongside a passenger train as it slows to cross a bridge over the *Río Salado*, pleading with the passengers to "tirar diez" (throw ten cents). This section of the film goes beyond any purely documentary intentions to introduce to Argentine cinema a previously unseen point of view, that of the social class that inhabits the margins of the city and lacks the means to travel on the railway. From this subject position grounded in the experience of these children, the train ceases to connote an abstract but desirable modernity, and instead represents a possible source of subsistence.

The children's point of view is intercut with shots from the perspective of the middle-class passengers, creating a shot-countershot dynamic in which each gaze corresponds to a social class on either side of the inclusion–exclusion opposition that recodes Sarmiento's civilization–barbarism dichotomy as a tragically uneven modernization. Presented as it is after the first two parts of the film, the *tire dié* sequence underlines an awareness that the criteria for inclusion/exclusion are as much economic as ethnic or cultural (the three are shown to be inseparable here) and form a chasm across which mutual recognition seldom happens. The passengers show differing degrees of interest toward the children, some throwing them coins, others gazing at them, and still others sitting inside the train chatting or reading the newspaper, underlining the willful obliviousness to the presence outside on the land, the same obliviousness that was reproduced by the classical cinema's stubborn refusal to direct its gaze from the train outward toward marginal space. Neither the perspective of the children nor that of the passengers could be said to be privileged over the other in the editing of this sequence, which, while it reproduces classic divisions—bourgeoisie versus lumpenproletariat, civilization versus barbarism—does so not through a unidirectional eyeline-matched shot, but by way of the shot-countershot, a classic technique of mutual recognition used for exchanges of glances, conversations, fights, and so on, thus dramatizing an affectively powerful scene of communication previously absent in Argentine cinema. *Tire dié*, then, stages a face-to-face confrontation across the wide class division earlier articulated in the geographic separation seen in the bird's-eye shots that opened the film.[7]

Feature Films Outside the Industry

Birri's next film, *Los inundados*, is a fiction feature in which the titular *inundados* are the "flooded out" inhabitants of the *bajo*. Its principal characters are based on those interviewed in *Tire dié*, with some of the locals appearing as themselves, while most are played by theater actors and other local performers. This way of developing the script and characters represents a foundational break from the *costumbrismo* of classical Argentine films set in the interior of the country. As a result, the characters do not belong to the tradition of passive victims and noble savages, nor are they instinctual primitives in the mold of Facundo Quiroga, destined to perish with the rationalization of the national territory, but are instead individuals who form part of the complex social fabric of this particular place. From this conception, the film goes on to find formal solutions to represent rural space in ways that respond to its particularities, the most notable being its use of the train, to which I will return.

The making of *Los inundados* involved a struggle against established ways of making films in Argentina. According to Birri, obtaining a credit from the Instituto Nacional de Cinematografía (INC) to make the film obligated him to work with the industrial union, the Sindicato de la Industria Cinematográfica Argentina. Instead of being able to rely on the Escuela Documental's students and teachers to carry out the many tasks needed to make the film, regulations required that a union member be employed in each position. Birri was eventually able to negotiate an agreement by which each technician would have an assistant who was a student of the Escuela Documental. The film was finished, screened in Argentina, and invited to the Cannes Film Festival, but according to Birri the INC refused to send it because, in a belated answer to the calls for censorship by Pessano and Sánchez Sorondo three decades earlier, it considered it "indigna de representar a la Argentina en el extranjero" (unworthy of representing Argentina overseas) (Truglio 76). A synopsis of the film makes clear the reason for INC's apprehension in the context of the national cinema's treatment of the social margins up to that point.

The film tells the story of the displacement of the *inundados*, the struggle to find a solution and the futility of populist (read Peronist) politics. In doing so it indicts the use of the poor as a reservoir of mass political support. As we have seen, both in the cinema and in the real space outside of it the marginalized are usually banished from the visible realm, thus the greater irony when the *inundados* set up camp in a downtown train yard, visible to all in the modern city center. The flood is shown less as a contingency—as something natural and unpredictable—than as a rational outcome of a modernization process that has produced space for certain sectors of society on its margins, in this case the riverside plain that floods with a mathematically predictable frequency. For the middle-class city dwellers, the conceived space of the nation and its inhabitants is superseded by the sudden direct experience of the latter, numerous and boisterous, as the return to protagonism of the presences suppressed along with Perón several years earlier. But a simple synopsis that assumes the film could be reduced to its script does not address it sufficiently, since *Los inundados* does not observe a classical narrative economy: characters come and go, the camera follows one, then another, dialogue overlaps first with political, then commercial, slogans. A drunk shows up at a party and starts a fight, but the band plays on. Children light bonfires, dogs trot by, and into this rich jumble of people and place the conflict that structures the plot comes and goes, never quite displacing that which is contingent to it. Birri's explanation of his intentions is telling:

> Era una obra que tenía que tener repercusión local, no universal, y tenerla en ese momento en que se hacía. Esas eran las premisas básicas de nuestro trabajo . . . se trabajaba con conciencia de *ese* momento y de *ese* lugar, no para el futuro ni para la historia del

cine. Se trataba, de alguna manera, de aprender a operar en la contingencia. Lo formidable es que, operando en la contingencia, con la necesidad de responder a eso que flota en el aire, la obra, en un momento determinado, se carga de una serie de valores que terminan por trascender ante todo a las propias intenciones. (Truglio 70, emphasis in original)

It was a project that had to have local, not universal, repercussion and have it at the moment in which it was made. Those were the basic premises of our work . . . we worked with a conscience of *that* moment and *that* place, not for the future nor for cinema history. It was a matter of, in some way, learning to be prepared for any contingency. The fantastic thing is that, operating with contingency, with the necessity of responding to that which floats in the air, the work, at a certain moment, becomes charged with a series of values that end up transcending above all one's own intentions.

Birri's account reads like a manifesto of opposition to the national clichés, providing a model for a cinema that might question the official discourses that tend to subsume the contingencies of place into simplified conceptual oppositions or elide them. Especially telling is Birri's acknowledgment that by inviting the aleatory into the film the director's own intentions become secondary to the "values" provided by chance, an acknowledgment that also provides a theoretical basis for the use of trains in the film. The classical conventions, by which the land and inhabitants of Argentina's interior were seldom filmed, resulted in a narrative economy in which the landscape and rural society were rarely more than a backdrop to a conflict involving a protagonist played by an established star. *Los inundados* rejects the star system, and at key moments incorporates narratively dead time, taking advantage of film's documentary charge and the movement of the train in order to maximize its openness to contingency. It is here that *Los inundados* goes beyond the immediacy of politics into an exploration of the nation's rural space.

Flooded out of their *rancho*, having set up camp in a boxcar in the city center, the Gaitán family awakens one morning to find themselves linked, by virtue of a bureaucratic error, to a train rolling away from the city. They have no idea where they are going, and in the forgetting of their struggle to survive on society's margins, inflexible social relations and spaces are temporarily suspended. As a result they observe the rural landscape with a gaze capable of questioning conventional representations of the land as *barbarie* or as a desert. These tracking shots from the train are subjective, eyeline matched to the point of view of the members of the family, who are on the train not as part of its instrumental, modernizing function—that of efficiently moving goods and people from one place to another—but as uninvested observers, just along for the ride, going nowhere in particular. Showing the land in this way shifts the image from an instrumental mode of perception, in which a passenger on a train might reduce the landscape passing by the corner of his or her eye to a sort of abacus that measures the dead time between events and the empty space between places ("Luján . . . 8:15 . . . right on time") or calculate how many head of cattle could be grazed on it and the resulting profit, to a mode more open to the contingent, to that which is suppressed in the classic representations of the territory.

As theorized by Henri Bergson, the instrumental mode of perception "results from the discarding of what has no interest for our needs, or more generally for our functions" (23). Ronald Bogue expands on this idea in a commentary on Deleuze:

> Perception helps the living being control its environment not by adding something to things, but by *subtracting* from them, selecting those features of surrounding objects that interest and concern the living being and ignoring those that are irrelevant to its existence. In order to increase the scope of its action, the living being decreases the number of elements with which it must deal. (30, emphasis in original)

In their way of viewing that is temporarily disengaged from practical ends, the Gaitans' subjectivity suppresses this instrumental, subtractive mode of perception in the train shots. In addition (staying within Deleuzian terms), it could be argued that the subjectivity of those doing the perceiving—the Gaitán family—is made *fluid* due to the state in which they find themselves: on a pure voyage, in movement, their worldly cares suspended due to a bureaucratic accident, the contingency that linked them to a train without a known destination, thus suspending the usual instrumental, sensory-motor mode of perception.

The flood metaphor, or that of liquidity, is useful to address the flow created by the train journey's temporary unmooring of the subjectivities of the Gaitán family from their solidified roles in the social hierarchy and the resulting mode of perceiving the world. Instead of the hardened, fixed milieu that imposes a subtractive, sensory-motor mode of perception on them (since immediate survival—and thus utility—is an ever-present concern) they temporarily float freely, perceiving the world more openly. Where seen reacting to the passing landscape, their faces show wonder, as they observe, with open sensorium, objects and people on the landscape, contingencies captured on film that retain the richness of their meaninglessness within the terms of both the narrative of modernization and that of the film.

This mode of perception is reflected in the editing, which privileges observation. André Bazin famously discussed a similar use of time in Vittorio De Sica's *Umberto D*, in the shot in which the young maid is shown in the kitchen, which extends far beyond the amount of time needed to move the narration forward, displaying "the simple continuing to be of a person to whom nothing in particular happens" (69). In *Los inundados* a similar, also momentary, disregard for temporal economy is seen in the shots filmed from the train as it carries the Gaitán family across the landscape of the interior. The train does not merely leave one station to arrive at the next by way of an ellipsis or a rapid montage sequence, but rather the movement through the landscape is given time that would not be allotted it in the typical analytical editing mode of a more classical cinema, in which the spectator's gaze is disciplined, directed to look for information that will advance the narrative at the expense of that which is contingent to it. Given this excess of time and the liquid movement, that which is contingent—"The embarrassment of contingency is that it is everywhere and that it everywhere poses the threat of an evacuation of meaning" (Doane 144)—becomes available to perception.

With the train, Birri creates a line of flight—not for the modernizing project or for capitalist exploitation of the interior, since the railway serves these machinic assemblages as striations—but rather for the cinema, for which rural space had been absent. Instead of transitions that connect two urban spaces by way of charted, stable trajectories, Birri's train shots trace a line of flight into rural space. The camera's shutter opens to receive traces of what exists out there on the land but has been excluded from the cinema. Upon seeing the land in this subjective but uninvested way, the viewer, at least momentarily, sees an image that is allowed an opportunity to break through the conventional representations of rural space. In a contemporary review of *Los inundados*, Juan José Sebreli described the film's impact on his postulated Argentine viewer, referencing specifically the train shots:

> Birri nos muestra hasta qué punto era falso el gaucho legendario y apócrifo de Demare. Esos paisajes cinematográficamente

"invisibles" del interior argentino a fuerza de ser ignorados, se vuelven de pronto con *Los inundados* una presencia luminosa y flagrante, insospechadamente próxima: toda una parte desconocida de nuestro propio territorio se ha puesto de pronto a existir, ha adquirido solidez, densidad de cosa real y experimentamos la extrañeza y el reconocimiento de recordar lugares en los que sin embargo creemos no haber estado nunca. (n.p.)

Birri shows us to what point the legendary and apocryphal gaucho of Demare is false. Those cinematographically "invisible" landscapes of Argentina's interior, due to their being ignored, in *Los inundados* suddenly become a luminous and glaring presence, unsuspectedly close: a whole unknown part of our own territory has suddenly started to exist, has acquired solidity, density of a real thing and we experience the strangeness and recognition of remembering places where nevertheless we believe we've never been.

Sebreli, in addressing the unique way the film shows the landscape, was possibly the only critic of the time to recognize the illuminative power of the train sequences, which can now be recognized as a key moment in the shift in the way the interior of the country was represented, toward a type of gaze that has since become an important part of Argentine cinema.[8]

In the years immediately following the fall of Perón, the weakened industrial Argentine cinema had been opening itself to spaces that had seldom appeared on the screen, especially the *villa miseria*, but it had been slow to develop new formal strategies with which to do so. Birri is the filmmaker who most thoroughly reformulated the dominant tradition's conventions, through films that are marginal in a double sense, referring to both marginal spaces (and their people) and a marginal production model. An impoverished production model allows Birri's work to escape the static structures that conventionally put heterogeneous elements into a sympathetic cofunctioning in order to create a totalizing image of marginal spaces that works toward satisfying any curiosity regarding those spaces that the viewer might have. The corporatist logic of classical Argentine cinema resulted in its investment in certain images that could only be treated in very limited ways by the industrial apparatus of production, but the cinema of Birri and others, radically uninvested in such assemblages and their conventions, is free to explore formal solutions that allow it to represent the margins in other ways and which, instead of a totalizing gaze, both cultivate and respond to an inquisitive gaze.

The most obvious example is the use of the train. Where the dominant commercial cinema used the train to connect "civilized" spaces through a brief transition, the cinema of the inquisitive gaze is free to turn the camera toward rural space, and the train, as it had done occasionally a half-century earlier, again serves as a vehicle for tracking shots that show the rural landscape. If the previous restriction of the train to its syntactic function could be attributed to a tacit imperative to eliminate visual reminders of persistent or produced "barbarism," this turning of the camera toward the landscape represents both a will to foreground these same reminders and a diametrically opposed conception of the viewer's desires.

Deleuze and Guattari's account of nomadic movement through territory might illuminate how such uses of the train activate a new gaze by privileging the spaces between stations:

> A path is always between two points, but the in-between has taken on all the consistency and enjoys both an autonomy and a direction of its own. The life of the nomad is the intermezzo . . . the nomad goes from point to point only as a consequence and as a factual necessity; in principle, points for him are relays along a trajectory. (*A Thousand Plateaus* 380)

In the films of the inquisitive gaze, the duration of the train shots, which does not respond to narrative demands, starts to account for the in-between spaces, instead of privileging solely the "points" where characters, like the Gaitáns, will stop on their itinerant wanderings aboard the train. As these intermezzi "acquire solidity and density of the real" (Sebreli), rural space and its contingencies come forward, cease to be mere ground or setting, and the fact of the absence at the heart of Argentine culture becomes evident and consolidates a new spectatorial gaze.

Martin Lefebvre, in his discussion of landscape in the cinema as *parergon* and *ergon*—as marginalia or as object of the gaze, that is—writes that "it rests with the spectator to assure the movement from setting to landscape and, when possible, to make the space autonomous by interrupting for a moment its connection to the narrative" (2006, 48). I suspect that, in the Argentine context, the spectator who is able to transform a view of rural space as mere setting or ground into the object of the gaze emerged with the implied contract between film and spectator of this cinema, which assumed a viewer who would undertake the work to turn setting into landscape, and thus the cinema into a source for the revelation of a national reality that had been unattended to by the classical cinema. The spectator's cultural knowledge, which had for decades provided the condition of possibility for the continued use of the cinematic *cuadro de costumbres*, was undergoing a shift: instead of looking for a known image of the rural inherited from the national tradition, an inquisitive gaze now responded to curiosity about rural space and national reality.

That this gaze contributed to the reconfiguration of the cinematic apparatus in the following years is evident in the cinema's use of the train, which continued to be employed by filmmakers who followed Kohon and Birri's lead throughout the decade of the 1960s and into the '70s. They brought the camera to the margins and trusted that its documentary charge would reveal conditions more complex than a simple *barbarie* or *desierto*, in an operation that relied on a faith in cinematic transparency (at times supplemented by montage that juxtaposed the marginal with the central, underlining the injustices and social inequalities). The resulting films are of many types—militant, documentary, ethnographic, narrative—but all refute the conventional totalizations and expand the field of representability.

Nuevo Cine Narrative Feature Films

By the 1950s Leopoldo Torre Nilsson and Fernando Ayala, the most visible industrial auteurs and precursors of the urban variant of the Nuevo Cine, had also begun to engage with an Argentine reality to which the commercial cinema had long turned its back. Four years after Soffici's *Barrio gris*, Torre Nilsson set *El secuestrador* (1958) in a *villa miseria* and filmed much of it on location. In Ayala's 1963 *Paula cautiva*, a portrait of national and aristocratic decadence produced by Ayala and Héctor Olivera's relatively independent and occasionally adventurous studio Aries Cinematográfica Argentina, the *costumbrista* representation of rural folklore is satirized as commodified faux-authenticity.

Ayala's film centers on the romance of Paula Peña (Susana Freyre), daughter of a family of impoverished aristocratic landholders, and Carlos Sutton (Duilio Marzio), an Argentine expatriot who has found business success in New York, but who has taken renewed interest in Argentina. Ayala employs foreign gazes, most importantly that of Carlos, to defamiliarize an Argentine reality that at the time, eight years after the overthrow of Perón, had normalized constant tension and violence between military factions. This violence is documented in the film through television broadcasts both watched by the protagonists and seen on screen by the film's viewer. Unlike Paula, who reacts with indifference, each time Carlos sees this evidence of the conflictive state of Argentine society the shock is visible on his face.

Other foreign gazes more comically defamiliarize visual convention. Early in the film a group of North American tourists arrives, providing a brief but incisive account of how the national cinema (and the culture more generally) conceived of the national space. When an elderly tourist woman meets the charismatic urbane charlatan played by Lautaro Murúa, she exclaims "Oh, just like Valentino, I love these gauchos!," then continues: ". . . and now a little rest before lunch, and after lunch sightseeing around town. This pampa is exciting!" As she mentions the pampa, the image has already cut to the next sequence, a view of the kind of open landscape she refers to, bounded by trees in the distance. But after a moment the stasis of the fixed frame is broken by a pan to the left, and as the Edificio Kavanaugh—the skyscraping symbol of the capital city's modernity, built in the mid-1930s—enters the frame the pastoral landscape is revealed to be a small section of central Buenos Aires' Plaza San Martín, in an image carefully composed to leave the cement of the city off screen, just beyond the frame. Another, equally eloquent indictment of the culture's representational conventions soon follows. A series of vertical pans measures the city's most modern buildings in shots eyeline matched to the gaze of a Carlos in wonder after a fifteen-year absence. The sequence comes to a climax with a wide shot of the cityscape, with skyscrapers in the distance and the railroad tracks leading to the central Retiro Station in the foreground, a portrait of Buenos Aires as an unequivocally modern metropolis. But once again the illusion is shattered when the camera pans down, and we see that spreading below the cityscape is the Villa 31, a centrally located *villa miseria* that extends along the tracks behind Retiro. This hide-and-reveal camera movement will be increasingly seen in the Argentine cinema, even becoming a convention that both responds to and prompts the inquisitive gaze of the spectator who is encouraged not to trust the carefully composed image and to instead wonder what might lie beyond the frame of the national culture's field of representability.

When the film returns to its narration, it is revealed that in order to make the mortgage payments on their estancia, named La Cautiva, Paula's fallen aristocrat family has had to recur to *viveza criolla*, which could be translated as a kind of self-interested dishonesty often accepted as a necessary means of survival. The Peña patriarch rents out the family burial vault in Recoleta Cemetery to those who want to socially impress by holding services for their deceased in the aristocratic cemetery, then the viewer learns that the family also stages folkloric representations for visiting tourists. When the same elderly tourist heard earlier tells Carlos, "We're off to see the pampa, and gauchos, real gauchos!" the cut again comes early, and before she finishes her phrase Paula's half-brothers appear on screen dressed up in *ponchos* and *bombachas*, pretending to be gauchos. The tourist opines that they are "perfectly authentic gauchos," before a series of representations of gaucho folklore: prowess with the *facón*, horses, and dances.

Later, as romance blooms, Carlos, stricken with shame for Paula, pleads with her to discontinue the folklore shows and instead find a way to maintain the *estancia* without sacrificing the family's distinction. But little does he realize the extent of the strategies resorted to by locals to overcome economic difficulties: Paula has been working as an escort to maintain the family's lifestyle and status. Then, in an ultimate allegorical critique of the aristocracy's insistence on conserving past glory, the family patriarch is paraded on an antique carriage in a show at La Cautiva despite having just died. Defamiliarized by Carlos's perspective, these strategies of economic survival that exploit the clichés of Argentine identity become a humiliating farce. But eventually a hopeful ending is provided, as Carlos decides to stay and marry Paula, in a twentieth-century refoundational allegory that brings together the economic power of the new professional class (and foreign capital) with the distinction of the *terrateniente* aristocracy, to the conspicuous exclusion of the Peronist movement that was stubbornly retaining its electoral potential in the absence of its leader. Ayala's film, produced on the margins of the industry, engages with the political problems of corruption and instability in the period after Perón's overthrow and exile, and in doing so critiques conventional representations of national space, but it stops short of venturing to document the social margins. The younger generation of filmmakers known as the *Generación del 60*, however, deepened this engagement by often setting their work on the urban margins and inviting incursions of documentation into their fiction features.

In his 1961 film *Los jóvenes viejos*, Rodolfo Kuhn inserted a tracking shot as his urbane protagonists drive through a *villa miseria* on the way out of Buenos Aires. Kohon's *Prisioneros de una noche* (1962) contains a long sequence set on a train, from which the characters gaze at Buenos Aires' marginal neighborhoods passing by.[9] Kuhn set the opening sequence of

Pajarito Gómez (1964), which tells the story of a young man's meteoric rise to pop-music stardom, in rural poverty, portraying the singer's childhood misery as motivating his dream of moving to Buenos Aires. Leonardo Favio also set a large portion of his 1965 *Crónica de un niño solo* in a *villa miseria*. These are only a few examples of how in urban-set films the frame of representability had become porous and the presence of the urban margins was felt in the diegetic city.

At the same time, the *Generación del 60* began to represent rural space in unconventional ways, the foremost example being Lautaro Murúa's *Shunko*. Murúa was a Chilean actor who had worked with Torre Nilsson, Ayala, and others, and then turned to direction, making his first two films in 1960. *Alias Gardelito* was set in the urban criminal underworld, while *Shunko* was set and filmed in the province of Santiago del Estero. *Shunko* is not the first Argentine film to thematize a rural schoolteacher's predicament, since *Los afincaos* had done so in 1941, but where in Barletta's film the impediment took the form of a powerful local caudillo enabled by an absent state, Murúa chooses instead to center on the lack of responsivity on the part of the state to indigenous social structure and beliefs.

An openness to the local, then, characterizes Murúa's film. Already in the credits sequence it is clear that what he referred to as "un documental con argumento" (a documentary with a story) (García 197) is not a conventional piece of filmmaking. A tracking shot filmed from a moving vehicle opens the film with a perspective on rural space that is soon revealed to be subjective, that of the teacher played by Murúa himself en route to the rural community where he will work as the sole teacher in the local school. The shots, then, are matched to the gaze of a character who uncritically undertakes the modernizing mission and is seeing these spaces for the first time, but by the return trip his perspective will have been transformed. Jorge Sala points out how the film uses a near internal focalization, which "remite a una mutación en el modo de registro de los acontecimientos, que se desnaturalizan y pierden su carácter pintoresquista al pasar por el tamiz de la mirada crítica" (brings about a change in the mode of registering of the events, which are denaturalized and lose their picturesque character as they pass through the critical gaze) of the schoolteacher, who is "responsable de producir el choque entre su propuesta de desarrollo social y la realidad de los campesinos" (responsible for producing the clash between his proposed idea of social development and the reality of the peasants) (Sala 306). The film represents for its viewer the consciousness-raising process of a schoolteacher at the center of a conflict between the Sarmientine Eurocentrism of the state-driven education project and the resistant character of rural space and its inhabitants, whose hostility is apparent upon the teacher's arrival. But Murúa's schoolteacher soon manages to overcome local distrust, and he realizes that the problem lies in the state's own failure to respond to the cultural particularities of its inhabitants.

Although he starts out teaching the canonical version of national history as progress, his Western rationality is shown to be inadequate when faced with local epistemologies, a lack of understanding exemplified by his attempt to explain an eclipse to his students. The children suggest an alternative interpretation, one offered by an indigenous matriarch, and the teacher brings them to see her and listen to her explanation. Teacher and students come to an understanding in which each learns from the other, but the surprising side of the equation is of course the teacher's openness to local knowledge and the shifts this leads to in his outlook, a reciprocity unthinkable in the cinema of a mere decade earlier. The community's gratitude—especially for his medical attentions—is reflected in its helping him construct a schoolhouse. The efforts of Murúa's schoolteacher to overcome his cultural training include adopting the local dress—a *poncho*—and observing local beliefs, such as when he follows the students' suggestion to burn a book belonging to a deceased student, so that her soul can go free and stop haunting the schoolhouse. Where for Sarmiento's Enlightenment-inspired modernizing project the act of burning such a symbol of civilization would be little short of heresy, Murúa's more receptive teacher comes to recognize and respect the local significance of such an act. The film, then, rejects the usual glossing-over of the contradictions internal to the modernizing project—which had invariably suppressed local particularities—to explore the inevitable and seemingly unresolvable conflicts that arise from contact between cultures. This is metaphorized in the failure, remarkably unsentimentalized, of a romantic subplot. Murúa's teacher and a local woman exchange longing gazes throughout the film, but the conservative mores of the traditional society are more powerful than cinematic convention, and their love is not allowed to develop further.

These are only a few of the many notable treatments of marginal space in early 1960s Argentine film, upon which further elaboration will remain for another book. I will move to the later part of the decade, during Juan Carlos Onganía's dictatorship, under which political position–takes on film soon become more explicit and discourse on marginal space more militant.

Militant Film and Rural Space

As the 1960s wore on, military dictatorships alternated with brief periods of democracy. Especially under Onganía (1966–1970), oppositional culture became more confrontational, and by the last years of the decade militant culture had taken on heightened visibility. The Onganía regime, the most repressive in modern Argentine history up to that point, solidified the opposition through its authoritarian cultural policies and at times violent repression. Censorship became blatant, and as militancy went underground several clandestine groups developed film production and screening apparatuses. One of these was *Grupo Cine Liberación*, which, as Solanas and Getino wrote, addressed "the imperious necessity for the militant intelligentsia to root itself in Argentine reality and to contribute to the process of internal liberation of the movement of the masses" (qtd. in Pick 59). Where *Cine Liberación* was of a left Peronist position and included the middle class in its intended audience, another group, Raymundo Gleyzer's *Cine de la Base*, was associated with the Trotskyist Ejército Revolucionario del Pueblo, and aimed more at raising the consciousness of the proletariat to its own condition, in addition to diffusing information in the form of "comunicados cinematográficos" (cinematographic communiqués) that, among other things, publicized their organization's clandestine operations, such as the kidnapping of the British consul and representative of the Frigorífico Swift, Stanley Silvester, in the 1971 short *Swift* (Peña and Vallina 234–237).

In their landmark militant film *La hora de los hornos*, Solanas and Getino took up the dual strategies of critiquing the production of underdevelopment by the modernization project and creating a new, politically conscious and active spectator who would take part in the transformation of national reality. The film, then, sets out to reflect the interrelated disparities between the apparent modernity of the port city and the misery and violence of marginal spaces, an objective that makes necessary the documentation of those spaces excluded from canonical representations of the nation and results in the further development of the formal strategies that had been pioneered by Birri, Kohon, and others. In addition to the use of the zoom discussed at the beginning of the chapter, also notable are tracking shots filmed from a train and innovative uses of found footage and montage, such as the sequence that quotes *Tire dié*. The blond boy from Birri's film is shown from above, running alongside the train, palm outstretched in hope that a dime will be thrown. But Solanas and Getino edit this in continuity in a shot-countershot dynamic against views of Buenos Aires skyscrapers seen from street level, and the Kuleshov effect leads to the suggestion that from these monuments of capital no dimes will be thrown, so direct action is imperative. As the voiceover points out that "aquí un gaucho es tan exótico como en París, Londres, o Nueva York" (here a gaucho is as exotic as in Paris, London, or New York), the film brings spaces together that the culture has been careful to keep separate for fear of the type of conclusion produced here by associative montage. Since the innovations of Solanas and Getino's film have been extensively discussed elsewhere, I will move on to a discussion of how other militant films engage with the spatial margins.[10]

A very different film, in its production, reception, and form, of *Cine Liberación* is Gerardo Vallejo's *El camino hacia la muerte del Viejo Reales* (1971). Vallejo expands on Solanas and Getino's denunciation of the impoverishment and exploitation of sugar-plantation workers in his home province of Tucumán, which, despite being known as the "jardín de la república" (garden of the republic) due to its agricultural productivity, had become (and remains today), emblematic of Argentina's particular uneven modernization as the source of the nation's most shocking images of poverty. Fabiola Orquera writes of *Cine Liberación*'s "desplazamiento del punto de enunciación discursiva de Buenos Aires al 'interior'" (displacement of the point of discursive enunciation from Buenos Aires to the "interior") (2), a move that is fully realized with Vallejo's film, in which "[l]a Argentina rica y abundante deviene entonces una máscara que oculta a los sujetos que margina, representados en este caso por los trabajadores 'golondrina'" (the rich and abundant Argentina becomes a mask that hides those subjects it marginalizes, in this case represented by the migrant workers) (2–3). Orquera's final reference is the colloquial term applied to the migrant laborers who figure prominently in the film and whose subjectivity is represented in order to portray the harrowing experience of life in those areas kept in poverty to serve as a source of cheap resources and labor.

As Orquera recounts, Vallejo's film was relatively well distributed, both internationally and within Argentina, in part due to the fortunate timing of its release. As the legalization of Peronism became imminent, it was officially approved and given "special interest" status by the INC, which made its exhibition obligatory. In the provincial capital of San Miguel de Tucumán it was very well attended and continued to be shown for six months, becoming so prominent in the provincial and national media that Vallejo was appointed "Asesor Cultural" (Cultural Advisor) of the Tucumán provincial government during the brief Cámpora presidency. But the film also produced a fierce reaction in the opposed political sectors, and when in December of 1974 a right-wing group attacked the home of Vallejo's parents, the filmmaker went into exile (Orquera 9–17).

By opening the film with an image of text showing verses selected from *El Martín Fierro* that address first economic exploitation, then the legitimate violence that resists it, Vallejo links his protagonists—a family of cane plantation workers—to the traditional image of the resistant gaucho as a long-exploited popular figure who practices just violence. On the exploited condition the verses ironically mimick the official line on the gaucho: "Si uno aguanta es gaucho bruto/si no aguanta es gaucho malo/dele azote dele palo/porque es lo que él necesita/de todo el que nació gaucho/esta es la suerte maldita" (If he takes it they say he's a fool; if he doesn't, he's a bad gaucho. Lash him, give him a clubbin', since that's what he needs! For anybody born a gaucho, this is his damned fate) (Hernández 1974). Then the verses switch to the gaucho's perspective, from which violent resistance against state repression is legitimate: "Vamos suerte vamos juntos/dende que juntos nacimos/y ya que juntos vivimos/sin podernos dividir/yo abriré con mi cuchillo/el camino pa seguir" (Come on fate, let's go. Since we were born together, and since we live together and can't never be apart, with my blade I'll clear a path for us to follow) (Hernández 1974). This episode in which Fierro chooses violent resistance over submission to the state suggests an analogous condition that legitimizes resistance by the exploited protagonists.

El camino hacia la muerte del Viejo Reales centers on a single family, resulting in a narrower, more subjective focalization than the more epic *La hora de los hornos*. Instead of presenting a history of Latin American colonization, it aims to show the present-day effects of neocolonialism on minds and bodies in an isolated zone of Tucumán.[11] The film employs images ranging from wide shots of landscapes to the extreme close-up detail that transforms body into landscape, speaking volumes about neocolonialism through the marks it leaves on both the continent and its inhabitants. The industrial agriculture-based exploitation evident on the landscape—cane fields and shanties—produces fraught labor relations that drive scenes of alcohol-fueled domestic violence and state repression that scar the bodies of individuals. These scenes of violence are staged recreations that employ as actors individuals embedded in the places of the location shooting in these most absolutely marginalized of areas.

These characters exemplify various ways of relating to the community and illustrate the ethical implications of individual choices. Angel, Mariano, and "El Pibe" (the Kid) are brothers, sons of "el Viejo" (the Old Man)

Gerardo Reales. From a common beginning, the life trajectory of each leads them toward radically different relationships with the rural working-class community to which they belong. With a wife and four children, Angel lacks economic options and is forced to work as a migrant agricultural laborer. At several points he is shown traveling on the train to find work, and the landscape is seen in extended shots filmed from the train. As the train passes through stations, many more *golondrinas* standing on the platforms are documented. By contrast, Angel's brother, Mariano, is at first a union delegate, and then becomes a local policeman. In such a context as this, employment in the interest of the bosses to repress workers qualifies Mariano as a traitor to the *pueblo*, and Vallejo shows how his resulting shame and self-loathing are manifested in episodes of drinking and domestic violence.

The last story, of El Pibe, most incisively integrates the train into the cinematic apparatus. As a union delegate he had developed a lucid consciousness of the causes of the local working-class condition and, like Angel, he is repeatedly seen traveling by train, contemplating the passing landscape. He has evidently traveled these tracks many times in the course of his life, and the landscape seen through the window is imbued with memories, functioning as a sort of visual madeleine that triggers flashbacks to his union activist career—"It is the silence of these things put at a distance, behind the windowpane, which, from a great distance, makes our memories speak . . ." (de Certeau 112). The perspective is expanded horizontally through El Pibe's memories to become that of the *pueblo*: Individuals plead with him as delegate and tell stories of their own suffering, which are filmed in dramatic recreations of scenes of alcoholism and domestic violence, intimidation, and corruption, and, as the unions attempt to unite in order to better the conditions of the workers, violent revolt against the foremen. As we hear his voice and see the scenes it narrates, sometimes the image cuts to El Pibe's face as he recounts the events, and at others to the passing landscape in subjective shots that directly link views of the land to the memories they trigger. In part through this use of the train in combination with nonactors embedded in the setting to denounce the suffering and exploitation of the workers at the hands of an alliance between landowners and state power, *El camino hacia la muerte del Viejo Reales* became one of the most politically consequential films of Argentine militant cinema.

Argentine criticism has been quick to point out differences between the work of Jorge Prelorán and more militant filmmakers, and it has at times judged him harshly for a lack of an explicit political commitment (Derbyshire 7). These differences are often attributed to the nationality of Prelorán's mother—she was from the United States—and to the time he spent in her country of origin, during which he studied film at UCLA and was for a time in the military. Descriptions of him as "de formación anglicana y liberal, profundamente humanista" (of an Anglican, liberal, deeply humanist education) (Pérez Llahí 2011, La voluntad 311) and "de educación puritana" (of a Puritan education) (Taquini 34) are typical of the way he is differentiated from those filmmakers of his time who are considered to be more Argentine, and function to explain away Prelorán's self-avowed political agnosticism—"Yo no creo en la revolución, creo en la evolución" (I don't believe in revolution, I believe in evolution) (qtd. in Taquini 41)—and reluctance to answer the call to militancy in the way that did Solanas, Vallejo, Gleyzer, and so many others of his time.

After early collaborations with Gleyzer on the short films *Ocurrido en Hualfín* (1965) and *Quilino* (1966), Prelorán entered into a long association with the Universidad de Tucumán and the Fondo Nacional de las Artes (National Fund of the Arts). The films produced during the collaboration have caused him to be considered by many as Argentina's first ethnographic filmmaker. An inquisitive, rather than prescriptive, attitude toward images of the nation's inhabitants is revealed in the following statement:

> Nuestro país es increíble, del trópico al frío, y tenemos una gran variedad de argentinos. Tengo la certeza de que si uno pudiera conocer la forma de vida de un jangadero de Paraná, un pescador de Mar del Plata, un ovejero de la Patagonia, un minero de Catamarca, un puneño, un jinete de Corrientes . . . además de las realidades urbanas en las grandes ciudades o los pequeños pueblos, entonces recién conoceríamos qué es el ser argentino. (qtd. in Ruffinelli 167)

> Our country is incredible, from the tropics to the cold, and we have a great variety of Argentines. I am certain that if one could get to know the way of life of a *jangadero* from Paraná, a fisherman from Mar del Plata, a shepherd from Patagonia, a miner from Catamarca, a person from the Puna, a horseman from Corrientes . . . in addition to the urban realities of the big cities and the small towns, only then would we know what it means to be Argentine.

With this enumeration of the varied ways of life of inhabitants of his birth country, all defined by their relationship to specific geographies and most by their livelihood, Prelorán could be replying to the limited imagination of the gaucho-centric *cuadro de costumbres* notion of Argentine identity. He referred to his own filmic work as "etnobiografía" (ethnobiography), because of its explorations of subjectivity through the use of long-term collaborations with his subjects (to whom he refers as "co-directors") and the use of their first-person voice as a central thread that determines the content and sequence of the images. This method distinguishes Prelorán's work from classical expository ethnography with third-person voiceover narration that tends to use images as evidence to support an argument, in a practice Bill Nichols refers to as "evidentiary editing" (2001, 107).

Prelorán's usual working method was to start by getting to know well an inhabitant of the Argentine interior, then recording a long, unfilmed interview, which was then edited and used as a soundtrack. The subject's principal contribution to the collaborative aspect of the film is the personal perspective provided by these interviews, on which Prelorán would then base his own decision making during the filming. Through the resulting responsivity of the images to the words of the subject, Prelorán claims to avoid imposing his own authorial will on the images (92–93), which is, of course, only partially possible, since in the interview itself, the filming and the editing, his input is inevitable. Prelorán provokes the encounter with the subject and elides the provocation, thus rendering his presence implicit.

He does not theorize about or analyze the political causes of his subjects' conditions in his own voice. Where there is a political analysis, it is done by the subject of the film in the voiceover, such as Cochengo Miranda's complaints of the state's neglect of the rural western pampa where he lives, but of course both the provocation and the selection of what to include is again Prelorán's own. Despite this self-erasure, Prelorán's strategies are vastly different from those of the third-person voiceover of much political cinema of his time, and the autobiographical, first-person voice of his subjects injects his films with political potential at the same time that it avoids some of the problematic aspects of more conventional forms of ethnography, as Louis Werner notes:

> Many scholars criticize conventional ethnography for seeming to take place outside the passage of time, as if the subjects exist in some kind of primitive "never-never" land without history, as if they live from generation to generation in a state of suspended development. Prelorán's biographical films all recognize that history's forward movement is the great equalizer, creating the common ground upon which modern and traditional peoples meet. (52)

Although Werner's egalitarian conclusion here seems somewhat overly optimistic, he cites a historical dimension that is indeed lacking in many more classically expository documentaries in which a guiding consciousness—Nichols's "voice of documentary"—imposes meaning on the images through selection, editing, and voiceover. In Prelorán's work the guiding voice of the documentary subject neutralizes this effect, although only to a degree, since Prelorán's filmed images and editing can be as eloquent as the voiceover. In *Quilino* (1967) and *Chucalezna* (1969) for example, he introduces images of the train as a symbol of modernity, which are intercut with scenes of children in schools, a montage that functions, as Werner remarks, to "underline modernity's intrusion into a quiet landscape that nonetheless remains stubbornly isolated from city life" (51).

With this use of voiceover in mind, in considering Prelorán's work the notion of vernacular, as opposed to official, landscape might be useful. As described by Rob Nixon, a vernacular landscape

> is shaped by the affective, historically textured maps that communities have devised over generations, maps replete with names and routes, maps alive to significant ecological and surface geological features. A vernacular landscape, although neither monolithic nor undisputed, is integral to the socioenvironmental dynamics of community rather than being wholly externalized—treated as out there, as a separate nonrenewable resource. By contrast, an official landscape . . . is typically oblivious to such earlier maps; instead, it writes the land in a bureaucratic, externalizing, and extraction-driven manner that is often pitilessly instrumental. (17)

It could be argued that the images of the land in Prelorán's films move toward vernacularization by virtue of the director's technique of allowing, first, his protagonist's presence to focalize the narration and thus to determine which spaces he films, and second, the same protagonist's voiceover to subjectivize the images, rendering these affective spaces.

But this way in which Prelorán and his subjects work together toward the production of vernacular landscapes does not exhaust his films' complexity, since these character-focalized images are supplemented by the less frequent images shot from modern forms of transport that provide an additional perspective that does not necessarily claim objective or scientific knowledge of these spaces, but instead serves the inquisitive gaze of the spectator by supplying visual information on these culturally invisible spaces of the nation. In *Hermógenes Cayo* (also known as *Imaginero*, 1970), the filmmaker employs the train both as a metaphor for a voyage made to Buenos Aires by the protagonist two decades earlier and as a vehicle from which to document the landscape. The eponymous subject of what is probably Prelorán's most widely known film is a sculptor and painter of religious icons who lives with his wife, Aurelia, in an extremely isolated zone of the Argentine altiplano. Hermógenes, and occasionally Aurelia, provide the voiceover. The very limited narrative focus mostly confines the information provided to the perspective of the protagonist, until, that is, Hermógenes describes his participation in the Malón de la Paz, when, in 1946, 174 indigenous men traveled to Buenos Aires to reclaim the titles to their ancestral lands that had been taken from them as part of the vast dispossessions that accompanied colonization and the nation's modernization, and which have since been in the possession of large landowners. As we hear Hermógenes speak of the voyage, Prelorán represents it visually by filming from a train, and in doing so widens the range of narrative information, providing greater omniscience. First we see the train rolling through the rural landscape, and then we see the vast landscapes of Jujuy province filmed from the train. Like his later use of an airplane in *Cochengo Miranda*, the use of the train is an example of how Prelorán utilizes the material resources available on location, but in both films such a shift in narrative mode provides visual information about space that exceeds that of the protagonist and would otherwise be inaccessible to the viewer. These are of course spaces that had not been represented in the national culture in ways that reflected their realities.

Cochengo Miranda (1974) documents, with a degree of psychological depth through its use of first-person voiceover, the life of the eponymous *puestero*, or small farmer, who lives with his family in an extremely isolated zone of the dry western pampa. After an examination of his day-to-day life, scenes of gaucho tasks from the "tiempo de las yerras" (cattle-branding season) are seen as Cochengo tells of the difficulty of existence on this unforgiving landscape. Those carrying out the gaucho tasks are presented to the viewer not as *costumbrista* symbols of national identity, but as men and women with histories of scraping out subsistence by raising cattle on a dry landscape. Cochengo recounts that much of the younger generation has emigrated to the towns, leaving the aging population that remains in an ever more difficult situation, and then proceeds to specifically indict the absence of the state. Several of the film's formal strategies contribute to his analysis.

Unmentioned in most accounts of the film is Prelorán's use of an airplane from which he films the land. When Cochengo has to travel to a nearby town to complete a bureaucratic task, he hitches a ride in a truck, but Prelorán chooses to represent the voyage with shots of the landscape filmed from an airplane. This somewhat jarring decision produces one of the few moments in which the narrative focalization strays from Cochengo himself. It does so as he is criticizing the state for its absence in the western Pampa, where, according to him, there is very little help available and the state's bureaucracy even impedes the inhabitants' ability to provide for themselves in the already challenging environment. The focalization had been fairly consistent, with the camera following Cochengo, but the sudden cut to shots of the landscape filmed from an airplane introduces a far wider and more distanced perspective. If only momentarily, there is complicity between filmmaker and viewer, who have access to a perspective which the earthbound Cochengo does not share. While this perspective could be understood as an attempt to establish a more traditionally omniscient and objective scientific perspective, thus as betraying Prelorán's avowed strategy of allowing the subject to determine what is seen in the imagery, I would argue that this might be done in the interest of providing the viewer with documentary counter-information on the geography of the western Pampa, specifically the confirmation of the vastness and aridity, described earlier by Cochengo, of this space that has all too often been imagined in the national culture as a premodern idyllic background for the national symbol of the gaucho.

A final important aspect of Prelorán's films, one related to his claims of being apolitical, is their thematization of labor. The films explore the meaning of rural labor to both society and the individual who carries it out, but where Gleyzer, Solanas, Vallejo, and other militant filmmakers tend to be drawn toward the exploited worker, both urban and rural, in Prelorán labor is that of craftsmen, artisans, or subsistence laborers who, as the eponymous protagonist of *Cochengo Miranda* insists, are not part of the society to which the state responds. This permits another political dimension to come to the fore.[12] Work by rural subjects becomes, in Prelorán's films, labor as a potential commodity, a theme of central importance to a continent colonized, then neocolonized, in large part with the intent to appropriate the labor of its inhabitants, and where the dispossession of space and resources has continued unabated and even intensified in recent decades. The passage of time has thus located Prelorán as a prescient filmmaker who anticipated the increasing importance of capital accumulation by dispossession, the victims of which are not a proletariat already laboring under capital and wielding tools that are themselves capital owned by someone else. Prelorán's subjects are instead those whose labor, lands, and knowledge still belong to them, but who have since increasingly faced dispossession at the hands of capital with the expansion of monocultural export agriculture and extractivist economic policy. Thus it could be said that Prelorán's politics are not absent, but implicit and even deferred.

Fiction Films of the *Primavera Camporista*

By the early 1970s, as the series of military governments became ever weaker, the return of Perón appeared imminent. This political opening was accompanied by a reconfiguration of the field of representability in the national culture. On May 25, 1973, the elected Peronist candidate, Héctor Cámpora, assumed the presidency, and in August of that same year appointed Octavio Getino, the militant filmmaking partner of Fernando "Pino" Solanas, to head the state censorship board, which was quickly relaxed. Certain films that had until then circulated only clandestinely, among them *La hora de los hornos*, were legalized. The popular Peronist filmmakers Hugo del Carril and Mario Soffici were appointed to run the Instituto Nacional de Cinematografía; both production and attendance greatly increased, and politically engaged films were made, many of which were commercially successful (King 1990, 89). In narrative film there was an opening to themes that until then had been untouchable, as evidenced by *La Patagonia rebelde* (Héctor Olivera, 1974) and *Quebracho* (Ricardo Wullicher, 1974), which fictionalize historic rural labor conflicts. The *primavera camporista* ended abruptly. Cámpora left office on July 12, 1973, and in the ensuing election Juan Perón ran for the presidency, won, and quickly broke with his supporters on the left. When Perón died on July 1, 1974, his widow Isabel took over the presidency, and under the sway of her advisor José López Rega a quasi-state paramilitary apparatus, the Alianza Anticomunista Argentina (or Triple A), was set up to intimidate, hunt down, and eliminate opposition figures. In August of 1974 Isabel Perón put the notorious cultural conservative Miguel Paulino Tato in charge of film censorship, which returned with a force far greater than ever before.[13]

Such is the context of the production and distribution of Eva Landeck's *Gente en Buenos Aires* (1973), which contains one of the most incisive filmic engagements with the spatial aspects of the social conflict and state violence of the time. Landeck, who in a brief career made only three feature-length films, is one of the few women to direct prior to the breakthrough represented by the six feature films made by María Luisa Bemberg between 1980 and 1993. The effects of economic difficulties and state pressure are present both in the diegesis of Landeck's *Gente en Buenos Aires* and in the history of its production and exhibition. Landeck, who had studied filmmaking at the Asociación de Cine Experimental in Buenos Aires, made several shorts in the 1960s before turning to feature-length films. She wrote the script for *Gente en Buenos Aires* in 1972 and, unable to find financial backing, devised a cooperative funding plan. Since the film industry was in a period of reduced production, several technicians and actors agreed to her plan, which she describes:

> Nadie estaba filmando nada en aquel momento, y yo tenía un poco de dinero. Fui al sindicato, hablé con [el cinematógrafo Juan Carlos] Desanzo y [el actor Luis] Brandoni . . . Estuvieron ambos muy dispuestos a trabajar en sociedad. Todo marchó muy bien . . . Anunciaron el proyecto en la pizarra del sindicato, a ver quiénes querían trabajar en cooperativa. Respondieron muy bien; los puestos más sencillos se pagaron, pero los técnicos tenían que entrar en una especie de sociedad. Ellos cobraban semanalmente parte de su salario, y el resto quedaba en sociedad. (Trelles Plazaola 200–201)

> No one was filming anything at that moment, and I had a little money. I went to the union, spoke with (the cinematographer Juan Carlos) Desanzo and (the actor Luis) Brandoni . . . They were both very willing to work in a cooperative. Everything went very well . . . They announced the project on the chalkboard of the union, to see who wanted to work in a cooperative. The response was very good. The lower-earning positions were paid, but the technicians had to join a kind of partnership. They were paid part of their salary weekly, and the rest went back into the cooperative.

This innovative production model gave Landeck creative control over the project, and filming began and was completed in 1973 in the relatively open climate of the *primavera camporista*. But after completion indirect censorship began to be felt, as problems with distributors pushed the premiere back several months. According to Landeck, these problems were mostly due to competition from films made by large producers (she specifically names Sergio Renán's *La tregua*) that were given screening privilege over her film (Hardouin and Ivachow 49). By the time *Gente en Buenos Aires* opened in August of 1974, Isabel Perón was president and the censorship took on the more direct form of intimidation and threats.[14] The film opened well and, according to Landeck, continued to draw spectators, but it was finally pulled due to threats against Brandoni by the Triple A. As Landeck recounts, the film "[h]izo muy bien comercialmente; estuvo seis semanas en el cine, y la sacaron en el momento en que a Brandoni lo amenazaron de muerte y tuvo que abandonar el país, un mal momento—1974—fecha que no olvidaré nunca" (did very well commercially, screened for six weeks, and they took it down right when they threatened Brandoni and he had to leave the country, a bad moment—1974—a date I'll never forget) (Trelles Plazaola 200–202).[15] As a result of these pressures *Gente en Buenos Aires* vanished from view and has remained little known.

The sociopolitical context of Argentina in the early 1970s—a period of conflict during which state violence and political militancy were peaking—is represented in several ways in *Gente en Buenos Aires*. The film intercuts two different registers: black-and-white documentary and color narrative footage. The latter tells the story of a romance between Pablo (Brandoni) and Inés (Landeck's daughter Irene Morack), two young single middle-class migrants from the provinces to the capital who have precarious and unrewarding jobs. The city is portrayed as an alienating space that inhibits the kind of romance that drives most narrative films, including this one, due to the antagonistic interpersonal relations imposed by quotidian stresses and competition. Manners are brusque, interactions aggressive, and humiliation of the other is naturalized in daily social intercourse. Inés, under pressure from her colleagues, sharpens her incivility into a habitual cruelty toward the socially awkward Pablo during his sales visits. But when Pablo finds a certain Inés's phone number on a drawing she had made for the wife of a friend, he calls her, and through long nightly conversations they fall in love without realizing they have already met. Pablo realizes by chance who Inés is, and in an emotional final sequence they agree to meet. Despite an initial flight by an ashamed Inés they end up together, and as they walk hand in hand along the sidewalk this final color shot is intercut with black-and-white documentary footage of street protests and police repression, a rhetorical strategy to which I will return.

The narration is set entirely within the limits of the city of Buenos Aires, but despite its wholly urban setting the uneven modernization that has kept the inhabitants of marginal spaces economically subjected to the national elite is a central concern of the film. This uneven modernization and the social conflict it generates are manifested in several ways. First, their effects are shown to extend to Pablo's interiority, as he is portrayed as participating, albeit unconsciously, in militant operations. In two dream sequences he carries out direct actions as a member of the urban *guerrilla*. In the film's opening shot, unmarked as a dream until its end, he machine-guns a line-up of suit-clad men, and in a later dream he robs a bank to redistribute funds to the inhabitants of a *villa miseria*. These dreams portray what many at the time saw as socially just violence (following Frantz Fanon and other anticolonial theorists as filtered through militant films like *La hora de los hornos*), suggesting that Pablo's unconscious desires have been mediated by the surging "popular spring" but that active participation in militancy has been repressed by the alienating reality of his immediate surroundings.

The social conflict also appears in the use of documentary evidence. The setting of the film in 1972 is made explicit by a glimpsed newspaper headline reading "Fugaron Guerrilleros del Penal de Rawson" (Guerrillas Escape from Rawson Penitentiary), a reference to the Massacre of Trelew in which, on August 22, 1972, nineteen escaped political militant prisoners were recaptured and summarily executed on a military base in the south of the country. The headline contextualizes the intercut montage sequence mentioned above and several others in which the black-and-white documentary footage interrupts the color footage of the fictional narrative. These montage sequences show urban scenes, football matches, a newspaper headline reading "Más detenidos por actividades extremistas" (More Detained for Extremist Activities), but mostly protests and police repression. Not only do they situate the narrative in the conflictive political reality of its time, they also produce montage effects—like those so powerfully used in *La hora de los hornos* five years before—that imbue the film with a political charge unique to its historical moment by juxtaposing the political struggle with activities, such as spectator sports, which are often seen as distracting the population from its immediate reality. Such montage effects produced in a narrative film set in the present work in direct opposition to what was widely considered to be the escapist function of commercial narrative (or "first") cinema, by juxtaposing spaces that are usually separate, thus suggesting relations of causality that implicate national elites in the perpetuation of uneven modernity and structural violence.

The use of archival news footage of popular uprisings and their violent repression at the hands of the state was common in the militant films of the period, most notably in *La hora de los hornos*, but also in *Ya es tiempo de violencia* (Enrique Juárez, 1969) and *Argentina, mayo de 1969: el camino a la liberación* (Realizadores de Mayo, 1969). While it could be argued that the mere inclusion of these sequences in *Gente en Buenos Aires* does not explicitly lay out a political position, the ideological charge is unequivocal. The Cordobazo had taken place only five years before the making of the film, and other popular uprisings had followed in the years since. The historian Luis Alberto Romero refers to the resulting optimistic climate in somewhat epic terms as the "primavera de los pueblos," describing it as

> un coro múltiple, heterogéneo pero unitario, regido por una lógica de la agregación . . . Según una visión común, que progresivamente iba definiendo sus perfiles y simplificando los matices, todos los males de la sociedad se concentraban en un punto: el poder autoritario y los grupos minoritarios que lo apoyaban, responsables directos y voluntarios de todas y cada una de las formas de opresión, explotación y violencia de la sociedad. Frente a ellos se alzaba el pueblo, hermandad solidaria y sin fisuras, que se ponía en movimiento para derrotarlos y resolver todos los males. (243–244)

> a chorus of protest of great diversity, heterogeneous but in unison, ruled by an inclusionary logic . . . According to a common vision gradually gaining currency as it simplified the complexity of the situation, all of society's afflictions were concentrated in a single problem: the dictatorship and the small groups that supported it, the direct and willing culprits of each and every form of oppression, exploitation, and violence in society. Confronting them were the people, rising up in fraternal solidarity and without divisions, mobilizing to defeat the oppressors and resolve all of society's ills. (Romero 2006, 183–184)

Romero describes a sharply polarized society in which the chorus, unified in opposition to economic power and the state that acted in its interest, was reaching a climax as *Gente en Buenos Aires* was in production. Documentary footage of events like the Cordobazo seen on the relatively young medium of the television contributed importantly to the resonance of the political movement throughout Argentine society, as Jessica Stites Mor explains:

> [I]t is clear that the journalists, photographers, and news media that documented the Cordobazo and participated in its unfold-

ing meant to invoke the social memory of heroics from a past moment of solidarity and glory among the laboring classes. The journalist Roberto di Chiara's televised images of the assault on the city center and the subsequent military repression were a significant point of inflection in this struggle, unique in Argentina's history because of the way that the conflict was captured by and broadcast over the national media, almost in real time. His footage captured a specific narrative of the conflict that celebrated the worker and emphasized the repressive nature of the state's intervention, a triumphalist vision that suggested an opportunity for radical action to make real change. (27)

The rapid and massive diffusion of di Chiara's footage—including a charge by mounted police that suddenly shifts into a retreat in the face of the protesters, taking on a powerful allegorical charge—spurred optimism and further mobilization against state repression. Landeck's use of footage of the Cordobazo and other episodes of repression and protest is, then, politically a highly charged choice, one that locates *Gente en Buenos Aires* in sympathy with this climate of optimism on the left and with openly militant films that employed the same footage:

> Mass media images of the Cordobazo . . . circulated a utopian political vision of popular rebellion that was easily recycled as stock footage for documentary and political filmmakers who had previously had to rely more heavily on propagandist newsreels for historical images. The television and print media manufactured an expansive collection of audiovisual material that filmmakers could use to reflect on and then represent the lived experiences of the period. This synergetic relationship would feed a hungry audience of leftist intellectuals, university students, labor activists, and their allies . . . (Stites Mor 28)

While such borrowing of this footage was common among militant filmmakers of the time, as a narrative fiction filmmaker Landeck may be unique among the borrowers. In *Gente en Buenos Aires*, the black-and-white imagery is of a different order than the color sequences of the fiction film they interrupt, and as such are clearly marked as documentary registrations of the kind of political militancy that had seldom been referenced in Argentine fiction film. The documentary footage anchors the story of urban alienation and romance to a very specific moment in national history and a tense climate of political violence, in contrast to the more atemporal, escapist films that had dominated local commercial screens for decades. This inclusion of footage proper to "third," anticolonial cinema makes *Gente en Buenos Aires* unique as a film that was screened in commercial theaters that more typically showed the "first cinema" of the commercial industry or auteurist "second" cinema.

The relationship to third cinema is further consolidated by an exploration of the possibilities, advocated in militant cinema, of cross-class solidarity and the revolutionary potential of the popular classes. *Gente en Buenos Aires* elaborates on cross-class commonalities by portraying both middle and working classes as victims of the entrenched economic power that led the country through a flawed modernization and imposed an alienating economic order. For the middle-class protagonists, then, the class struggle can represent a possible source of salvation from the existing order. While the filmmakers of the *Generación del 60* had exhaustively explored the theme of urban alienation, *Gente en Buenos Aires* widens the focus to include the relationship between rural and urban spaces and the resulting political violence. Rural space is present, though always off screen, and despite its dystopian portrait of the city the film does not indulge in the easy antimodern nostalgia for rural space that characterized much of Argentine culture, and especially cinema, throughout the twentieth century. Like the urban setting, the off-screen rural space is a site of human suffering due to exploitation at the hands of economic power, as is revealed on several occasions. In one instance, during a phone conversation between Inés and her mother, we learn that her family had owned a tract of land in the provinces but were forced to sell it during a drought, after which they were hired as caretakers of the same land in the employ of its new owner. The transformation of Inés's family from owners of land to laborers employed by capital suggests that this is accumulation by dispossession, not the kind of change that might facilitate greater production of the land and be legitimately considered modernization.

The critique of uneven modernization and structural violence is made more explicit in the direct discourse of Pablo's neighbor, Torres, a migrant from the rural interior, popular philosopher of social justice and possible political militant. Torres's discourse is an example of what Gonzalo Aguilar calls "exterioridad," in which a character who represents "la posición moralmente correcta, la mirada que interpreta más adecuadamente lo que sucede" (the morally correct position, the gaze that most adequately interprets what occurs) (26), pronounces a discourse that "baja línea," or imposes an authoritative interpretation on the film. The usual exterior perspective is urban, either that of an intellectual or a member of the working class, but Landeck's use of Torres provides a rural-based perspective less often seen in Argentine cinema. Through Torres's brief but lucid account of class relations in Argentine society, rural space becomes the source of a social consciousness otherwise inaccessible to the more alienated urban protagonists. He lays out a simple but cogent account of the economic injustice brought about by uneven modernization and an implicit justification of political militancy in a response to Pablo's specifically urban complaint about his lack of free time, saying that

> Sin embargo en el campo sobra el tiempo, y eso tampoco está bien. Al campo y a la ciudad hay que transformarlos para que la gente que trabaja tenga una vida humana. El hombre necesita tanto la naturaleza como la compañía de la gente. Y a nosotros nos toca vivir en un mundo de veinticinco millones de habitantes, y más de cincuenta millones de vacas.

> But in the countryside there's too much time, and that's not good either. The country and the city have to be transformed so that people who work have a humane life. Man needs nature as much as he needs the company of other men. And we live in a world of twenty-five million inhabitants and more than fifty million cows.

Torres links back to the resistant *gaucho malo* of the nineteenth-century literary tradition, in which rural poverty is brought about by the modernizing process. To Pablo's subsequent complaint, ". . . yo no tengo ninguna vaca" (. . . but I don't have any cows), Torres responds: "Y yo tampoco, las vaquitas son ajenas" (Me neither, the cows belong to others). Meanwhile, the filmmaker participates in the diagnosis by intercutting the shots of the conversation with documentary footage of the Sociedad Rural, thus identifying economic power with the association of traditional wealthy livestock producers. Footage of protests and state violence is also shown, which anchors Torres's discourse in national reality and resonates unavoidably with *La hora de los hornos*, in which the landowning class of the Sociedad Rural is blamed for Argentina's uneven modernization and ridiculed as Eurocentric and superficial.

The most disturbing and prescient implications of the film, however, are not reached until the viewer, along with Pablo, sees Torres abducted violently by what appears to be a paramilitary group. Pablo calls Torres's lawyer, whom he had met briefly, but is rebuffed, and the likely assumption is that the lawyer either works with the abductors or is too fearful to pursue the case. Even as the romantic storyline is resolved, Torres's fate is left open, like that of many of the historical disappeared. By 1973, although not yet at the levels it would soon reach, the abduction and torture of citizens was already an established state practice, but one that had not been referred to in narrative films set in the present. Keeping in mind that the theatrical run of *Gente en Buenos Aires* took place during the presidency of Isabel Perón, with an already active Triple A, this episode would likely have been immediately resonant with the social reality in which its first viewers were immersed. Through these varied strategies, *Gente en Buenos Aires* denounces the persistence of uneven modernization and the related state violence and implicates the landowning elites of the Sociedad Rural.

In certain aspects, *Gente en Buenos Aires* is in continuity with many of the narrative films of the independent cinema of the preceding fifteen years, but its representation of the intersection of space, economics, and state violence goes further. Landeck diagnoses the nation's uneven modernization and directly addresses the use of state violence to perpetuate economic injustice in the interest of the economic elites, but in addition to these themes, common to many films of the time, Landeck extends the critique beyond the conflict between capital and labor, into the dynamic of dispossession that has since become central, as addressed by David Harvey in his account of "accumulation by dispossession" (2004). As Maristella Svampa wrote in 2015, the dynamic of dispossession has gone unaddressed even on the left:

> A large part of the Latin American Left and progressive populism has maintained a productivist vision of development, which tends to privilege the conflict between capital and labor, minimizing or giving little attention to new social struggles concentrated on territory and the commons. In this political-ideological framework dominated by the productivist vision, the current dynamic of dispossession becomes a nonconceptualizable blind spot. (Svampa 2015, 70)

This blind spot is addressed by Landeck with the dispossession of Inés's family's land, which is linked throughout the film to the larger dynamics of capital, state violence, and resistance at a historical moment in which these themes were uniquely immediate, before state repression neutralized the political struggle and rendered social issues unrepresentable. Partly as a result of its prescience in foreshadowing the violence of the dictatorship, Landeck's *opera prima* was the beginning of the end of a very promising filmmaking career.[16]

If a single film might function as a symbolic culmination of the cinema of the inquisitive gaze, it could be *La Raulito*, shot on the streets of Buenos Aires in 1974, while Isabel Perón was president and the Triple A abducted and killed militants, labor activists, and others. By the time of its October 1975 premiere, nonconventional culture was under suspicion and the military dictatorship was not far off. Although the film was screened to great commercial success, its director, along with the actors Marilina Ross, Duilio Marzio, and Luis Politti would soon be blacklisted and exiled (*Los nombres prohibidos . . .*). Ross's title character is based on a real-life Raulito (María Esther Duffau), who exists between genders, in part, as she says, in order to stay alive on the streets. In the film the character Raulito "actúa por instinto, procede con la inmediatez del impulso, incapaz de medir las consecuencias de sus actos" (acts by instinct, proceeds with the immediateness of impulse, incapable of considering the consequences of her acts) (García 207), a lack of self-control that results in a life on the streets of Buenos Aires. Condemned to a constant back-and-forth movement between state institutions and precarity on the streets, Raulito is marginal even when in the city center. Life for her progresses in cycles, which justifies that the film does not so much narrate linearly as cyclically, as she is repeatedly captured and institutionalized, only to escape and again be captured. When on the streets, Raulito sleeps in a camp of street children near Retiro Station, so although she is trapped in a seemingly inescapable cycle, present all the while is the linear form of a train track that offers a potential line of flight to a dreamed-of freedom.

When Raulito finally sneaks onto the train with her young friend Medio Pollo at the film's climax, it proves to be just such a line of flight, a vertiginous liberation from seemingly inescapable social bonds. While on the train she gazes overwhelmed at the rural landscape zooming past, which for her, if it is possible to judge from her expression, signifies freedom from the cyclical bind. An arrival to the coastline appears to confirm this liberation as Raulito and Medio Pollo gaze out at the breaking waves ruffled by an offshore breeze, but this liberation proves all too subjective and fleeting when, once again unable to escape her own impulses, she breaks a store window to steal a soccer ball in her beloved Boca Juniors' blue and yellow. She finds immediate joy playing on the beach, but soon police sirens announce an imminent fall back into institutionalization and precarity. An allegorical interpretation of the time of the film's making is difficult to avoid, since the possibilities of social change that had fueled the inquisitive gaze were becoming illusory as all imagined lines of flight were cut off in an increasingly authoritarian Argentina.

Commercial Cinema Responses to the Inquisitive Gaze

The commercial and new cinemas have generally been studied as separate, even mutually exclusive phenomena. While this division is justified to a degree by their distinct thematics and apparatuses of production and exhibition, as well as a somewhat differentiated viewership, an unexplored question remains: How did the themes and formal innovations of what I have called the cinema of the inquisitive gaze—as well as the somewhat distinct entity of the New Cinema—impact the more commercial cinema of its own time and after? I will reframe this question slightly as a way into the final section of this chapter: How did the commercial cinema during the most politically conflictive years of Argentine history respond to an increasingly inquisitive gaze of a spectator curious about what lay beyond the frame that bound the field of representability? The films discussed thus far in the chapter contributed to the opening of the cinema to spaces like the *villa miseria*, the Tucumán sugar plantation, and the slaughterhouse, while representing the violence that results there from national power relations and economic inequalities, and the commercial cinema appears to have then engaged with these same spaces by depoliticizing their representation. With the modest goal of opening a line of inquiry into the little-studied commercial cinema of the conflictive period running from the dictatorship of Juan Carlos Onganía through the end of the most recent military dictatorship, I will analyze two such responses.

Civilization, Discontents, and Scopophilia

Prime examples of the commercial narrative cinema's appropriation and depoliticization of the representation of spaces that had been brought into the national cinema with the inquisitive gaze are found in many of the over two dozen films directed by Armando Bó that star Isabel Sarli. In these films, especially those made during and after the late 1960s, marginal spaces often situate sexual encounters, at times violent, in which Sarli's character is victim. But unlike the explorations of marginal spaces that catered to an inquisitive gaze, in Bó's work such spaces are not represented as autonomous landscapes that capture the gaze, but as what Martin Lefebvre calls *setting*, a space "subservient to characters, events and actions" (2011, 64). The use of marginal space in Bó's films as setting for spectacle prompts a shift in the gaze from inquisitive to scopophilic (the Freudian "pleasure of looking" that Laura Mulvey sees as motivating the commercial cinema's male gaze that objectifies women) and thus works to neutralize the politicization of such spaces. Possibly most apposite is *Carne* (1968), set in a *villa miseria* and made after the cinema of the inquisitive gaze had helped to bring the urban margins to the national consciousness.

Bó first worked as an actor, then producer, in the era of the classical cinema, before moving to direction at the industrial studios' demise. He made his final film, *Una viuda descocada*, in 1980. Bó began to use marginal space as a setting for sexualized spectacle in the late 1950s, with *El trueno entre las hojas* (1958)—a film best known for introducing female nudity to the Argentine cinema—and continued, with varying explicitness, through the Onganía period, the upheaval that followed, and well into the last military dictatorship.[17] The political contexts of Bó's directorial production, although differing through time, were often authoritarian and characterized by a strong state presence in regulating and censoring film, with which his work came into frequent conflict. He made *El trueno entre las hojas*—his first film with Sarli—as the studios were closing, a period in which commercial film was forced to develop new strategies in order to compete for audiences with television. While some of these were technological advances, such as wide-screen formats, others involved pushing against limitations on nudity or sexual themes.

Bó's films exemplify the latter more consistently than any other director's work. Resolutely scopophilic in their gaze, they are described by David William Foster as "el grado cero de la explotación machista del cuerpo de la mujer" (the zero degree of *machista* exploitation of woman's body) (2). The sequences in which Sarli appears as spectacle are clearly the most carefully conceived and directed in Bó's work, the mise-en-scène designed as if the director had productively misread Mulvey's "Visual Pleasure and Narrative Cinema" as prescriptive rather than critical. When Sarli as passive object of desire is seen by the male characters with whose gaze the spectator is invited to identify, the resulting spectacle momentarily suspends the forward movement of the narration. But an account of their scopophilic gaze does not exhaust the film's complexity, since a tension between such scopophilic attraction and socially committed narrative runs through Bó's work, of which *El trueno entre las hojas* is perhaps the foremost example.

The film is based on a short story, written and adapted for the screen by Augusto Roa Bastos, that thematizes the plight of indigenous laborers exploited by the violent henchmen of a cruel plantation owner. In addition to the famous naked bathing scene, Sarli's character is raped by a group of mestizo, Guaraní-speaking rural laborers in an act of violence carried out indirectly against her significant other, the plantation owner. The violation takes place at a river surrounded by a visually impenetrable forest that ensures the act is hidden from the diegetic social realm as well as from the prying eye of the camera, at this point not yet permitted to serve up the spectacle of violation to a mass public. But in the subsequent trajectory of the pair's filmography, social concern cedes ground to scopophilia and Sarli's nudity and sexual humiliation become increasingly graphic. Such spectacle eventually becomes the *raison d'être* of films like *Carne* even as gestures toward the social remain, perhaps as attempts to persuade censors and public that these films are more than mere sexploitation. Such superficial justifications persist even as Bó's films become increasingly formulaic, as in *Fuego* (1969), which sheds crocodile tears for the tragic consequences of the Sarli character's nymphomania even as it devotes ample screen time to the manifestation of the condition's symptoms.

Referring to these apparently contradictory intentions, Rodolfo Kuhn calls Bó's cinema "pornografía moralista" (moralist pornography), arguing that "su seudopornografía no deja de apelar constantemente al 'humanismo cristiano' que tanto nos vapuleó desde niños . . ." (its pseudopornography constantly appeals to the "Christian humanism" they beat into us since we were kids) (9). The pure spectacle of Sarli's body as attraction, then, is tempered at times by a humanist message, at others by more Catholic appeals to feminine virtue: "Es notable como ella pasa por la vida sin alterar su cara. Su tono de voz es siempre monocorde y es evidentemente la mujer a la que le 'pasan' cosas. Y cuando ella las genera lo hace por su exuberancia sexual, por su ninfomanía, o en última instancia sin querer" (It's notable how she goes through life without changing her facial expression. The tone of her voice is always monotone and she is clearly a woman to whom things "happen." And when she initiates things they happen because of her sexual exuberance, her nymphomania, or as a last resort against her will) (Kuhn

39). With certain exceptions, like the sexually forward Flavia in *El trueno entre las hojas*, Sarli's characters are not so much autonomously desiring subjects as they are victims on whom sexual contact is inflicted in a seemingly inexhaustible catalog of ways by a seemingly endless cast of aggressors, thus her sexuality need not be punished in the diegesis. In Kuhn's view, the Catholicism of these films differentiates them from European and North American sexploitation films, in that it serves to justify them by appeasing the moral discomfort of a Latin American–wide public not ready for the kind of guilt-free female sexuality seen in foreign cinema: "El público necesita el castigo y el arrepentimiento de los personajes de Isabel" (The audience needs the punishment and repentance of Isabel's characters) (53). While Kuhn's hypothesis may seem somewhat reductive, especially in its account of Latin American cinema viewers, the concept of moralistic pornography will be a useful tool with which to examine the spatial dynamic seen in many of Bó's films.

The sexual encounters of the Bó-Sarli films are often set in those marginal spaces whose existence could, by the 1960s, no longer be denied by the national culture.[18] But unlike Birri or Solanas, Bó does not denounce economic injustice or structural violence, and instead employs the urban margins along railroad tracks, slaughterhouses, and other spatial detritus of the modernizing process as settings in which the imperatives of social solidarity or national projects are absent. Freed from such demands, Bó instead offers his spectator identification with a scopophilic gaze of the male protagonist upon the erotic spectacle of Sarli's sexual humiliation, with increasing explicitness toward the late 1960s as his films found success on the burgeoning international sexploitation market.

Such displacement of the social by the spectacle of sexual violence arguably reaches its furthest consequences in *Carne* (*Meat*), made under the Onganía dictatorship. Despite being filmed on location in a *villa miseria* and inside a meat-packing plant, the film dodges issues of poverty and labor exploitation to instead thematize inter-male violence among the proletariat and spectacularize the violation of Sarli. In order to understand the depoliticization of space in *Carne* it is worth returning to the cinematic uses to which the space of the *matadero-frigorífico* had previously been put. A source of immense wealth for the beef-exporting elite after the invention of technology to keep meat frozen for shipping across the Atlantic, as well as a site of frequent labor unrest, several landmarks of political cinema have focused on it. In 1919 *Juan sin ropa* documented the workplace of its title character and fictionalized a strike and its repression by police, while

Humberto Ríos's 1960 short *Faena* documented it and was then quoted in *La hora de los hornos*' famous sequence counterpointing glossy print ads with bovine slaughter. In light of such a tradition, *Carne*'s use of the *villa* and the slaughterhouse as settings for spectacularized sexual violence becomes a particularly stark depoliticization of the gaze on marginal space. Declining to denounce any temporal cause, the film suggests that blame for the *villa*'s *miseria* rests on the universal—thus both incorrigible and forgivable—condition of male sexual desire and is exacerbated by the sublime yet saintly object played by Sarli.

Delicia—the name as subtle as the *décolletage*—fulfills the traditional criteria of feminine virtue, at least if we take her at her word: "Yo solo quiero casarme y dedicarme a mi casa, a mi hogar" (I just want to get married and dedicate myself to my house, my home), she claims to her gossipy *compañeras* on the meat-packing line. Delicia does not acknowledge feeling sexual desire, claiming instead to want a man because only with one present does a *casa* become an *hogar*. In light of such a lack, although the female body is defiled the soul remains pure, allowing the pornography to claim a Catholic morality. Male desire, by contrast, is the driving force in Bó-Sarli's universe as a primitive—universal and irrational, that is—force that underlies civilization and disturbs the peace along its margins, a kind of manifestation of a Schopenhauerean Will accompanied in the film by a Dionysian leitmotif performed by an organ and drum combo. Whenever a male character intensely desires Sarli—every time one sets eyes on her, that is—this insistent rhythm reinforces the implacability of the resulting desire.

The first setting of violation is a railroad track on the edge of a *villa miseria*. Sarli, walking to work at the *frigorífico*, is first attacked by one man, then rescued by another, who upon getting a better look at her decides to take her for himself. This episode makes clear the universality of male desire for Delicia-Sarli, since no real *macho* could possibly resist being swept into an encounter of such irresistible forces as heterosexual desire and Miss Argentina 1955. Since this violence takes place among inhabitants of the social margins, the state is absent and diegetic punishment takes not a judicial form, but rather that of further violence exerted by males as they in turn stake their own claims over Sarli's body. A barbaric marginal masculinity on a Darwinistic model is thus proposed: in order for the economically challenged to possess the object that all males have a duty to desire (insofar as they aspire to normativity) violence is necessary, to eliminate both the competition from other males and the obligatory resistance on the part of the female (which allows her to remain a good Catholic, apt for monogamous coupling, reproduction, and child raising). The setting of such a scene needs to be an asocial space in which both violation and individualistic inter-male violence can take place far from the meddling of the state with its monopoly on violence, a space of natural freedom of the id in which pure violence can determine who wins the sublime prize, at least until a more worthy rival fixes his gaze on her. But since a film can only be so long, there has to be a final male, one large and strong enough to retain possession of Sarli when the film ends. In *Carne* this final male is Antonio—played by Bó's own ne plus ultra-macho son Víctor—a man both sufficiently invincible and forgiving of Delicia's nonconsensual sexual encounters so that a compliant spectator just might be convinced by the film's ending. Maybe the couple will find continuity beyond Delicia's next violation on the tracks or in the meat freezer, in a barbaric happy ending that is nonetheless the best that could be hoped for in such a hopeless place, where social solidarity is futile and the only cohesion possible is that of the heterosexual nuclear family.

The final dialogue of the film, when Antonio finds out that Delicia has been raped and asks why she didn't tell him, elucidates this moral:

ANTONIO: ¿Por qué no me lo dijiste antes? (Why didn't you tell me before?)

DELICIA: Tenía miedo, [los hombres] son capaces de todo. Y tenía miedo de ti. (I was afraid, men are capable of anything. And I was afraid of you.)

ANTONIO: No digamos nada a nadie. ¿Para qué? Total, yo te quiero lo mismo. (Let's not tell anyone. Why would we? Anyway, I love you all the same.)

DELICIA: ¡Qué bruta es la gente! ¿Qué ganaron con eso [las violaciones]? (People are such brutes! What did they get out of that [the rapes]?)

ANTONIO: Satisfacer el instinto animal, que todos llevamos adentro. (Satisfy the animal instincts that we all have inside.)

DELICIA: Es la desesperación de la carne, el deseo brutal, sanguinario. (It's the desperation of the flesh, brutal, bloody desire.)

ANTONIO: Pero sin alma, sin amor. (But without a soul, without love.)

DELICIA: Yo fui una cosa muerta, que nada sintió, nada más que asco y repulsión. ¿Me perdonas, Antonio? (I was a dead thing that felt nothing, nothing but disgust and repulsion. Will you pardon me, Antonio?)

ANTONIO: ¿Cómo no he de perdonarte, querida? (How could I not pardon you, my love?)

Despite the animalized men and victimized women, this conversation manages to articulate a comforting message, teaching that love can indeed flourish if sin is forgiven.

But the representation of the male proletarians as irrational beings incapable of forming part of a social body prepares the viewers for a text that appears immediately after the above dialogue and just before the final credits roll. It reads "El verdadero amor puro, sin concesiones, y la bondad de Dios triunfarán sobre la violencia y la ola de terror que invade el mundo" (True pure love, with no concessions, and the goodness of God will triumph over violence and the wave of terror that is invading the world). It must be assumed that this apparent non sequitur is a condemnation of late-sixties political militancy designed to appeal to Onganían film-critical sensibilities and counter the constant problems with the censor faced by Bó's work, but it also provides one pole of an opposition that resonates more deeply if the marginal setting of *Carne* is taken into account. This opposition is between a working-class male homosociality based on the cohesiveness that binds political and militant movements, that of class-based solidarity, in stark contrast to the agonistic, radically individualistic and depoliticized homosociality of the marginal spaces in the film, from which the only possible refuge is the family *hogar*. This is a masculinity in no way compatible with calls to solidarity or militancy, and thus one that does not threaten the status quo. Such a place prompts no inquisitive gaze, since it is *la barbarie*, a place long understood in the national culture.

Faith: In the Father and the Son and the Culture Industry

Another response by the commercial narrative cinema to the inquisitive gaze is seen in *Yo tengo fe* (1973). Produced as the return of Juan Domingo

Perón was imminent, the film contains a moralizing allegory that lays out two diverging paths available within Peronism. One is a conservative model compatible with the right-wing sector of the movement that would soon dominate, the other an amoral delinquency that the film manages to associate with political militancy.

The film's director and star, Enrique Carreras and Palito Ortega, had worked together extensively since before Onganía took power, making *El club del clan* (1964), *Mi primera novia* (1965), *¡Viva la vida!* (1969), and *La sonrisa de mamá* (1972), among other titles. These films, targeted at youthful consumers of pop culture, were part of the cross-platform marketing strategies of a rapidly modernizing culture industry of which Palito Ortega was the most visible product, an object of feverish adoration of a mass fan base who had previously seen him on the relatively new medium of television. Peña argues that Carreras, Ortega, and the producer of *Yo tengo fe*, Atilio Mentasti, were as a filmmaking team opportunistically compatible with the values of the authoritarian right, and particularly with those of the Onganía dictatorship. The three "reprodujeron en su cine todo el catálogo de valores reaccionarios de ese gobierno, como ya lo venían haciendo desde años antes" (reproduced in their cinema the whole catalog of the reactionary values of that government, as they had been doing for years) (195). This ideal reflection of the cultural politics of an authoritarian state resulted in the remarkable continuity of Ortega's success in the decades punctuated by military takeovers. The pop singer's

> vacío absoluto de sustancia lo transformó en el intérprete ideal del cine promovido por el Estado durante la dictadura iniciada por Juan Carlos Onganía en 1966. Mientras las películas de alguna inquietud renovadora no recibían créditos ni subsidios públicos, Ortega protagonizó una extensa serie de films que encontraron simultáneamente el éxito público y el apoyo oficial. (199)

> total absence of substance transformed him into the ideal performer for the cinema promoted by the state during the dictatorship begun by Onganía in 1966. While films with a restlessness for change didn't receive credits or state subsidies, Ortega starred in an extensive series of films that enjoyed both popular success and official support.

Ortega's success with both film consumer and state bureaucrat did not wane in Onganía's absence from the Casa Rosada, and he continued to work in film through and beyond the dictatorship that ended in 1983. He moved to Miami in 1985, then returned to Argentina, where, allied with the President Carlos Menem in the Peronist Partido Justicialista, he was elected as governor of Tucumán Province in 1991.

But to return to the context of *Yo tengo fe*, after the cinema's increasing engagement with the social margins, Carreras's film recuperated the strategies that had been devised to represent the causes and consequences of uneven modernization and the production of marginal spaces. As we saw in the cases of *La hora de los hornos* and *El camino hacia la muerte del Viejo Reales*, earlier filmic denunciations frequently referenced the plight of workers on the sugar plantations of Tucumán province. *Yo tengo fe* responded in total ideological opposition to such representations through a reactionary recuperation of the settings and formal devices of Vallejo's film.

Yo tengo fe opens with a Palito Ortega concert in Tucumán. As he sings "vivir con alegría significa vivir más . . . ," his backup singers wear loose long-sleeved, ankle-length dresses, an image of chasteness that would soon be enforced on the nation's screens by Miguel Paulino Tato, head of censorship under the government of Isabel Perón and the first years of the dictatorship.[19] During an intermission the cheerful singer is interviewed in his dressing room and begins to narrate his life story, at which point the viewer learns that instead of Palito this is the fictional Martín Ríos, although the life stories of both are similar enough to make this a fictional biography of the former.[20] His story is told in a long flashback that opens during what is shown as the idyllic national interlude of the Perón presidencies of 1946 to 1955. The first shot of the flashback sets the nostalgic tone by showing Martín, his brothers, and father riding in a picturesque rustic horse carriage to the local train station. The father, like Gerardo Reales, is a Tucumán cane worker, but here no bosses, enforcers, or police are evident. Despite the absence of a repressive apparatus, Martín has decided to migrate to Buenos Aires, less as an attempt to escape poverty than to satisfy an abstract thirst for travel that he describes as "aquella obsesión de los trenes, aquellas ganas de irme lejos, lejos" (that obsession with trains, that desire to go far, far away). Seen from Martín's perspective, the train is recoded; no longer a carrier of agricultural products that facilitates the exploitation of cheap labor, here it becomes a symbol of individual freedom. After an emotional but expressionless, unequivocally masculine farewell—a lack of outward emotion reinforced by the father's admonition, "sin llorar compañero, no me gustan los hombres que lloran" (no crying, partner, I don't like men who cry)—Martín boards the train for a voyage that results in shots that could be seen to recuperate, and repoliticize, those of Vallejo's film, to which I will return.

The family in *Yo tengo fe* is a costumbrized version of those seen in Vallejo's film and in another, Rodolfo Kuhn's *Pajarito Gómez* (1965), which was a satiric fictionalization of Ortega's own early years as invented by culture industry publicists for its eponymous protagonist. In both *Pajarito Gómez* and *Yo tengo fe*—though thoroughly ironic in Kuhn's film and solemnly earnest in that of Carreras—rural poverty (at least under Perón) is ennobling and edifying, rather than stultifying of intellectual and physical formation, as it is in the militant films. In Carreras's optimistic version the father never loses his stoicism, turns to alcohol, nor strays from a strict exemplary compliance with the law, and as such is yet another return to the ethos of the *costumbrista* peon gaucho. Likewise, *Yo tengo fe*'s Martín could be seen as a similar reworking of El Pibe, the union delegate-turned-militant of Vallejo's film, but Martín is never tempted to turn to militancy nor to the criminality that the film associates with it as resulting from a lack of faith in the traditional pillars of society. Such activities are left to his childhood friend and dramatic foil, Ezequiel, characterized as lazy and morally corrupt from the very beginning of the film, when as a child he (sensibly) refuses the available work—"Yo quiero trabajar como un hombre, no como una bestia de carga" (I want to work like a man, not like a beast of burden)—then later steals a priest's lunch and sells a used train ticket to a gullible *golondrina*.

After Martín and Ezequiel arrive in Buenos Aires together, the latter gradually engages in more serious infractions, from petty theft to armed robbery and beyond. By contrast, Martín sets out to work hard at the worst of jobs—his boss in a restaurant does not give him time off and locks him in the basement each night—and keep to a straight and narrow path despite hardships and temptations, because, as he states repeatedly, he has faith, both in religion and in his personal trajectory. As the cynical marketing expert played by Federico Luppi in *Pajarito Gómez* had stated, a pop star must display consumer-friendly traits: "machito, buen hijo, tiene un coche veloz pero maneja con prudencia. Gana mucha plata pero la usa bien . . . no se mete para nada en política. Dice cosas tales como 'Si todos somos buenos y sentimos mucho amor el país saldrá adelante'" (a tough kid, good son, has a fast car but drives carefully. Earns a lot of money but uses it well . . . doesn't get mixed up at all in politics. Says things like "If we're all good and feel a lot of love the country will get better"). The description snugly fits Ortega's character in *Yo tengo fe*. After working as a waiter, then selling coffee on the street, he will eventually find the success as a singer that the viewer was never allowed to doubt since the film's opening concert sequence. The resonances with Hollywood's self-made-man storylines are unavoidable, but the film specifically engages with the Argentine cultural field, an examination of which demands an expansion of several details of the synopsis.

After being robbed upon arrival in Buenos Aires' Retiro Station, Martín and Ezequiel are detained for lacking identity documents. As a panoramic shot surveys those in the jail—who include prostitutes both female and male—an interior monologue by Martín is heard in which he underlines the film's antimodern opposition between urban and rural spaces:

> Y así toda la noche y la madrugada, un constante desfile de miserias humanas, un muestrario alucinante de todo lo más bajo y todo lo más sucio, lo más triste y canallesco que puede vomitar la vida. ¡Cuánto hubiera dado en ese momento por estar allá lejos, en mi pueblo, con mi gente, con mis hermanos, con mi padre!

> It continued like that all night and into the morning, a constant parade of human misery, a mind-boggling collection of the lowest and dirtiest, the saddest riff-raff that life can vomit out. What I would have given at that moment to be far away, in my town, with my people, with my brothers, with my father!

When faced with this urban jail, a cyclical destiny as a cane-cutting son of a cane-cutting father appears desirable. Further memory adds a moralizing dose of folk wisdom, when his father is heard saying (as sound internal to Martín's subjectivity) "Lo único que puedo hacer es arrimarle un buen consejo: Elija siempre el buen camino" (The only thing I can do is offer you a good piece of advice: Always choose the right path). The suggestion is clear: life in the city may be horrible, but rocking the boat through laziness, crime, or political militancy can only make it worse.

The two friends are released from jail to Ezequiel's brother, an assistant to a Peronist politician who lodges them in the local party headquarters. A wall calendar indicates the date as June 14, 1955, and before long the bombing of the Plaza de Mayo and the overthrow of Perón take place. After the coup, with Peronism banned and its leader in exile, the two find themselves once again without work or lodging. An allegory is articulated in which each character follows one of two diverging options within the movement as seen from the Peronist right wing, with Martín representing a conservative Peronism that would soon take power and Ezequiel an amoral lawlessness that the film equates with militancy. They eventually go their separate ways, as Ezequiel turns to crime and Martín finds the restaurant job before eventually opting for the discouraging work of an ambulant coffee seller, which he nonetheless livens up by singing a catchy song: "Yo voy cantando mientras vendo mí café. Café, café, bien calentito yo lo sirvo para Ud . . ." (I go singing as I sell my coffee. Coffee, coffee, I serve it nice and hot for you . . .). Here the music detains the narrative, bringing relief to the spectator at what might otherwise be the most dishearteningly realist moment of the film. The suggestion is presumably that songful escapism is always a better choice than organized labor, militancy, or crime. Predictably, singing leads to Martín's lucky break. He sells coffee in a television studio, which turns out to be his first step in achieving mass success as a pop singer.

But while the plot and the many pronouncements by its characters are the most obvious ways the film articulates its edifying message, it also responds more directly to the inquisitive gaze in a way that demonstrates that the classical conventions used to represent marginal spaces had, at least for a time, been rendered obsolete after the culture's politicization of the nation's economic margins. The surge in inquisitive filmmaking and viewing had already contributed to the modification of the cultural field in which *Yo tengo fe* was made, and I would suggest that the spread of such a gaze had obligated the commercial cinema to not only acknowledge and attempt to depoliticize marginal spaces and peoples, but even to counter inquisitive formal strategies. First the settings.

The setting of part of the film in a *villa miseria* would have been unthinkable for such an optimistic commercial product even a mere decade earlier. Martín enjoys a chaste romance with a young fellow internal migrant, Delia, but although their love is clearly blooming, she refuses to invite him to her family home, so one day he follows her bus and discovers that she lives in a *villa miseria*. In the following sequence, filmed on location on the edge of the Villa 21, the conventionality of the clichéd storyline is equaled by the depiction of space, in which the homes have picket fences, kids play happily on a soccer field, and plentiful green space and public transport are readily accessible. The inhabitants are healthy, active, and apparently pleased to be living in this *villa* that the film represents through the tropes of a more classic *arrabal*. As in the Tucumán cane fields of the same film, here poverty does not result in suffering, unless it is due to a more arbitrary tragedy—an epidemic eventually strikes the *villa*, killing Delia. Recalling

Klimovsky's *Suburbio*, *Yo tengo fe* locates the site of communicable disease in poor communities, but here it can be assumed that the potential solution proposed is the return of Perón.

Themes and settings alone do not exhaust the engagement in *Yo tengo fe* with Vallejo's film. Carreras's film also recuperates its formal strategies to invert their meaning, as seen in the example of Martín's train journey. As in *El camino hacia la muerte del Viejo Reales*, the train is used as a platform from which to film tracking shots in which rural landscapes are seen. Where in that film the gaze of El Pibe upon a landscape from a moving train evoked memories of scenes of familial abuses brought about by poverty and repressive state violence that checked the possibility of social progress, in *Yo tengo fe* the subjective train shot is put in the service of a counter-revolutionary message, as memories of poverty that edifies, instead of causing suffering, and which is naturalized as lacking a societal origin. Workers in the cane fields, horses, and a wagon pass through the frame. Soon, much like El Pibe in Vallejo's film, Martín appears in close-up and his thoughts are heard, but instead of remembering exploitation and state repression, his memories are purely nostalgic: "El tren seguía alejándome de aquel pueblo tucumano que había sido todo mi mundo, y como si quisiera aferrarme a todo aquello que iba quedando atrás, cerré los ojos y empecé a recordar . . . a recordar . . ." (The train kept taking me further from that Tucumán town that had been my whole world, and since I wanted to hang on to what was being left behind, I closed my eyes and began to remember . . . remember . . .). Thus begins a flashback within a flashback in which Martín's childhood in rural poverty is inflected more by nostalgic longing than hunger and violence. Martín's food security is made explicit in the flashback when he tries unsuccessfully to decline his father's offer of a sandwich, and apparently satisfying work abounds in this Tucumán.

Regarding both the inquisitive uses of the shots from the train and their commercial recuperation, if these shots are considered as purely documentary, thus as objective shots, it might be claimed that Carreras's film demonstrates the inquisitive use to be ineffective, a mere stylistic choice. But this objection would fail to consider the shots' rhetorical framing as subjective, and subjectivity's power to instrumentalize the filmic image. As images seen through the eyes of the labor activist El Pibe, the Tucumán landscape of fields, workers, and horses is one of produced poverty and crushing labor. By contrast, in the eyes of Palito's Martín Ríos, it is a space of nostalgic longing whose timelessness helps him to maintain his faith while enduring the harsh modernity of Buenos Aires. Despite the lesson taught by Lev Kuleshov a half-century earlier, the effects of a subjective gaze are easy to overlook in favor of film's much-vaunted indexicality.

As an exemplary fiction, Carreras's film proposes that the suffering caused by poverty on the Tucumán plantation and in Buenos Aires' *villa miseria* is not as militant film represented it, and recommends that the rural poor attempt to overcome a lack of economic opportunity not through political militancy, which is equated with criminal delinquency, but instead by keeping faith—in tradition, Perón, and oneself—and playing by society's rules. This message is delivered through an allegorized construction of biblical simplicity: two friends leave the province, one keeps to the straight and narrow path and returns triumphant, while the other takes that of dishonesty and crime, and, predictably, ends up badly. Near the film's end, its message is summed up by a repentant Ezequiel, when Martín offers him work but he again refuses, now for a different reason: "No. Para cambiar se necesita algo que yo no tengo y que a vos te sobra: Fe. Fe y voluntad, por eso llegaste donde llegaste." (No. In order to change one needs something that I don't have and you've got plenty of: Faith. Faith and will, that's why you got where you got). The faith here is in tradition, Perón's return, and the trajectory of the individual, exemplified by a character played by and identifiable with Argentina's most successful product of the modern culture industry, a destiny far less readily attainable than winning a lottery jackpot. Such faith is merited only in a fictional universe in which one can look to a rural space of mythic traditional values, not one maintained in service of the interests of capital as a reserve of cheap labor and raw materials, because in such a space faith would be better invested in the just violence of a social revolution.

Chapter 4

Contemporary Cinema and the Neoliberal Social Margins

Recent decades of economic crises and rapid neoliberalization brought major changes to national spaces and the regime of visibility, as well as a renewal of film production. The most notable development in terms of space has been the increase in extension and visibility of the *villa miseria*, especially after the 2001 crisis, when its inhabitants were seen in most parts of the city as *cartoneros*, searching the streets for cardboard or other recyclables. This new visibility of the *villa* and its inhabitants extends to the cinema, where, as Aguilar writes, at present "la cuestión no pasa por mostrar o no mostrar, sino por cómo hacerlo" (it's not about whether to show or not show, but rather how to do so) (Aguilar *La representación de las villas en el cine*, n.p.). The media, especially television, have tended to stereotype the inhabitants of the *villa*, whose identity took on a sharper definition and became associated with criminality, as a kind of internal social other to be feared and excluded from an increasingly illegible social contract. The *villa* itself is generally portrayed on film from an exterior, middle-class perspective, as a chaotic and hopeless place, although there are exceptional films that problematize such a perspective. But first, a brief account of the cinema since the dictatorship should go some way toward contextualizing both these conventions and the exceptions.

By the early 1990s the country nearly ceased producing films, as few as five in 1994, but nearer the end of the decade the Menem administration, through the imposition of neoliberal policies that favored production capital over more independent filmmakers, was encouraging an industry that attempted to compete on the terrain of the Hollywood blockbuster and managed to produce some commercially successful films with relatively high production values. Those favored production companies, like Patagonik and Pol-ka, were mostly owned by multinational media conglomerates such as Telefónica and Disney. But while the INCAA, the state institution that was remodeled by the 1994 *Nueva ley de cine* (New Cinema Law), favored this more commercial production model, it did not completely abandon nonindustrial filmmaking (Falicov 2007; Andermann 2012, *New Argentine Cinema*). It sponsored a competition for short films, whose winners formed part of what became known as *Historias breves (Brief Stories)* (1995), a feature-length compilation that was very positively received by the public and critics. This project is seen today as one of the first signs of activity of a new generation that would employ alternative production models and eventually renew the national cinema. Several of the initial participants went on to direct features that would find international success and subsequently be grouped by critics under the label *Nuevo Cine Argentino* (NCA, New Argentine Cinema). Many of these films involved multiple sources of funding from different countries, which aided their festival access and subsequent international distribution, but most found lesser commercial success within Argentina, where Hollywood imports continued to dominate the market.

Films made by directors referred to by Falicov as "industrial auteurs"—the most notable are Juan José Campanella, Fabián Bielinsky, and Damián Szifron—have occasionally enjoyed commercial success both within Argentina and internationally, and eventually some of the original NCA directors moved closer to their production model and attracted funding from the media conglomerates. A notable example is Pablo Trapero, who progressed from the micro-budgeted *Mundo grúa* (1999) to far larger productions like *Elefante blanco* (2012), produced by Patagonik (controlled by the media giant Clarín Group) and featuring established stars both Argentine and international, including Ricardo Darín and the Belgian Jérémie Renier.[1] Other, far lower-budget production models allow for more directly politicized treatments of the *villa*. Solanas's *Memoria del saqueo* (2004), *La dignidad de los nadies* (2005), *Argentina latente* (2007), and subsequent documentaries venture often into the *villas* as they denounce the corruption of the Menem years and urge Argentines to action in defense of national industry and a more equitable distribution of power and wealth. These are made on video, on a budget that frees Solanas from the need to appeal to a wide public. Similar, but even less costly modes of production include activist video, *cine piquetero*, and even some films that originate in the *villas* themselves.

The most innovative examples of filmic engagement with marginal spaces are seen in the films of the NCA, whose rejection of the kind of allegorical messaging that had been prevalent in the cinema since the fall of the dictatorship contributed to the renewal, both formal and thematic, of Argentine cinema. Various other factors helped bring about this renewal, but critics have mostly agreed on several points that are contained in a passage by Jens Andermann, who writes that the NCA

> can be thought of as the contingent and heterogeneous outcome over the last decade and a half of the profound changes in film circulation and consumption—boosted by festivals and film journals—with the resultant emergence of new, diversified audiences, the possibilities offered by cheaper, lightweight technologies such as digital video and editing software, the consolidation of film schools raising levels of formal and technical expertise, the introduction of new, fragmentary and improvisational rhythms of production and, last but not least, the ways in which these have made cinema contemporaneous with, and curious about, its own present. (2012, 10)

The causes mentioned in Andermann's account are important and generally agreed upon, but for my purposes the outcome he insightfully identifies, a curiosity about the present, merits further discussion.[2] Joanna Page examines the ways in which this curiosity has focused the new cinema's gaze on Argentina itself. The new cinema set out, as Page writes, "to present contemporary Argentina as a territory in need of charting, dissecting and recording and to present film as a tool ideally suited to the construction of social knowledge (or perhaps more accurately) . . . to the representation of a *crisis* in social knowledge" (36, emphasis in original). This is a cinema, then, that opened toward the marginal places and peoples of the nation with a high dose of skepticism toward its own capacity to represent them. Unlike the impulse behind the first films of Kohon, Birri, and others, who believed more firmly in film's capacity to document excluded sectors of society and their problems, the current new cinema has privileged epistemological crisis and rejected the notion of transparency so dear to Birri's generation. As a result, they

> do not "deliver" the social knowledge apparently promised by their semidocumentary or neorealist styles. Indeed, these borrowings are often undertaken with the paradoxical effect of *frustrating* the epistophilic desires usually associated with documentary spectatorship. They draw on structures and discourses of knowledge to

explore the limits of epistemology and deconstruct the relationship between visibility and knowledge. (36, emphasis in original)

Instead of the more transparent window onto the social used to satisfy the inquisitive spectator half a century before, these recent films introduce a reflexivity that "suggests that the real subject of these films' analyses is not society so much as the gaze itself" (36). Like the earlier generation, today's NCA filmmakers ask questions about the people and places on the national territory, yet here the form of questioning reveals the limitations of the cinema's capacity to provide knowledge and, importantly, of the spectator to possess knowledge, of such peoples and spaces. But this shared impulse toward epistemological crisis is as far as similarities go in the NCA films, which veer off in very different directions.

It must be emphasized again that this new cinema is in no way the dominant mode of production in Argentina. Among the small percentage of screens afforded to the national cinema (Hollywood still rules), the more commercial local cinema continues to dominate. In terms of thematics, and especially of form, the commercial cinema follows mostly on the Hollywood model. But even in this cinema the existence of the social margins, especially the *villa miseria*, is less frequently denied than in the past, although its role is more often as a source of middle-class fears within the context of an economically polarized neoliberal society. These fears include not only the potential violence of its inhabitants, but also the possibility of a fall of members of the middle class into precarity, an anxiety created by the downward mobility that became more common with the increased labor flexibility and the severity of the periodic economic crises in neoliberalized Argentina.

Rural spaces, by contrast, have faded into the background of the national imaginary with the increased visibility of the *villa*, despite the fact that many have undergone rapid, often violent, transformations due to corporate extractive and monocultural agricultural practices and the resulting environmental destruction and dispossession of rural communities. But despite the decreased cultural visibility of rural space, contemporary films have on occasion examined how it is conceived in the distant metropoli and documented economic exploitation and violence.

In general terms, contemporary film has engaged fully with the social margins through such a variety of ways to form a cultural field so diverse that it is impossible to make sense of it in a single chapter. My goal, then, in this chapter is to make a modest contribution to scholarship on recent Argentine film and space by extending the book's thematic study to the present through an examination of a limited selection of films. Some of these engage with spatial configurations that have resulted from specifically neoliberal impulses, such as the middle-class will to enclosure that results in the opposition of the *villa* and the gated community known as the *country*, while others formulate novel approaches to the representation of rural spaces. In the limited scope of a single chapter, many relevant films need to be excluded, but fortunately many of these have been intelligently analyzed elsewhere, especially by Page, Andermann, and Aguilar. Since my interest here is to explore in depth a few distinctly contemporary approaches through which to consider recent shifts in the place of the social margins in filmic (and video) culture, this chapter samples not only the NCA, but also more commercially conceived as well as more explicitly political films. The first selections center on the spatial opposition of relatively recent centrality to Argentine culture, that of the *villa miseria* and the *country*, while the latter engage specifically with metropolitan conceptions of the rural.

The Cruel Optimism of *Country* Life

While the classical cinema took part in the national culture's erasures by denying the existence of the social margins, certain contemporary films have brought into the light a related denial, one more proper to the neoliberal present. Upon the national culture's acknowledgment of the nation's internal others, the displacement of the denial onto the individual level is manifested spatially in the contemporary opposition of the *country* and the *villa miseria*. The *country* is an exclusive, wholly privatized neighborhood removed from urban dangers yet insulated from rural economic conditions. In it a relatively privileged collection of individuals dominated by fear seals itself in a space that recreates a reassuring illusion. Such social isolation has produced contradictory conceptions of the *country*. Have neoliberalism's winners found in it a synergetic solution that allows them to materially accumulate despite an increasingly jealous and hostile world? Or has the neoliberal economic regime produced conditions that have scared the middle class into a space of irresponsibility and class endogamy, a new instantiation of the Sarmientine opposition and a return to the nineteenth-century ethos of carving out a space for *civilización* in the midst of *barbarie*? While the former conception is most visible in the discourse of marketing, the films that have engaged with the *country* and its effects on the individual have mostly done so from the latter. I will discuss one of these, *Los Marziano*

(Ana Katz, 2011), which is set in a *country*, and another, *La mujer sin cabeza* (Lucrecia Martel, 2008), which engages with a similar kind of self-enclosure. Both employ the trope of sensorial impairment to engage with the phenomenon of enclosure through exemplary protagonists.

In the proliferation of gated communities in the last few decades, the sociologist Maristella Svampa sees a symptom of a social fracture, a "brecha urbana" (urban rift) exacerbated by the privatizations of the 1990s and the accompanying increase in social inequality (2004). Svampa tells the sweeping tale of the Argentine middle class, which, encouraged by the state throughout most of the twentieth century, had expanded to occupy the public spaces of the neighborhood, the *plaza*, and the school. But the more recent decline of the middle class has seen private space displace public, and the resulting exclusions, along with the increasing cultural visibility of the *villa miseria* and its inhabitants, have generated distrust and fear. As the *villa* plays its role as the imagined source of barbaric invasions—of *piqueteros* at the gates—the middle class is caught in the breach between the dream lifestyles of the rich and the nightmare presence of the *villero*—neoliberalism's winners and losers. Those who flee to the *country* are unified in a fear-based community whose most pressing imperative is that of reducing the danger faced by those whom an ever more unbalanced distribution of resources has left surrounded by have-nots of varying degrees of acquiescence. But security is not their only motivation: the *country* also offers distinction, symbolic confirmation that one has indeed managed to become a winner. Where fear of violence is answered with physical barriers and private police forces, fear of downward mobility produces a turn toward the assurance provided by amenities like swimming pools and golf courses.

So beyond being *just* a securely gated community, the *country* also functions as a desired symbol that generates consent for the perpetuation of neoliberal economics. While the business class of the Menem years might have marketed the *country* as a modern synergetic solution that allows one to more intensely accumulate without compromising the well-being of his or her family and possessions, from a less enterprising, more critical perspective it could be seen as the repository of a "cluster of promises" that draws the subject into a pernicious relationship of what Lauren Berlant calls "cruel optimism." Berlant theorizes cruel optimism as "a relation of attachment to compromised conditions of possibility whose realization is discovered either to be impossible, sheer fantasy, or *too* possible and toxic" (24). She goes on to specify that the desired attachment "might involve food, or a kind of love; it might be a fantasy of the good life, or a political project" (1). Or it could involve a *country*. But how can a gated community be an obstacle to the flourishing of its residents?

Berlant writes that "[t]he conditions of ordinary life in the contemporary world even of relative wealth . . . are conditions of the attrition or the wearing out of the subject . . ." (28). In recent films, we often see how the kind of individualist optimism that attaches the subject to the *country* generates a tolerance and even oblivion toward a condition in which ordinary life is far less than optimal. Such attrition can of course take on many forms, but in these films it could be said that the socially mediated desire that affectively attaches the subject to the promise of the *country* wears out this same subject through "autotelia," the state of being self-contained and sense-dead, as Susan Buck-Morss writes. Such autotelia results in an inattention to and a lack of care toward the relations between the self and society, and the passive cruelty of the sin of omission that takes the form of a letting-violence-happen (as long as it doesn't happen to me) becomes ordinary, and violence is naturalized as the driver of neoliberal spatial relations through the threat of the *villa* and the promised safe haven of the *country*.

The relation between self and society is played out in the films in diverse ways. Ana Katz's comedy *Los Marziano* explores the contemporary predicament at the level of the subject by opposing the fates of two estranged brothers, both in their fifties, both in crisis. One is an inhabitant of a *country*, while the other is one of those many individuals made obsolete by neoliberal economic design. Its plot is split into two separate but converging lines, each following one of the brothers, and the distance between the two dramatizes the cruelty of the promise of the *country*. Elder brother Luis is a well-off *paterfamilias*, his tribe ensconced in the apparent safety of a gated community. He is fully committed to the normativity proper to the *country*, to the point of obsession with the maintenance of its effectiveness as phantasmagoria, or "reality as narcotic" (Buck-Morss, after Marx). As a result, Luis's present is inflected by the kind of leaning toward the future that characterizes cruel optimism by "enabl[ing] a concept of the *later* to suspend questions of the cruelty of the *now*" (Berlant 28, emphasis in original). Thus is care suspended in favor of the promise, the mechanism of cruel optimism that explains why, for Berlant, "people are not Bartleby, do not prefer to interfere with varieties of immiseration, but choose to ride the wave of the system of attachment that they are used to . . ." (28).[3]

The commitment to *country* normativity, then, requires the sacrifice of any ethical commitment toward the non-normative in the present. In Luis's case, to stave off affective susceptibility that might cause his own conscience to suffer, he turns to golf as a technology of patience.

Golf serves Luis as a microcosmic distillation of the phantasmagoric function of the *country*, shutting out a corrosive reality through the sublimely conventional promise of the hole-in-one, which offers the kind of infinite room for improvement so useful for occupying an overabundance of leisure time. The golf course itself enforces an impoverishment of the corporeal sensorium. A monocultural space—*Cynodon dactylon*, Bermuda grass—cleared of anything autochthonous, which henceforth ventures in at its own risk, as a weed, the unwelcome barbarian of the links. This space must be cleared of anything that might introduce chance, any variation that would invite the sensorium to open, to fix on anything peripheral to the hyperbolically distilled telos of striking a small ball in such a way as to make it enter a distant hole. The course is rendered as temporally uniform as possible—no blooming or fruiting plants that might attract birds and bees or other wandering distractions—all in the name of what history might someday deem the most autoerotically insignificant telos of the modern world, repeated, with controlled variations, eighteen times over. And all in the service of those unwilling to recognize the productive openness of boredom, who instead opt to fill time to reduce the risk of the appearance of that uncomfortable question: "Why?" But golf's hyperbolic focus that annuls the present is only a microcosmic figure for the comfortable predictability that is the utopia of the *country*: Nature, and as a result, chance, are exiled from the space claimed as property by what Buck-Morss called "sense-dead autotelic man."

But the tranquil oblivion that Luis has found on the links is thrown into crisis when, on the course near his home, he falls into a two-meter-deep hole dug and concealed by mysterious vandals who apparently roam the *country* by night. The event of the fall neutralizes the phantasmagoric effect of the golf course, transforming it into a space of unpredictability that brings a need to improvise, to open the sensorium, and with this the possibility of a return to the present and to a more ethical sociality. But this kind of opening is, however, not the only possibility, and Luis reacts by putting himself on a war footing, a state of exception in which every aspect of life is subjected to the paranoia of an army-of-one's war on terror. He opts for the nonreflective response of obsessive persecution of those who dug and covered the hole, thus sinking into an even more destructive form of autotelia.

Meanwhile, his brother Juan is suffering from a different type of sensorial impairment, an incipient neurological disorder that makes it impossible for him to aspire to much beyond survival and condemns him to economic precarity. He first notices the onset of his condition when, riding a motorbike on a country road, he stops to read a sign. In close-up, as he struggles to make out the letters, an insect-like buzzing is heard just as the focus shifts from his face to the background vegetation, then back again. It can be readily assumed that this alteration in focus and sound is an exteriorization of his sensorial perturbation, manifested on screen for the viewer through filmic free indirect discourse.[4] As Juan's ever-more dysfunctional sensorium fails him, he comes to represent a potential burden to Luis, and as such, that which the older brother must sacrifice in order to preserve his own cluster of promises. Juan is not wealthy enough to aspire to *country* life nor to have recourse to specialists, and for him the future holds no promises toward which to incline. His exacerbated sensorium is instead subjected to the buffeting overstimulation of immediacy in a harsh urban reality. As he stumbles past middle age, losing his very ability to orient himself physically in the world, he finds himself estranged from an elder brother who fears the threat he represents to his own increasingly fragile cluster of promises.

The issue at stake thus becomes the ethics of Luis's stance toward his brother, who, under a neoliberal order that has privatized risk by eliminating the social responsibilities of the state, faces the immediate possibility of falling out of the bottom of the middle class. But Luis chooses to abandon him to precarity rather than risk being dragged down himself. In the post-Progress predicament, individual success appears the easiest option, and utopia means freedom from the demands and visible presence of those left without resources, a desire Luis obliquely addresses when he declares to a meeting of his fellow *country* dwellers that "la paz es la garantía obligatoria de este lugar, la razón por la que hemos mudado aquí" (peace is the compulsory guarantee of this place, the reason why we have moved here). The condition of possibility of *country* life is the exclusion of the nation's internal economic other, but at the end of the film the two brothers are brought together and the door to a more caring relationship is opened, and the *country* is suddenly transformed into a place where, away from danger and discomfort, familial harmony is facilitated and promises are fulfilled. But the falseness of this prosthetic happy ending betrays the looming presence of the multimedia conglomerate Grupo Telefé, the film's producer, which is owned by the multinational Telefónica. Insofar as the falsity of the ending can be dismissed as a condition imposed by such corporate backing—after all, Telefé's corporate slogan is "Siempre Juntos" (Always Together)—the film retains a critical edge and the *country* comes out looking like a central promise of the cruel optimism that afflicts many of those who today still possess the resources to lean toward the future, beyond the immediacy of survival in the present. *Los Marziano* is a quirky film, which has become a genre of sorts with the internationalization of work by Wes Anderson and others, and given its corporate production it is no surprise that the film delivers its critique from well within generic conventions. But other films, especially those more independently produced, have articulated related critiques in a far less conventional form.

Lucrecia Martel first came into prominence within a cinephile context with the short *Rey muerto*, which was part of *Historias breves* in 1995. Her first feature, *La ciénaga* (2001), earned high acclaim on the festival circuit and international theatrical releases. David Oubiña refers to its "insidious realism" (2007), a formula that captures the film's attention to aspects less easily represented by the medium, those underlying forces that bubble to the surface in Martel's work to disrupt a decadent but superficially stable quotidian normalcy. *La ciénaga*'s attention to the differing ways in which children and adults relate to domestic and marginal spaces gestures to what would come in Martel's subsequent films. Andermann points out that "the film's two generations entertain radically different relations with the location; the adults languishing in the confined space of house and garden (with the putrid swimming pool at its center), the children and adolescents opening up lines of flight towards the natural surroundings . . ." (2012, 78). The adults' often desperate attempts to castle themselves into a secure domesticity removed from the less-predictable realities of the surrounding spaces prefigures *La mujer sin cabeza*.

The protagonist of *La mujer sin cabeza*, Vero, hits something or someone while driving on a country road, but doesn't stop to find out what it was. The shock throws her out of her ordinariness of dentistry practice, home, family, and friendships, and reveals how much, in her effort to maintain the status quo, she had closed off her body as a sensitive interface with the world and become unable to recognize and respond to the precarities of her historical moment, the situations of those both inside and outside her immediate circle of loved ones. The trauma of the accident is, then, also an opportunity, one of those moments when, as Berlant writes, "life could become otherwise, in the good sense" (48). It opens Vero's sensorium and returns her to the present, thus potentializing her for a more ethical sociality. But, as Berlant also writes, "affective atmospheres are shared, not solitary" (15). Since the accident shakes Vero visibly, this same circle of loved ones—family, friends, relatives—mobilizes quickly to repair the torn fabric of ordinariness, closing around her to mediate the pressures of the moment on her sensorium and enable a return to normalcy. The tragedy is that normalcy is eventually restored and the possibility of ethical sociality is foreclosed, but the film, by staging an impasse in which an individual is ethically potentialized then subsequently depotentialized, brings into relief the mechanism that forecloses the possibility of ethical sociality.

But how does Martel's film do this? Its narration is fairly subjective: the information provided to the viewer is mostly restricted to that available to the protagonist, whose embodied perturbation is made visible in the image and sound through what Pier Paolo Pasolini called cinematic free indirect discourse, in which the filmmaker's stylistic decisions are based on the interiority of a character who focalizes the narration. In the resulting variation from cinema's "objective" formal norms the protagonist's subjectivity is expressed even when she is seen in the frame (not just in point-of-view shots or dreams, fantasies, hallucinations, etc.). Pasolini was concerned with the effects that social class has on perception, and he privileged the society-changing possibilities inherent to the subjectivity of the peasantry in contrast to the more conservative subjectivity of the bourgeoisie:

> the "gaze" of a peasant, perhaps even of an entire town or region in prehistoric conditions of underdevelopment, embraces another type of reality than the gaze given to that same reality by an educated bourgeois. Not only do the two actually see different sets of things, but even a single thing in itself appears different through the two different "gazes." (177)

In contrast to Pasolini, Martel explores how a middle-class gaze contributes to the conservation of the status quo. By placing a bourgeoise in crisis she is able to explore the temporary breakdown, and eventual efficacy, of the mechanisms of forgetting that make cruel optimism possible.

Vero is the narrative focalizer, and the crisis-driven lucidity she suffers is reflected in the variation of the image and sound from an objective norm. While the notion of an extrinsic stylistic norm in today's cinema is problematic, in Martel's film an *intrinsic* norm is easy to identify, since there is a clear moment of trauma that triggers the crisis suffered by the protagonist, separating a before from an after. The before is ordinariness. The opening minutes of the film offer a relatively omniscient narration in which social classes are clearly differentiated: the running dark-skinned boys, subject to constant near-impacts—a truck looks like it will hit one boy, another cartwheels off a water pipe into a ditch—are contrasted with the automobile-reliant and apparently secure middle-class women. The concerns of the latter are for their children's activities and trivialities like false eyelashes and face creams, and the most serious threat to their well-being of which they seem aware are aquatic turtles in a swimming pool.

Relative to the rest of the film, in this sequence Vero does not focalize the narration: the story information provided is not restricted to that known to her. The images are as close as Martel gets to conventional mise-en-scène, as is the sound, the sources of which are easily identifiable in the diegesis. But then, while Vero is driving along a rural road, she hits something or someone, a dog or a dark-skinned child, or both—neither she nor the viewer can be sure—but does not stop. Soon after the accident there is a cut to black and a title card reading "La mujer sin cabeza." This turning-point between a before and an after marks the alteration of Vero's subjectivity and, consequently, of the stylistic norms of the film. The accident brings about what Berlant calls a *situation*: "a disturbance [that] forces one to take notice, to become *interested* in potential changes to ordinariness" (195, emphasis in original). Vero is disconnected from the phantasmagoric effects of her quotidian existence, in an embodied perturbation that pulls back the veil of illusion that seems to have enabled her to exist in comfortable ignorance of the generalized precarity. Disoriented, she drifts as caring friends and family try their best to reassure her back to normalcy, laying bare for the viewer the device of denial that makes optimism possible. For both Vero and the viewer, the guilt of privilege and the generalized precarity have passed into the world of phenomena, resisting the efforts of other characters to reassure them away, and the crisis-driven defamiliarization of Vero's reality motivates the film's visual and sound design from this point on.

Parts of the widescreen visual field are left illegible, but fleshed out by acousmatic sounds—those the viewer hears without seeing their source. Sometimes these seem momentarily to be internal to Vero's mind, but a source usually appears in the frame after a few seconds. In one sequence, as Vero is walking for exercise around a schoolyard sports field, we hear examples of such sound, along with what might be called free indirect illumination, in an oddly disorienting causal relationship between the sunglasses Vero puts on and the suddenly increased exposure of the film that results in a washed-out image. As she walks around the playground along with several other women, a loud crash is heard. None of the other women react or show any indication of having heard it, but Vero stops and looks to her left. The following eyeline-matched shot reveals the cause: a young man playing soccer has run into the chain-link fence that separates the sports field from the space in which the women walk. While these techniques make Vero's lucid disorientation available for the viewer by creating short-lived illusions and false continuities, they also reinforce the film's intrinsic norm under which all sound can be attributed to a source within the diegesis and exterior to the protagonist's mind. Having established this norm, a noise-scape consisting of deep roars and hums punctuated by beepers, buzzers, and sirens becomes Martel's most effective tool for exposing the mechanism by which the subject in a potentially productive crisis is brought back into the middle-class comfort zone. The free indirect aspect comes into play with the distortions that correspond to Vero's ever-changing psychological state: these sounds sharpen with her crisis, but when she is reassured or distracted they fade into the degree zero of background murmur that filmmakers call "room tone." In a sequence that demonstrates this functioning of noise-scape in the film, she meets her cousin at a hotel restaurant. As the two characters later enter a hotel room, a continuous urban roar is heard. This noise-scape is sharpened well beyond room tone, but when Vero initiates physical contact and they begin to make love, the sounds fade. The momentary distraction from psychological crisis provided by the extramarital incest does not last long, however, since immediately after the act a cell phone's ring brings back Vero's crisis and with it the invasive noise-scape.

This is one of several instances in which people or events distract Vero, which lead up to a final sequence that displays the eventual efficacy of the mechanism that restores her more optimistic, sensorially closed condition. The vigilance of friends and family has enabled Vero to begin forgetting. Hotel and hospital records are made to disappear, the dent in her car is fixed, she is told that a boy found in a canal had not been killed by a car, but had drowned. Then the *juntada* (get-together) announced earlier in the film takes place. This sequence begins in the same hotel, where Vero asks at the front desk about her own earlier stay and is told that on that night no one was in that room. She reacts without visible emotion and enters the restaurant where the *juntada* takes place. Seen through glass doors that soften the sharp edges of Vero's post-accident world, music covers the noise-scape as family and friends comfort her through physical contact and conversation. Berlant writes of "the optimism of recuperative gestures" (2011), and by now it is clear that such gestures have pulled Vero out of her crisis and allowed for a happy ending, on an individual level, at least. But from a more collective view, this represents the foreclosing of the possibility of a post-optimistic response and the restoration of a politically nullified subject.

In Martel's films the contact between middle and popular classes does not work toward an expanded consciousness of class relations. This missed encounter is representative of a shift in Argentine cinema that has taken place over recent decades, which Page addresses when she argues that films of the 1980s and 1990s

> had often revolved around an encounter between representatives of two different social classes, usually for the benefit of the middle-class characters, whose contact with the "earthiness" of life at the city's margins restored a vitality they had lost and provided the inspiration they were seeking. Such encounters are extremely rare in more recent films, which portray a city increasingly divided along class lines. (180)

Page goes on to ask about the new cinema's frequent isolation of middle-class characters in their own neighborhoods, insulated from the marginalized and the violence with which they are associated in contemporary culture. As we have seen, *La mujer sin cabeza* rejects the earlier cinema's redemption-by-way-of-the-popular, but does not shy away from contact between middle and working classes. When Martel's middle-class heroine experiences the presence of the latter in the most proximate, sensorial terms, her guilt is manifested in immediate disorientation and even pain felt by both her and the viewer, an effect of yet another kind of "largo muro" built by the economic order of the neoliberal age.

Rural Space in Contemporary Film: Inquisitive Gazes on an Opaque World

Unlike the relative immediacy of the *villa*, for most of today's urban film viewers rural spaces remain entirely mediated spaces. The rest of this chapter examines two films that take contrasting approaches to the problem of mediation. One problematizes the impression of epistemological certainty through a radical use of casting and mise-en-scène, while the other updates an earlier mode of *denuncia* and its prescription for action in response to the political and economic practices of the neoliberal age and beyond. The first is Lisandro Alonso's *Los muertos* (2004).

In an article that discusses Alonso's film, Jens Andermann activates Martin Lefebvre's distinction between *setting* and *landscape* in order to theorize the break between classical and modern Argentine cinemas. Lefebvre defines setting as a "scenic background to which can be entrusted various rhetorical functions of exposition, emphasis, or counterpoint in relation to the plot or to specific characters" (2014, 52), while landscape, by contrast, "represents the excess or remainder of this subordinate function of space. Landscape interrupts, as place, the narrative continuity" (Andermann 2014, 52). In the classical Argentine cinema, rural space was generally represented through *costumbrista* conventions, in which the land itself was a relatively undifferentiated setting for the gaucho, his accoutrements, and tasks. After the break discussed by Andermann, by the 1960s many films began to reject the exclusive use of rural space as setting—and with it the dehistoricizing classical conventions—to instead focus on the most pressing questions of the national present, using screen space "as constantly suspended between setting and landscape . . . to stage [a] dialectical critique of neocolonial oppression and the complicity of classical narrative cinema" (2014, 53). These films "forced out the historicity of places beyond their diegetic function as settings of the action" (2014, 51), thus inviting their spectator to perceive the inscription of a far less official history on the land. But between the cinematic modernity of the 1960s and '70s and the present lies the radical transformation of the dictatorship period and the subsequent neoliberalization, the two most important of the factors that shut down the kind of filmmaking Andermann refers to.

Decades later, Alonso takes yet another approach to rural spaces, one that centers on the particularity of his characters' relationship with the land. *Los muertos* (2004) is Alonso's second feature-length film. His first, *La libertad* (2001), was set in the interior of Buenos Aires province, in what was once the habitat of the gaucho, while *Los muertos*' forest lies to the sparsely populated north. Alonso casts "ready-made" actors—preexisting individuals embedded in the space in which the film is set—a choice that contributes to an inversion of cinema's usual script-based production of images, which have to pass through linguistic concepts. As Nathaniel Dorsky lamented, "language can point out, direct, specify, and describe the world, but it doesn't *see* the world" (29). Bypassing the script can allow for a more immediate responsivity to the reality of the ready-made actor's relationship with a specific place.

In *Los muertos*, once Vargas is released from prison—where he spent an unspecified length of time for apparently murdering his brothers—he appears to be radically adrift, his long absence having apparently erased all affective relationships with nonincarcerated inhabitants of the modern world. But ties soon become apparent, as Andermann points out. In his first films Alonso cast

> a native character who literally stands between the viewers and the landscape, thus denying us a view of the latter independent from the temporality of the character's actions (which initially appear to be set in "the time of nature" itself, only to reveal their own profound engagement with the polis and the market) (Andermann 2014, 52)

Andermann's insight on the impossibility of any attempt by the characters to disengage from these larger forces of the polis and market identifies what is certainly a key aspect of Alonso's films. I hope to complement this insight by turning the focus to the particulars of the engagement of Vargas with the riverine landscape, in order to explore how the film productively collapses the distinction between setting and as landscape in order to foreground the particularity of the character's relationship with the land, thus reconfiguring the spectatorial gaze into one that transforms the barbaric void into plenitude.

Although the back stories of the protagonists of Alonso's films are never very explicit, unfulfilled promises and broken dreams seem to make up their pasts. They return to rural spaces of Argentina attempting to exile themselves from the modern spaces that remain mostly off screen, but these are not romantic accounts of individualist returns to a welcoming nature. In *Los muertos*, once Argentino Vargas is released from prison he appears to be cut off from all affective relationships and community he might have had years earlier, and returns to a forest that, at least to the viewer, appears hostile. But the film then proceeds to problematize the spectatorial gaze, calling attention to the incomprehensibility of Vargas's relationship with rural space for the viewer, for whom it might prompt a recognition of their own inability to comprehend it. The sublimity of *barbarie* for the usual civilized gaze of a long tradition in Argentine culture of observers blind to the complexities of traditional rural society, to whom it appears simple, rudimentary, and even primitive, is of central importance to my reading of Alonso's film.

Vargas enters the semi-tropical forest of the province of Corrientes after the long stay in prison that resulted from the killings, which are elliptically narrated (as possibly a dream) in the film's opening sequence. In this long take, the forest is a sinister setting for a brief, ambiguous series of events surrounding the murders, but as the film progresses, what is at first glance a hostile nature is transformed into a space of more complex relations between a subject and an environment, as it is revealed that the actor-character possesses a set of skills uniquely suited to life in this specific forest. Such casting combines with an observant mise-en-scène to transform the barbaric "void" (in Sarmientine terms) into a space of potential plenitude through a reconfiguration of the spectator's gaze. Vargas is portrayed in observational long takes that meticulously describe the knowledge and manual skills that constitute his relationship with the natural world—he rows a canoe downstream, extracts honey from a beehive, kills and guts a goat he happens across—which activates a documentary charge proper to films that elicit "the story from the raw material of life rather than subjugating the raw material to (a story's) preestablished demands" (248), as Siegfried Kracauer wrote in a somewhat erroneous description of Robert Flaherty's 1922 *Nanook of the North*.

Los muertos' mise-en-scène runs counter to what most narrative film language is designed to do. Its nonchalance regarding story allows it to instead observe the movements and pauses of this solitary figure in the forest and thus create a fiction of radical alterity: a character whose practical orientation toward his world is so different from that of the film's viewers that he can only appear as a cipher, an individual whose embeddedness in this place—the way he perceives and acts upon this forest—is so radically unreadable that a common reaction is that in the film nothing happens. Due to this radical use of film form to access alterity, one is forced to recognize that Argentino Vargas possesses specific perceptual and bodily skills that he or she lacks. The key to this realization is Alonso's use of the circumstances in which his actor is situated, his heritage in this space, and the limits and possibilities these impose on him. This is evidenced by the meticulous depiction of Vargas's ready-to-hand relationship—how "a stonemason or a sculptor meets up with a rock" (Steiner 89)—with his world, one of such radical alterity that the relationship of the viewer to Vargas runs the danger of forming a contemporary version of Sarmiento's dismissal as *barbarie* of all that was unable to be readily identified by a subject trapped within the privileged culture. Alonso's cinema thus problematizes the historic characterizations of the rural in the writings of Sarmiento, Lugones, and others. Instead of linguistic representations in terms of ideas such as *barbarie* or a gauchesque pampa, Alonso explores with the camera a radical alterity on the land that is capable of triggering doubts about the universality of the viewer's own epistemological assumptions. In the resulting doubt lies the importance of Alonso's casting and mise-en-scène.

While *Los muertos* could not be considered an observational documentary, due to Alonso's control and elaborate mise-en-scène, it does borrow from direct cinema its centering on the particular—the individual subject—its long takes, and its lack of master shots and voiceover that leave the work of interpretation to the viewer. But Alonso's rejection of a conventional relationship with the viewer goes further, to a refusal of the usual analytical-editing mode in which directorial decisions regarding framing and shot length are based on criteria that privilege the provision of information that forwards the narrative. Since these decisions at the same time respond to and form conventional viewer expectations, the result in Alonso's film is often the impression that nothing is happening, and as a result the viewer might feel that he or she is being forced to tolerate long stretches of dead time and boredom. But this reaction, I would argue, is due less to an absence of narrative drive on the part of the film than to the radical otherness of Argentino Vargas's world, in which he, unlike the viewer, knows how to do things and why they are done that way. This radical otherness results in the viewer's incapacity to perceive what *is* happening.

The spectator is made to assume the worst about Vargas from the opening sequence, in which two murdered children are seen lying on a forest floor, before a man, likely assumed to be Vargas, passes by, machete in hand. After the sequence ends in a fade-to-green, Vargas is seen in prison, presumably as a result of the murders. His subsequent release casts him out of his prison community and he then moves off into the forest, off the island of relative modernity that is the prison and the town of Goya. Once in the forest, Vargas and his relationship to the land are filmed in a way that maximizes the documentary charge, through mise-en-scène and editing that invite the viewer to instead recognize Vargas's relationship to this space as one of nonfictional, very real, and life-sustaining knowledge of how to do things in this particular corner of *barbarie*.

Of great importance, then, is the fundamental difference between the manual skills shown in *Los muertos* and the specialized technical skills of a Taylorized economy of production.[5] This difference is illustrated by a comparison of Vargas's killing of the goat with the analogous actions of workers in a typically Argentine site of hyper-rationalized labor, that of the slaughterhouse, a location documented in several landmark films of the national tradition, as early as 1919 with *Juan sin ropa*, and taken up again by Humberto Ríos in 1960 with *Faena*, which was quoted in *La hora de los hornos*. The actions of modern slaughterhouse workers are the Taylorized, impersonal, and interchangable tasks of a hyper-rationalized economic system in which each movement is meaningful for a production system that tolerates no loss or excess. By contrast, Vargas's actions—at least those he performs after returning to the forest—are what make possible his survival and thus create his particular identity and world.

While in the modern spaces of the film—the prison and the town—Vargas and his actions belong to a rationalized economy: he is replaced by another prisoner at his task of making a chair, who tells him "Tomate un mate, andá tranquilo que yo voy a continuar" (Have a drink of yerba mate, go ahead, I'll take over here). The items he purchases, even the business-like copulation with a prostitute, could all be seen as rationalized components of modernity. Once in the forest, however, his actions appear to leave this civilization behind for a more direct relationship with the natural world. As such, they require a particular disposition, an attunement of the corporeal sensorium, which must seek out opportunities or dangers. The senses are open to the contingencies of the surroundings, rather than closed as they would necessarily become in more rationalized, task-specific surroundings such as the slaughterhouse, or as a defensive reaction to the shocks inflicted by the modern city more generally.[6] Although Vargas's forest existence was interrupted by a long prison term, his necessary skills have not been lost. The question of how the relationship with his family and community will turn out remains to be answered, but the skills Vargas offers are not without benefit to this potential community.

The sequences that show Vargas's skills in long continuous takes are not used in the context of *Los muertos* as elements of a strong central conflict that would serve to raise narrative tension (of which there is very little in the film), and in the temporal economy typical of a more commercial film they would be considered mostly dead time. In these moments plot recedes and the documentary charge asserts itself. Instead of being used as a mere narrative event in support of a central conflict—"Vargas's Odyssey," for example—the action of extracting honey from a beehive is shown mostly in real time, far in excess of what a script might indicate as sufficient to provide the information necessary to forward filmic narration.[7] The forest sequences prompt a sensory openness that conditions the mise-en-scène. Free of modern rationalization, lacking routine and regularity, to film this protagonist Alonso's camera does not use a fixed, centripetal frame. Instead of a routine that happens in the same place each day, Argentino Vargas's highly mobile life in the forest necessitates improvisation, and an openness of the body to its surroundings in turn requires a corresponding openness on the part of the camera. The camera is mobile both in its placement (tracking shots from a truck and from a canoe on the river) and in its pans that follow the protagonist. Shots often begin by panning slowly over a green forest, only to find Vargas, and end by panning away from him across the forest where, it soon becomes obvious, he can perceive opportunities and dangers that remain hidden to a viewer's more civilized corporeal sensorium, which is (only) virtually exposed to this forest.

The space of this film, then, is not Sarmiento's flat, featureless pampa, nor the classical historical films' setting for a conflict based on a figure-ground binary, but rather a forest of uncountable shades of green that for Argentino Vargas (but not for the spectator) is pure feature, recalling Stan Brakhage's question: "How many colors are there in a field of grass to the crawling baby unaware of 'Green'? . . . Imagine a world before the 'beginning was the word'" (12). His perception of features is what allows Vargas to survive, but the viewer can only recognize them through Vargas's resultant actions as, fully reliant on his corporeal sensorium, he interacts with his forest context in a relationship that is not merely conflictive. On the contrary, he is part of it, and to a degree works *with it*, further problematizing the discourse of civilization and its characterization of man's relationship with nature as necessarily agonistic. In *Los muertos* the human can belong to both nature and society, and although Argentino Vargas is the point of interest, he is inseparable from his context—and importantly, its status as bearer of contingency—which ends up being as much an object of observation as he is, as the gaze is suspended between landscape and setting, as Andermann points out (2014, 63).

The manual skills of Vargas have no meaning in the modern sense of the word. They possess it only in terms of Vargas's particular understanding of this space, in which community as the shared experience of tradition, memory, and collectivity is deteriorated, if not absent. But while Vargas's skills are required for individual survival, they also produce objects for the symbolic exchanges present in the relationships he has with others—including his family, which appears somewhat disintegrated after the long absence implied by the completion of Vargas's jail term—with whom community urgently needs to be created. Gifts abound: the canoe, the half-full *damajuana* given to Vargas by the good-natured fish-gutting character—with whom he, in the moment of passage into the forest that disrupts the typical viewer's sensory schemata, exchanges some words in Guaraní that go unsubtitled—as well as the gifts that Vargas himself carries. He has a letter to be delivered to the daughter of his fellow inmate, candies—purely symbolic gifts it seems, for whomever he may meet in the forest—a shirt he buys in town, hoping it will fit his daughter, and, most significantly in terms of manual skills, the goat. All are objects or actions that form bonds between individuals. Offerings such as that of a freshly slaughtered goat in the middle of a territory sorely lacking in slaughterhouses but evidently abounding in fruit trees and honeycombs may be the only possible community-creating actions for the newly returned Vargas, even if the community is as small as that of a grandfather and the grandson he encounters upon his return.

The conventional historical narrative shares certain expectations with the cinema. Much as the latter sets up spectatorial expectations of continuity, history sets up the expectation of a linear narrative continuity. *Los muertos* problematizes these expectations by bringing an apparently primitive man out of the past and placing him firmly in the present, not in modernity's center, but rather in what lies apparently beyond its bounds, showing him in terms in which he is neither modernity's loser nor destined to perish in the present. Andermann writes of *Los muertos*' forest shots that

> narrative is . . . suspended by a kind of image that constantly forces the narrative gaze to revert to the spectacular, observant viewing that is attributed by Lefebvre to the landscape shot, but solicited here by way of a constantly stalled or suspended narrative progress. The image, in other words, or rather our own viewing relation with it, is forever suspended, left hanging, between the narrative and the spectacular. (2014, 63)

I agree fully with Andermann's observation, and wonder if its implications could be taken even further by arguing that these shots manage to move the boundary between narrative and spectacle toward the latter for the spectator, expanding what could be called narrative to include what one could imagine to be Argentino Vargas's notion of meaningful encounters and events, which for the spectator might not otherwise be meaningful or even perceptible. If identification with Vargas can change a viewer who, optimally, might perceive this space through the character, then it might be possible to overcome the "forever suspended" viewing relation described by Andermann, as the viewer responds to the prompt to recognize his or her own epistemological insufficiency regarding the relationship between space and character, and thus the radical incommensurability between the two forms of inhabiting space, that of the viewer and that of Vargas. In an enactment of what might be the only possible instance of competent viewership of the film, Vargas appeared again in Alonso's 2006 film *Fantasma*, in which he watches himself on screen in *Los muertos*. In *Fantasma*, Vargas is the sole spectator, but one could also imagine a different viewing scene, in which an enraptured Vargas is surrounded by bored *porteños* who, one by one, walk out on the picture.

In the first chapters of *Facundo*, Sarmiento described the land and the customs of its inhabitants as a sort of resistant barbaric national essence against which the civilizing project would have to struggle. In doing so he paid special attention to the skills that bound these inhabitants to the land in a typically romantic organic unity, but he nonetheless went on to categorize this as barbarism. Carlos Altamirano discusses this vision:

> El saber, las destrezas—la del caballo o la del cuchillo, las del baqueano o las del rastreador—, así como los valores de los habitantes de este mundo elemental, son los requeridos por las faenas rudimentarias de la estancia ganadera y una vida sometida permanentemente al peligro. Nada estimula allí la asociación, y la notoriedad de los hombres no proviene de la vida pública, que no existe. Lo que produce reputación son las habilidades estimadas por los gauchos y las pruebas del coraje físico. Éste era el ambiente de la barbarie . . . (Altamirano 47)

> The knowledge, the skills—that of the horse or that of the knife, those of the guide or those of the tracker—like the values of the inhabitants of this elementary world, are those required by the rudimentary tasks of the horse ranch and a life permanently subjected to danger. Nothing there stimulates association, the fame of men does not spring from public life, which does not exist. What produces a reputation are the skills esteemed by the gauchos and the tests of physical courage. This was the environment of barbarism.

Sarmiento was fascinated by the skills of the gaucho, but failed to recognize them on anything but his own terms. Incompatible with civilization, they remained for him barbaric skills, condemned to the past in the narrative of modernity. *Los muertos* inherits Sarmiento's fascination with rural skills, but instead of an imagined backwardness compared unfavorably to urban civilization as lacking opportunity for social interaction, these skills make possible a birth of community in *barbarie*, however minimal it may be, in Vargas's reencounter with others in the forest—a boatman, the family of a fellow inmate, his own grandson.

One hundred fifty years after the death of Facundo Quiroga, in a neoliberalized society in which dreams of civilization have lost meaning, Vargas's *barbarie* can take on another significance. No longer a signifier of a devalued mode of existence destined to disappear so that something more evolved might replace it in an optimistically linear history, it is rather a return to a space which, insofar as it continues to be considered a binary opposite of the modern or whatever other term might be used today, begs reexamination. Where Facundo Quiroga had been condemned to the past to make way for a new kind of world, in a less optimistic age Argentino Vargas is very much alive in the present. For Sarmiento, according to Altamirano, rural space "dispersa a sus habitantes y sus energías" (disperses its inhabitants and their energies), thus not offering places where people could commune and civilization could develop, while the city offered "sitios regulares de interacción entre los hombres, que son los que moderan los impulsos del hombre natural y generan el sentido y el interés de lo público" (regular sites of interaction between men, which are those that moderate the impulses of natural man and generate the feeling and interest in the public sphere) (Altamirano 52–53). But in *Los muertos* the human interactions of the civilization so highly valued by Sarmiento are reduced to a pure economic exchange, while in the forest, Vargas's unscripted knowledge and skills make possible the birth of a community.

Pino Solanas and the End of the *Pueblo*

While many recent Argentine filmmakers, as we have seen in the cases of Martel and Alonso, have engaged with the nation's marginal spaces by rejecting the notion of transparency to instead privilege epistemological crisis, other filmmakers have taken an approach closer to that of the 1960s political cinema's reliance on filmic transparency in combination with strategies intended to create a sense of authenticity. The foremost example is Pino Solanas, a filmmaker of that earlier era who had remained visible, but took on greater national prominence after the crisis of 2001. In the late 1960s, with *La hora de los hornos* and the manifesto *Hacia un tercer cine*, his work with Octavio Getino provided a model and theoretical foundation for a formally avant-garde, anticolonial cinema and some of the most resonant moments of the cinema of the inquisitive gaze. In the five decades since, national politics has remained central to Solanas's life and filmic production. His most recent films have focused on extractivist economic practices and environmental destruction, and have looked beyond the national scope toward the establishment of translocal alliances that might resist the depredations of capital.[8] I will examine *La guerra del fracking* (2013) as an example of this recent turn.

After nearly three decades in which he made only narrative features, Solanas's work since *Memoria del saqueo* (2004) constitutes a return to a militant documentary mode for which he first became known, now in the context of the economic crises of the first years of the millennium. Solanas's return to documentary was presaged in 2002 with his foundation of a movement that advocated the re-nationalization of the public resources sold off or leased in the 1990s, which he had been in a privileged position to witness as senator and member of commissions on Culture, Energy, Communications and Environment from 1993 to 1997. His subsequent filmic work employed the resulting insight to denounce the corrupt selling-off of the Argentine patrimony and the exploitation by foreign capital of the territory's natural resources.

Solanas's tone has become less optimistic through time, since the metanarratives that guided his first works are long shattered after the dictatorship's violence and the neoliberalism of the 1990s. He states in *Memoria del saqueo* that the enemy—neocolonialism and its wealthy local enablers—has remained constant, but its reach has gone further than was imaginable forty years before. Solanas traces this disaster to the sabotage of state-owned industry and the burden of odious debt contracted by the dictatorship. Subsequent pressure from the IMF for austerity measures enabled the government of Carlos Menem in the 1990s to justify selling off the two state energy companies, YPF and Gas del Estado. According to Solanas they were sold for a fraction of their value to foreign corporations, in a deal approved through bribery of elected officials. In later films Solanas interviews experts on hydrocarbons in Argentina who describe the problems brought about by corporate ownership, most notably the refusal to run the risk of investing in exploration. They tell him that in the years since the privatizations already known reserves of oil and gas were heavily extracted, mostly for export, seriously depleting the nation's reserves and resulting in today's high fuel prices and unemployment.

In *Tierra sublevada: Oro impuro* (2009), *Tierra sublevada: Oro negro* (2011), and *La guerra del fracking*, Solanas went on to further connect the dots between the privatizations and social and environmental crises, showing how, due to a lack of incentives and regulatory enforcement, along with an indifference toward the commons that local populations depend on for survival, the companies cut corners, pollute watersheds, and in turn inflict violence on indigenous and other rural disadvantaged communities that rely on surface and well water. Expanding the frame, Solanas ties the whole process to global warming, climate change, and other effects of the consumption-driven economy, and proposes that Argentina move beyond the neoliberal economic model to a more environmentally sustainable and socially just management of resources, the necessary first step of which he sees as the total re-nationalization of natural resources and utilities. In the *Tierra sublevada* films, as a counterweight to economic power, Solanas returns to his insistent calls for popular sectors to rise to historical protagonism, locating, in *Oro impuro*, the origin of the *piquetero* movement among the unemployed of Cutral-Có, an oil town impoverished by the effects of the privatizations. In that film a mass of protestors armed only with slingshots is shown in June of 1996 blocking highways, battling police, and emerging victorious.

Solanas now works in a less conspicuously avant-garde mode than he did in *La hora de los hornos*—both politically and aesthetically, to follow Robert Stam's classic analysis of the film—and now employs his own presence as a rhetorical device within his films, in what Bill Nichols calls a "voice-of-authority commentary," in which "the speaker is heard and also seen" (105). This mode is distinct from that of many recent documentary makers who utilize their own presence to undermine classical pretensions to objectivity or to privilege subjectivity over conventional truth claims, in that Solanas's presence is employed to more effectively authorize the truth claims made in his films.[9] His productions have shifted from the use (in his militant films) of the more impersonal "voice-of-God" narration to the inclusion of his presence in the image, which activates Solanas's own now-iconic status as authorized mediator between national reality and his viewer.[10] A passage in which Joanna Page discusses the shift in the use of voiceover in twenty-first-century Argentine film elucidates the contrast between Solanas and the bulk of current uses of the first-person in documentary today:

> The use of voice-over, so favored by Solanas in both fiction and documentary films, has been all but abandoned in contemporary Argentine cinema. This reflects a typically postmodern unease with a monologic, didactic perspective that confers a single narrative on disparate events, but it also suggests a growing reticence to

imagine the nation in a homogeneous sense or to 'speak for' the citizens of an increasingly segregated society. (24)

Los rubios (Albertina Carri, 2003) is the most noted filmic example of unease with the conventional rhetoric of politicized cinema. It questions the monologic perspective by insistently undermining the authority and expectations conventionally invested in the children of the disappeared. Solanas, by contrast, does not to forego the use of the authority conferred on him by his militant past, employing it to construct a narrative voice that Page calls the "national we" (24). Long a nationally recognized figure since his return to Argentina in 1983 after exile in France during the last dictatorship, Solanas has stayed very active in national politics, and his authority as a key figure of the left was consolidated in the 1990s after he was shot several times in the legs in an attempt to put a stop to his denunciations of the corrupt privatizations. This episode earned Solanas much respect, especially after the illusory boom of the 1990s went bust in the economic crisis of the early 2000s. He served as *diputado nacional* between 1993 and 1997, founded the Proyecto Sur movement and ran for president in 2007, and then was elected as *diputado* again in 2009. In 2013 he was elected to the national senate.

Solanas employs the authority earned with these experiences to forcefully instrumentalize the images and sounds of his films. As Emilio Bernini writes, in *Memoria del saqueo* "el autor es quien forja todas las imágenes y la fuente única, o última, de todo sentido. . . . [L]a experiencia popular de esos días de diciembre de 2001 es filtrada por una lectura en primera persona que excluye cualquiera otra de las hipótesis políticas que se han elaborado sobre ella" (it is the author who forges all the images and the sole, or ultimate, source of all meaning. . . . The popular experience of those days of December of 2001 is filtered by a reading in first person that excludes any other of the political hypotheses that have been formed about it) (Bernini 2004, 44–45). Solanas's political past and present enhances the authority of his voiceover far beyond that of both a typically subjective voice and of the currently devalued disembodied voice-of-god narrator, but does so, as Bernini points out, to the exclusion of other possible readings of the Argentine crisis.

Despite such critiques of the use of his own authority, Solanas remains for many one of the most trusted figures in Argentine politics. While this may signify very little in the context of a cast of characters like Menem and Palito Ortega, it is remarkable that such a figure makes documentary films in the first person. Solanas's visibility and ethos makes these documentaries possible by permitting him access to places and individuals that a lesser-known filmmaker would likely not have. He uses such access to provoke productive encounters with both experts and lay-people, allies and enemies, and with victims of violence who tell of their experiences while addressing him familiarly as "Pino" and treating him as a trustworthy *compañero*. In addition to his past political involvement, Solanas's filmic identity, or "enacted self" (Spence and Navarro 234), is based on markers of national popular authenticity. In one symbolically charged sequence, Solanas and Cristina Fernández Kirchner face off, her image on a computer screen in front of the seated director. In his hand is a steaming *mate*—containing yerba mate, stimulant of the masses—which serves to symbolically authorize him in this populist confrontation. The next shot, an unmotivated close-up on the *mate*, seems designed to leave no doubt about his status as man of the people.

Later, dressed rhetorically in impeccable white, he is seen in friendly banter with the common people (and their dogs), interviewing experts and victims, complimenting the *malvones* blooming on their patio, documenting misery and exploitation with a video camera mounted on a "fig-rig"—an economical device used to steady a hand-held camera—and interpreting events in his own voice, advocating for the exploited and disdaining the exploiters, while often glossing over the subtleties. Meanwhile, the second camera, which films Solanas, is kept carefully off screen and unacknowledged, a choice that limits the film's reflexivity, thus keeping intact the illusionism upon which the documentary image's credibility traditionally rested.

The interviews, carefully chosen and edited, function to reinforce the message communicated by Solanas's voiceover, at the same time that they put into question the conventions of credibility that have traditionally rendered certain sectors invisible in Argentine culture. In the social hierarchy the indigenous continues, as always, to occupy the bottom rung of the ladder, represented as sublimely barbaric not only in the nineteenth-century liberal tradition, but even in texts that revised national history to exalt the gaucho, such as *El gaucho Martín Fierro*, in which the brutal Indian character kills his white captive's baby son and binds her hands with his intestines. Such representations of spectacular violence in turn legitimized counterviolence against the indigenous as a necessary means to eliminate barbarism and advance the civilizing process, but in *La guerra del fracking* Solanas employs his own credibility to question these conventions of legitimacy, choosing to rely on the indigenous as witness and victim of forms of violence that otherwise resist representation. Rob Nixon, in *Slow Violence*, comments on the intersection of race and authority:

> To address violence discounted by dominant structures of apprehension is necessarily to engage the culturally variable issue of *who counts as a witness*. Contests over what counts as violence are intimately entangled with conflicts over who bears the social authority of witness, which entails much more than simply seeing or not seeing . . . if it's bloodless, slow-motion violence, the story is more likely to be buried, particularly if it's relayed by people whose witnessing authority is culturally discounted. (6)

When Solanas interviews indigenous victims of slow violence, the respect with which they are treated authorizes their testimony, which works toward making present a violence that goes unrepresented in the traditional, spectacular sense.

This role of Solanas as conspicuous mediator, instead of as absent maker of "objective" documentary, follows on a consequential recent development in his intellectual trajectory, in the shift in the historical function envisioned for the *pueblo*. Solanas's long career had been marked by faith in the protagonism of the popular classes—the *pueblo argentino* so central to the tradition of Peronism and *Cine Liberación*—and as recently as *Memoria del saqueo* he interpreted the post-2000 popular insurrections in a redemptive, epic key (Bernini 2004, 45). But in his recent films on hydrocarbons extraction Solanas has engaged critically with the recent uses of the idea of the good of the *pueblo* to justify the "commodities consensus" and underpin the neoextractivist developmentalism of the center-left governments of the "marea rosada" of the early twenty-first century. Instead he grounds his calls to action on the commons as contributing to the well-being of the planet by slowing the climate change brought about by massive fossil fuel consumption.

Distinguishing between common goods and the public good, Maristella Svampa explains that "in Latin America struggles for the common are usually marked by the defense of seeds, the protection of water, and generally natural goods and territory as a space of collective life and the ecosystem" (2015, 76). This definition leads to the key conclusion that "common goods are not understood as *commodities*, as pure merchandise, nor are they understood as *strategic natural resources* or *the public good*, as different progressive governments seek to define them" (2015, 76, emphasis in original). Svampa puts the notion of common goods in sharp contrast with the idea of the public good as defined on the level of the national *pueblo*, since ownership of specific common goods is limited to the level of a particular community, and as such they are kept outside the market. Public goods, by not belonging to the particular community, are subject to a very different set of uses and can be converted into commodities if in the interest of the national community. According to Svampa, such commodification of common goods has opened the way for large-scale accumulation by dispossession—even under progressive governments that might be expected to act to counter such economic violence—as goods enter into the dominion of the state and are therefore "subject to states exercising their jurisdiction without obligation to consult communities" (2015, 77). This destructive dynamic has been driving popular environmentalist movements—such as in the case of TIPNIS in Bolivia—in response to neoextractivist policies implemented by several progressive governments in recent years.

As Svampa argues, the recent political commitment to predatory extractivism has inflicted both immediate and slow violence on communities across Argentina while criminalizing resistance in the name of the public good of the *pueblo argentino*. According to Svampa, under the Kirchner governments the idea of the public good had been used to justify the use of coercion to force the common goods of particular communities to pass into the category of public goods under the dominion of the state. In the case central to *La guerra del fracking*, the water, land, and other common goods of the indigenous Gelay-ko community are destroyed in the name of the public good, as fracking is allowed to take place so that the state can earn money to be spent for the benefit of the national community. Needless to say, the members of the Gelay-ko community are not consulted about this extraction, and their attempts to protest it are criminalized and violently repressed by agents of the state. The common goods of this community are as a result destroyed and the long-term effects of slow violence are unleashed.

In *La guerra del fracking* Solanas never speaks the word "pueblo" himself. It is only mentioned near the end of the film by two interviewees, and even then more nostalgically than exhortatively. Solanas seems to recognize not only the improbability of social change being brought about by popular insurrection, but more importantly, he appears conscious of the dangers associated with the very notion of the *pueblo* in the context of the present political commitment to extractivism. For a viewer familiar with his *Cine Liberación* work, the absence of a rhetorical use of the concept of the *pueblo* in Solanas's devastating denunciation of this dynamic under the Kirchners is striking. But in his 2013 film Solanas takes care to clearly differentiate his own political position from that of the Kirchners, who had operated under "the central wager that progressive governments place on the citizen-consumer model, based on the hegemonic imperial mode of living, [which] reinforces the refusal to consider any hypothesis or scenario of transition and gradual exit from extractivism" (Svampa 2015, 72). As seen in the case documented in *La guerra del fracking*, the risk, in the context of a national population taught to aspire to the consumption patterns of the imperial mode of living, is that this population could expect, or even demand, that the state dispossess the Mapuche's common goods in order to utilize them for the benefit of a national *pueblo*. Notions like the rights of nature, *el buen vivir*, and indigenous ways of conceiving the relationship between humans and the natural world would be hard pressed to compete against a *pueblo* mobilized to consume what it considers its own and thus blinded to the possibility that it might be committing an act of dispossession.

An important aspect of Solanas's attempts to overcome the above-mentioned blindness of the *pueblo* is his efforts to represent slow violence, which Nixon describes as "a violence that occurs gradually and out of sight, a violence of delayed destruction that is dispersed across time and space, an attritional violence that is typically not viewed as violence at all" (2). Such representational obstacles render slow violence invisible in terms of the conventional modes in which film has represented violence. While the filmic image is surely second to none in its capacity to spectacularly depict what we customarily think of as violence, slow violence is not nearly so spectacular and has been relegated to near absence in the cultural archive, prompting new imperatives for those who would denounce it:

> In an age when the media venerate the spectacular, when public policy is shaped primarily around perceived immediate need, a central question is strategic and representational: how can we convert into image and narrative the disasters that are slow moving and long in the making, disasters that are anonymous and that star nobody, disasters that are attritional and of indifferent interest to the sensation-driven technologies of our image-world? How can we turn the long emergencies of slow violence into stories dramatic enough to rouse public sentiment and warrant political intervention, these emergencies whose repercussions have given rise to some of the most critical challenges of our time? (3)

I will briefly examine the rhetorical strategies with which Solanas has tried to counter the representational challenges slow violence presents and to narrativize its effects, thus to neutralize the inherent qualities that make it a weak candidate among the ever-stiffer competition for eyes and ears in the media universe.[11]

One strategy employed in *La guerra del fracking* to represent slow violence involves the use of scale. An emphasis on scale is a common strategy in oil documentaries since, as Imre Szeman notes, it "permit[s] a direct visualization of environmental destruction" (38). Solanas films, often from the air, arrays of fracking rigs, a city of cars consuming hydrocarbons, and other images that reference the sheer volume of hydrocarbons extraction and consumption. He juxtaposes this sublime scale of planetary change with the human scale of the victims, a movement from the general toward the specific that points to how the vastness of fossil fuel consumption has altered the landscape of the Argentine south and inflicted violence on its inhabitants. The local landscape filmed from the air—with its engineered filigree of extractive capital rendered temporal by the spreading stains of the slow flows of its externalities—is followed by the faces and testimony of those struggling to live brief lives down on these spaces produced by extractive practices that accord them so little acknowledgment, making visible the connection between the recent stains on the geological time of the landscapes and the immediacy of the suffering visible in the faces of the victims. That the slow flows produce visible suffering on those faces is testified to in an interview, one that generously employs close-ups, with the grieving family after the death of Cristina Lincopán, the young Mapuche woman interviewed earlier in the film. The close-up of the face is for Deleuze an *affection-image*: "It is the face . . . which gathers and expresses the affect as a complex entity, and secures the virtual conjunctions between singular points of this entity" (*The Movement-Image* 103). Here the close-ups of their faces carry, with piercing affective power, the suffering produced by the overwhelmingly destructive power of capital over dispossessed individuals.

The film's stark lack of optimism, though a relatively new development in the context of Solanas's documentaries, is likely a result of a recognition on the part of the director of what Szeman identifies as a central contradiction faced by contemporary documentary films on petroleum extraction and consumption:

> Generating an awareness of the structuring role of oil in civilizational processes, and so, too, its obscene primacy over both human needs and ecological ones, produces on its own no resolution, even as it indicts the poverty of the present . . . In the end, what is incomprehensible is not the scale of our action

on the world, but that our social world has as its foundation a substance demanded by our quotidian infrastructures, an input whose time has come, and soon will be gone. It's unclear what action one could take, even if one wanted to. (Szeman 38–39)

In their renouncing of the possibility of a hopeful investment in the Argentine *pueblo*, Solanas's recent documentaries leave the realm of the nation to join the transnational documentary field's inevitable recognition that the intersection between hydrocarbons and their consumers—all of us—represents a problem with no readily imaginable solution, one far more complicated than neocolonialism as it was conceived of nearly a half-century earlier in *La hora de los hornos*. Whereas the villain indicted in that film was identified through a simple opposition between foreign capital allied with local enablers against the *pueblo*, contemporary society's reliance on hydrocarbons is a bind that cannot be imagined in such Manichaean terms since, first, the enabler state is controlled by the very political force in which many had placed hope after the neoliberalization in the 1990s, and, second, any "us" that might be defined will inevitably be so reliant on hydrocarbons that it will be under intense pressure to disregard the interests of the particular. Since the redemptive promise of the *pueblo* can no longer be the basis for calls for action, Solanas steps back, to instead return to the objective of consciousness raising. The film strongly suggests that humanity's current course is not a viable long-term one, but it stops short of imagining a clearly defined resolution (not to mention a revolution), and gestures more toward the need for action than its possibility, describing a planet in which the kind of suffering seen on the faces of the Gelay-Ko community members may be universalized before any change can happen. Solanas's film communicates, in large part through its affective appeal, an obligation brought about by desperation, one in which the only hope possible lies beyond the nation, in a more universal, utopian alliance, which today seems as difficult to imagine as it is necessary, against a violence that is both economic and environmental.[12]

To briefly conclude, the last hundred years of cinema have seen a vast evolution in modes of production and consumption, but the gulf—both geographic and economic—between the sites of production and consumption of Argentine film and the marginal spaces it often represents remains wide. *Estrellas* (Federico León and Marcos Martínez, 2007) is possibly the contemporary film that most reveals the challenges faced by any centrifugal impulse to produce films outside established circuits.

As a television interviewer affirms in the film, in the contemporary audiovisual field "está de moda la marginalidad" (marginality is in fashion). In this trend the perspicacious protagonist of *Estrellas*, Julio Arrieta, saw an economic opportunity for himself and his fellow inhabitants of the Villa 21. Arrieta is an ex-*puntero*, or "low-level political fixer" (Andermann 2012, 103) turned representative of *villero* actors. Arrieta uses the astuteness and status he gained in barrio politics to run a casting agency that specializes in non-professional actors who live in the *villas* and thus bring something that, according to Arrieta, professional actors cannot possibly bring to a role: the authenticity that comes with being a "portador de cara" (face bearer) marked by an experience that cannot be simulated. But these are not roles originating with ready-made actors, but scripted "malos, guardaespaldas, ladrones" (bad guys, bodyguards, thieves) for which Arrieta supplies the faces. As Andermann puts it, Arrieta "attempts to negotiate and exploit to his own advantage [film professionals'] quest for reality effects" (2012, 130), thus participating more pragmatically than critically in corporate commercial spectacle. But León and Martínez present Arrieta's talent agency in a way that ironizes its role in the national spectacle, making it "a film about casting politics in present-day Argentine cinema" (2012, 130).

Arrieta's pragmatic discourse is understandably double. On the one hand, he justifies his business serving the corporate audiovisual use of the *villa*, while on the other he voices a complaint about how the same has represented the social margins. *Estrellas* expands on Arrieta's complaint through the inclusion of a sort of "making-of" of the narrative film *El nexo* (Sebastián Antico, 2007), which tells the story of a Martian landing in the Villa 21 and the successful repulsion of the invasion by the *villeros*, led by a character played by Arrieta. At one point Arrieta poses a deceptively relevant question:

> ¿Acaso los villeros no tenemos derecho a tener marcianos? Es muy fácil robarle una imagen a un chico con los mocos colgando, una mujer con las patas sucias, eso se ve todos los días. Sobre la villa se han contado . . . historias de bandas de chicos drogadictos y ladrones, de bandas de prostitutas, de mujeres golpeadas, de miserias humanas, pero nunca se mostró el villero desde el punto de vista de la ficción.

> Don't we villeros have the right to have Martians? It's very easy to steal an image of a kid with snot hanging, a woman with

dirty feet, you see that every day. About the *villa* stories have been told of gangs of child drug addicts and thieves, gangs of prostitutes, beaten women, human misery, but the *villero* has never been shown from the point of view of fiction.

Regardless of the accuracy of his final assertion, Arrieta speaks from a perspective little acknowledged by even the inquisitive cinema in the 1960s: those who live on the margins of society have seldom been creators of audiovisual culture, an exclusion apparently rectified by *El nexo*, which was based on a story written by Arrieta himself. Another lengthy passage from Arrieta expands on his unique perspective and demand for inclusion:

¿Adónde está escrito que no puede haber extraterrestres en la villa? Por lo general . . . los extraterrestres bajan en un barrio de plata, donde hay gente de plata . . . hasta los marcianos tienen plata. Siempre me pareció que los extraterrestres no bajaban en la villa porque tenían miedo de que los robemos. Y hoy con esta película, se van a dar cuenta de que no es así, que lo que queremos es . . . tener amigos extraterrestres.

Where is it written that there can't be extraterrestrials in the *villa*? In general . . . extraterrestrials land in a rich neighborhood, where there are rich people . . . even the Martians have money. It always seemed to me that extraterrestrials didn't land in the *villa* because they were afraid we'd rob them. And today with this film, they will realize that it's not like that, that what we want is . . . to have extraterrestrial friends.

Arrieta's unique view addresses the functioning of the frame of representability, by which certain things can happen only in certain spaces, and it is undeniable that classical genre fiction seldom takes place in marginal neighborhoods. Whether the little-seen *El nexo* (which was not shown in a cinema until 2014, and then only briefly) or its production model will have any real impact on the cultural field remains to be seen, but when, in *Estrellas*, *El nexo* is screened in the Villa 21's Primer Festival de Cine Villa (First Festival of *Villa* Cinema), it appears that its production model is doomed to marginality. While in theory such a festival might signal an emergent form of cultural production and consumption, Arrieta's mention that he promised a showing of *Mission Impossible* to entice the locals to come reveals its limitations. At least at present, there is little organic impulse behind such a festival and a cinema he calls "del barrio y para el barrio" (by the barrio and for the barrio).[13]

In a certain way, *El nexo* closes a circle that opened nearly a century earlier, when the motion-picture camera was employed to film a diversity of national spaces and film production was open to larger sectors of society. In 1915, Jose A. "El Negro" Ferreyra made the first of over forty films, *Una noche de garufa*. A radically independent filmmaker, described by Jorge Miguel Couselo as a bohemian from the poor Buenos Aires neighborhood of Constitución, Ferreyra's films often told local stories filmed in the *tanguero* scene, where he often cast nonprofessional actors. *El nexo* could be considered an heir to Ferreyra's production model, in its return of the camera to the hands of those without economic resources, but where the earlier director's work was commercially viable in a cultural field in which seeing local images on film was still an attraction, the cultural field in which *El nexo* finds itself is dominated by spectators eager to watch Tom Cruise's adventures in a far-off universe, illustrating yet again the limitations faced by a cinema that seeks to engage with the local.

Notes

Introduction: A History of Erasures

1. The poem opens Lugones's 1917 collection *El libro de los paisajes*.

2. From Juan Bautista Alberdi, *Bases y puntos de partida para la organización política de la República Argentina* (1852), chapter XXXII. An earlier depiction of America as desert can be found in the opening verses of Esteban Echeverría's 1837 poem *La cautiva*.

3. For an illuminating reading of the painting as allegory see Andermann (2007, ch. 5).

4. Another source of rural images is that referred to by William Acree as "quotidian visual culture." He discusses postcards, postage stamps, paper money, cigarette packs, matchboxes, and print advertisements of the 1880–1910 period, many of which feature images of gauchos.

5. A few early uses of film participated in the knowledge-gathering gaze Andermann refers to as the "optic of the state" and the project it served. Examples of this are discussed in Marrone; Cuarterolo 2016, 2015, 2013, 2011, 2010.

Chapter 1: National Modernization and the Production of Marginal Spaces in Early Feature Films

1. During the 1920s the cinema boomed as a commercial enterprise. The decade saw the most prolific construction of movie theaters in the history of Argentina, with over one hundred new *salas*. By contrast, the 1910s saw forty-six and the 1930s forty-seven new constructions (García Falcó and Méndez).

2. Di Núbila lists 221 silent Argentine films, from the early *prises-de-vue* of the late nineteenth century through the narrative features of the early 1930s. Slightly under half are feature-length films of the 1910 decade. Due to the precari-

ous state of film preservation in Argentina and the fact that much of the material remains in private collections, it is impossible to know how many silent films exist today.

3. This autonomy is confirmed by Peña (15–47) and Kriger: "Durante las dos primeras décadas de siglo XX, la relación entre el sector [cinematográfico] y el estado fue reducida y se desarrolló exclusivamente en el marco de los controles de la exhibición, dado que la producción cinematográfica se realizaba de manera discontinua y con características artesanales" (During the two first decades of the twentieth century, the relationship between the [cinema] sector and the state was limited and developed solely in the framework of exhibition controls, since film production happened sporadically and with artisanal characteristics) (27).

4. A related factor is the advent of sound cinema in the early 1930s, which complicated film production and made it less accessible to artisanal filmmakers, facilitating the development of the more industrial production. See Cook (275–281) and Thompson and Bordwell (213–232).

5. On the Argentine studio system see Félix-Didier (2002).

6. These conventions are those of an early continuity editing that could be considered transitional between the early cinema *tableau* and the more modern analytical editing of the feature film to come.

7. On the *film d'art* see Abel, 246–277.

8. Even the words of the gaucho's song are written in an impeccable Castilian, which is striking since most gaucho poetry mimicks rural linguistic particularities. The gaucho: "¡Qué bonito es su semblante/por el llanto humedecido!/¡Qué bonitas son las flores/salpicadas de rocío!" (How beautiful is her countenance/with its teary weeping!/How beautiful are the flowers/sprinkled with dew). The "Respuesta de la gaucha" (Response of the gaucha) follows: "Gotas parecen mis lágrimas/gotitas de agua de mar/en lo amargas, en lo muchas/y en que al cabo me ahogarán" (My tears seem drops/droplets of water of the sea/in their bitterness, in that they are many/and that in the end they will drown me).

9. The filmmakers are the playwright José González Castillo, Camila Quiroga, a foremost actress of the popular theater, her husband and actor Héctor Quiroga, and a technician from France named Georges Benoît.

10. On the pre-*Centenario* consolidation of the state, see chapter 5 of Sorensen Goodrich.

11. On positivism in Argentina see Terán.

12. The theme of mass psychology was popularized in Argentina by José María Ramos Mejía. His *Las multitudes argentinas* (1899) dealt with the recent immigrants to Argentina as a problem to be solved through the application of scientific knowledge, and undertook to identify the psychological traits of the immigrants as a group.

Chapter 2: The Classical Cinema and the Perpetuation of a National Fantasy

1. There were attempts by Argentine studios to cultivate a wealthier national public, such as the 1940s formation of the "comedia burguesa" (bourgeois comedy) (Kelly Hopfenblatt 2016) and the "comedia familiar" (family comedy) genres (Kelly Hopfenblatt 2014).

2. Félix-Didier discusses the shift to urban themes, commenting that the large studios "prosperaron gracias a la fuerte identidad local de sus films, identidad que es fundamentalmente urbana y específicamente porteña . . . dibujaron una mitología de lo porteño a partir de elementos característicos como el tango, el fútbol, la vida nocturna, el cabaret, el bar y el barrio" (prospered thanks to the strong local identity of their films, an identity that is fundamentally urban and specifically that of Buenos Aires . . . they depicted a mythology of Buenos Aires from characteristic elements like the tango, soccer, night life, the cabaret, bar and neighborhood) (2002, 82). On the "danger" associated with rural location filming, Félix-Didier cites a telling comment from the co-director of the foundational militant film *La hora de los hornos*, Octavio Getino, in which he writes that Argentine cinema in the early 1940s "sustituyó los escenarios naturales por gigantescos estudios hollywoodenses. Redujo también el espacio exterior, condenando la imagen a los interiores lujosos, inmensos y cerrados—pero seguros" (substituted natural scenery with gigantic Hollywood-like studios. It also reduced exterior space, condemning the image to luxurious, immense, and closed—but safe—interiors) (2002, 90).

3. The pressures that cause this cinema to conform to preexisting discourses on the nation are discussed in Bernini's reading of several "criollista" filmic adaptations of literary works in the 1930s. The alterations to the stories result in their conforming to the political climate of the decade and to viewer expectations. "El cine del período no puede sino narrar historias desde ese imaginario exigido por la industria y por la demanda . . . la lectura que el cine hace de la literatura, entonces, no tiene grado posible de autonomía . . . la interpretación que los cineastas o los guionistas hacen de las historias que leen y eligen para narrar está presumida, como si no fueran a la literatura sino a hallar lo que ya de antemano saben está en ella. Se trata de una lectura orientada, muy selectiva, dirigida indudablemente a encontrar más material para continuar reproduciendo ese gran imaginario" (The cinema of the period cannot but narrate stories from that imaginary required by the industry and by demand . . . the cinema's reading of literature, then, has no possible degree of autonomy . . . the interpretation that filmmakers and scriptwriters make of the stories they read and choose to narrate is predictable, as if they looked to literature to find what they already know beforehand is in it. It is an oriented reading, very selective, directed undoubtedly to find more material to continue reproducing that imaginary) (2007, La transposición política 121–122).

4. The term *indexical* refers to Charles Peirce's definition, that of a sign that has a physical relationship to the object it designates, and thus retains a trace of that object. This differs from the *iconic*, in which the relationship is one of similarity, and the *symbol*, in which the relationship is established by convention.

5. Bernini and others use the term "criollista" to refer to this genre, the most prominent examples of which are the gaucho-themed films of Lucas Demare, such as *La guerra gaucha* (1942) and *Pampa bárbara* (co-director Hugo Fregonese, 1945). See Lusnich (2007) and Bernini (2007, *La transposición política*) for accounts of how nationalist pressure produced, from a heterogeneous body of literary texts, an ideologically homogeneous body of films during the classical period. On Soffici's "social-folkloric" films and FORJA, see Falicov (1998).

6. As in the rest of the world, modern modes of transport were quickly imbricated with the emerging medium, not only as subject, but also through the cinematic use of the new perceptual opportunities they created: "Railroad travel . . . profoundly altered the human sensorium and produced a specifically modern perceptual paradigm marked by what Wolfgang Schivelbusch calls 'panoramic perception'—the experience of passengers looking out of a moving train window—. . . The cinema in Latin America developed a similar natural affinity with this panoramic mode of perception within its first decade; the railroad 'view' became the logical predecessor and producer of early traveling shots" (López 53). The related concept of "attraction"—the function of the cinema to show, rather than to narrate—is discussed by Tom Gunning in his 1990 article "The Cinema of Attractions: Early Film, Its Spectator and the Avant-Garde," and is also described by López: "Instead of the narrative forms that would later become hegemonic, the cinema of attractions . . . was based on an aesthetics of astonishment; it appealed to viewers' curiosity about the new technology and fulfilled it with brief moments of images in movement" (52).

7. Félix-Didier specifies 1933 as the year of the appearance of the classical Argentine cinema, due to the move from artisanal to industrial production with the rise of the large studios, and 1955 as its eclipse. Specific traits of the period she mentions are serial production, the star system, and the use of genres as a commercial strategy (2002, 81).

8. Such use of the train in transitions is seen in a surprisingly large number of films of the period, and extends back into the late-silent period, as seen in *Mi alazán tostao* (Nelo Cosimi, 1923).

9. Ballent and Gorelik discuss the problematic aspects of the projects.

10. Sasiaín examines the lack of distance between the Argentine state and documentary film production during the same period, which is seen in films that portray the state as successfully modernizing the nation's territory. Spadaccini discusses the pressure exerted by Carlos Alberto Pessano as both critic and, after 1936, as director of the Instituto Cinematográfico Argentino.

11. Andermann discusses the design of the Llao Llao as the central focus of Nahuel Huapi National Park, in an organic integration between the landscape, architecture, and the modernizing state (2017).

12. Graciela Silvestri describes further nationalistic motives behind the development of Nahuel Huapi: "En el caso de Nahuel Huapí, el problema no era sólo de límites, sino del famoso tópico argentino de la 'penetración chilena'; en efecto, la mayoría de los trabajadores del área eran chilotas, y de Chile venían los primeros emprendedores, muchos de ellos de origen norteamericano y alemán. En ambos casos, se imponía la misión de 'argentinizar'" (In the case of Nahuel Huapi, the problem was not one of borders, but rather the famous Argentine topic of "Chilean penetration." In fact, the majority of the workers in the area were from Chiloé, and the first entrepreneurs came from Chile, many of them of North American and German origin. In both cases, the mission was to "Argentinize") (129–130).

13. In December of 1937, Amorim published a text in the magazine *El Hogar* dedicated to the landmark (Ballent 109).

14. Martínez Estrada had written quite similarly several years earlier:

En el fondo de los campos estaba la miseria y la ignorancia, que es la verdad y no la mentira.

Desde el tren toda esa verdad parece un juego de palabras; hay que verla con los ojos del que se queda cuando el tren se va. Hay que mirarla desde afuera del coche, que es lo de adentro, las vísceras y órganos de un cuerpo de tres dimensiones, que parece en las cartas una red de líneas negras sobre un fondo blanco. La verdad y la vida están en ese fondo blanco que es nuestro interior, donde están las entrañas y los hijos de mañana" (69).

In the depths of the countryside there was misery and ignorance, and that is the truth and not the lie.

Viewed from the train, all this truth appears to be a game of words, but it must be seen with the eyes of those who remain when the train departs. One should contemplate the railroad from the outside and realize that it is a living three-dimensional body and not a net of black lines on a white background as it appears on the maps. That white background is our countryside; full of truth and life, it is the guts and the source of the children of tomorrow. (Nouzeilles and Montaldo 262)

15. Melina Piglia describes the network of service stations set up by the collaboration between the ACA and YPF in the 1930s as a key element of the public works initiative of that decade.

16. Pedernera shares a family name with Adolfo Pedernera, the premier Argentine soccer player of the 1940s and, as such, a foremost representative of a more acceptable form of urban masculinity.

17. Christensen was in constant conflict with Peronism and left Argentina permanently during Perón's presidency. In Ruffinelli's comprehensive account of the career of Christensen *Con el diablo en el cuerpo* goes unmentioned, although it does appear in the filmography at the end of the article.

18. Peña explains that "Argentina Sono Film fue la única productora con estudios propios que sobrevivió la crisis de 1955–1957 y lo hizo mediante una estrategia que combinó el habitual juego sobre lo seguro (en esta época representada por las películas de Lolita Torres) con una zona mayor de riesgo que apostó primero a lograr films que pudieran insertarse en el mercado europeo y después a obtener los premios más altos que anualmente entregaba el Instituto Nacional de Cinematografía" (Argentina Sono Film was the only producer with its own studios that survived the crisis of 1955–1957 and it did so through a strategy that combined a habitual production of the reliable [which at the time were films starring Lolita Torres] with an area of greater risk that first bet on making films that might manage to enter the European market and then on obtaining the biggest awards given out annually by the INC) (145).

19. An exception is *Puerto Nuevo*, directed by Luis César Amadori and released in 1936, which was set in an early *villa* but shot in a studio recreation that is decidedly not realist.

20. As Gionco writes, Demare is among the "directores-bisagra" (hinge directors) of the transition from industry to Nuevo Cine. The others she discusses are Leopoldo Torre-Nilsson and Fernando Ayala (271).

Chapter 3: An Inquisitive Gaze on the Nation

1. The gaze of *La hora de los hornos* could not be called exclusively inquisitive insofar as it is a militant film that communicates a clear, preexisting message on the legitimacy of revolutionary violence. As Emilio Bernini writes of the film, "la diversidad del material con que *La hora de los hornos* está compuesto responde a una gran coherencia ideológica y, en este sentido, la polisemia propia de la imagen es incesantemente reducida de acuerdo con el objetivo que los cineastas se plantearon de antemano" (the diversity of the material of which *The Hour of the Furnaces* is composed obeys a great ideological coherence and, in this sense, the polysemy proper to the image is incessantly reduced according to the objective the filmmakers proposed beforehand) (Bernini 2007, *El documental político* 24). I would argue that while the communication of such an *a priori* message often neutralizes the inquisitive gaze, in certain sequences, such as the one I analyze here, the gaze is resolutely inquisitive.

2. For a detailed account of the publications and *cineclubes* of the time see Félix-Didier (2003, La crítica).

3. The Ley de cine was gradually modified, and by 1963 the Consejo Honorario de Calificación, basically a censorship board empowered to demand cuts to films, was created. In 1968 the name of this organism was changed to the Ente de Calificación, at which point it took on the power to ban films entirely. This body was briefly disempowered during the "primavera camporista" in 1973, but was soon reinstated and lasted until 1983, the year of the end of the most recent military dictatorship.

4. The "Generación del 60" (Generation of '60) refers to a group of Buenos Aires–based filmmakers that includes David José Kohon, Rodolfo Kuhn, Lautaro Murúa, Manuel Antín, and others.

5. Paranaguá (1998) argues strongly for the importance of neorealism as the key formative influence on the new film cultures that appeared in Latin America in the 1950s and the creative filmmaking period that followed.

6. In Argentina there is an urban and a rural component to the more politicized aspect of the New Cinema. Key works of the former are David José Kohon's short *Buenos Aires* (1958) and Lautaro Murúa's *Alias Gardelito* (1961), while the latter includes Birri's work and Murúa's *Shunko* (1961).

7. That the existence of the poverty shown in *Tire dié* was not widely visible at the time is summed up well by Nicolás Prividera when he writes that the documentary "mostraba con crudeza la pobreza que nadie quería ver, y que cincuenta años después se ha convertido (como la película misma) en una realidad consentida que ya no parece inquietar a nadie" (revealed frankly the poverty that no one wanted to see, and that fifty years later has been converted into [like the film itself] an accepted reality that no longer seems to worry anyone).

8. In the same issue of *Lyra* in which Sebreli's essay appears, Agustín Mahieu criticized the use of time in *Los inundados*' train sequences: "Falta tal vez una depuración de montaje, sobre todo en relación con los tiempos" (A refinement of the montage is perhaps lacking, especially as regards the duration) (n.p.). Apparently Mahieu, unlike Sebreli, considered the editing to have created dead time.

9. I thank Sonia Sasiaín for calling my attention to this sequence.

10. On *La hora de los hornos* see, for example, Stam, or Podalsky (2004).

11. The Tucumán *zafra* was also shown in isolated sequences of *La hora de los hornos*.

12. For an analysis of the representation of labor in Prelorán's early collaborations with Gleyzer as "la desmitificación de la artesanía" (the demystification of artisan work) as a mere necessity for survival, see Pérez Llahí (2009, 398–399).

13. The name of Luis Brandoni, the male lead in *Gente en Buenos Aires*, appears among many on the dictatorship's secret blacklist of April 6, 1979 (released in 2013), under the category "Fórmula 4," which is defined as "registra antecedentes ideológicos marxistas que hacen aconsejable su no ingreso y/o permanencia en la

administración pública, no se le proporcione colaboración . . ." (has a record of a Marxist ideological background that makes unadvisable his or her entry and/or continuity in public administration, do not provide collaboration) ("Los nombres prohibidos por la dictadura," n.p.). In practice this meant that those on the list could not find work in Argentina either in state or private productions. Some other important figures of the cinema found on the list are Alfredo Alcón, Héctor Alterio, Norman Briski, Leonardo Favio, Delia Garcés, Octavio Getino, Cipe Lincovsky, Federico Luppi, Duilio Marzio, Bárbara Mujica, Lautaro Murúa, Marilina Ross, Pino Solanas, and María Vaner.

14. On the delayed premiere Landeck recounts that

> Teníamos asignado el cine Iguazú. Pero *La tregua* tenía una productora con mucha fuerza. Cuando mandaron *La tregua* en vez de *Gente en Buenos Aires* al Iguazú, yo pregunté en la distibuidora qué había pasado. Me dijeron que bueno, que fuera a ver al dueño del cine Monumental, que sus hijos le habían hablado muy bien de *Gente en Buenos Aires*. "¿Y por qué tengo que ir yo? Los distribuidores son ustedes." Igual, fastidiada, fui. Además yo soy un poco tímida, y era más tímida en esa época. El dueño del Monumental, que era un cine grande e importante, me recibió y me dio fecha de estreno . . . Finalmente la estrenaron. Pero estuvo cuatro semanas y, aunque cumplía la media, la sacaron. La mandaron al Lorraine. Cuando la sacaron del Lorraine . . . fui a hablar con Soffici, que era entonces director del Instituto [y] me hizo firmar una carta para hacer una protesta oficial. Luego, se inició un juicio a mi nombre. Fui a hablar de nuevo al Lorraine y me dijeron que fuera a hablar con Tato. "Para mi se terminó," pensé. Después recibí amenazas y me contaron que el juicio lo rechazaron porque debía presentarse la distribuidora, no yo. Después tuve que dejar el país. (Hardouin and Ivachow 49–50)

> We were assigned the Cine Iguazú. But *La tregua* had a powerful producer. When they sent *La tregua* instead of *Gente en Buenos Aires* to the Iguazú, I asked the distributor what happened. They told me to go see the owner of the Cine Monumental, whose children had spoken well to him of *Gente en Buenos Aires*. "And why do *I* have to go? You're the distributors." Even so, annoyed, I went. And I'm a bit shy, and was even more shy then. The owner of the Monumental, which was a big, important theater, met me and gave me a premiere date. . . . Finally they screened it. But it was on for four weeks and, although it was drawing enough spectators, they took it down. They sent it to the Lorraine. When they took it down there . . . I went to talk to Soffici, who was the director of the Institute [and] he had me

sign a letter of official protest. Then a case was opened in my name. I went back to the Lorraine and they told me to go talk to Tato. "It's over for me," I thought. After that I received threats and they told me they rejected the case because the distributor had to file it, not me. Then I had to leave the country.

15. For his part, Brandoni mentions the threats, but tells a slightly different story, speaking of a longer-term effort by the theater owner to replace the film with a foreign blockbuster:

> [*Gente en Buenos Aires*] tuvo un relativo suceso. Recuerdo que se estrenó en el cine Monumental, . . . estrenaron la película convencidos de que en una semana se la sacaban de encima. Y resultó que no. Pasó una segunda semana, ya definitivamente convencidos de que a la semana siguiente ponían otra película. Y resultó que no. . . . Se sostuvo en cartel una tercera semana y por supuesto, no soportó más la presión de los distribuidores. . . . Ese es el crimen que aún sigue vigente ahora, aunque el método es más sofisticado. (Garcete n.p.)

> *Gente en Buenos Aires* was relatively successful. I remember it opened at the Cine Monumental, . . . they screened it convinced that they'd get it off their backs after a week. But no. The second week they were definitely convinced that they'd move on to another film the next week. But no. . . . It stayed up for a third week and of course it couldn't take the pressure from the distributors any longer. That's the crime that still happens today, although the method is more sophisticated.

16. For an account of Landeck's career in the context of the gendered division of labor that had prevented women from directing films and of the specific political situations of the 1970s see Losada (2016).

17. According to popular film history, the most notable aspect of *El trueno entre las hojas* is female nudity the likes of which had never been seen before in Argentine cinema. The press and internet abounds with assertions that the first female nude shown in the national cinema was Sarli in *El trueno entre las hojas*, and some scholars make the same assertion, such as when Drajner Barredo writes, in an insightful article on gender in *Carne*, that *El trueno entre las hojas* "[e]s la primera película que tuvo como protagonista a una joven Isabel Sarli y la primera en contar con su exuberante cuerpo desnudo, el primer desnudo frontal de la cinematografía argentina" (is the first film that had a young Isabel Sarli as protagonist and the first to include her exuberant nude body, the first frontal nude of the Argentine cinema) (10). But such assertions must be qualified, since earlier in this same film several indigenous women are shown naked from the waist up, in unhurried shots

that last several seconds. How to explain such an oversight? Have the indigenous women been exempted from consideration as spectacle due to their race, which naturalizes their nudity and converts them from objects of a scopophilic gaze into objects of a National Geographic–type of pseudo-ethnographic, desexualizing gaze? Or could it be that, in continuity with the marginalization that extends from the nineteenth-century national literary classics, Sarli's privileged place in film history is due to the fact that the indigenous women are not accorded entry into Argentine culture? These questions are difficult to answer, but what is certain is that the scopophilic formal structure in which Sarli appears is absent in the shots in which these indigenous women appear. The diegetic males do not seem to notice their matter-of-fact nakedness, and the camera treats them no differently than any other element of the mise-en-scène, *qua* lamp or bowl of fruit, a formal treatment that renders Sarli's nakedness conspicuous by contrast.

18. These settings would presumably make a censor more willing to approve the films, since such acts would call into question the national image if they were to occur in recognizably national, or "civilized," spaces, rather than spaces that have remained untouched and continue to exist in a "barbaric" state.

19. At the end of the film Ortega/Ríos sings the film's optimistic title song, which refers to the imminent return of Perón: "Yo tengo fe, también mucha ilusión, porque yo sé, que será una realidad el mundo de justicia que ya empieza a despertar."

20. The events of Ortega's biography as depicted in the mass media are nearly identical to those of *Yo tengo fe*. An example is an article by García Melero published by the news agency *Agencia EFE*, which locates Ortega's childhood in Lules, Tucumán, as does the film. The six brothers, the migration to Buenos Aires, selling coffee, the job at the radio station and, above all, the unflagging willingness to work hard and keep faith, feature in both.

Chapter 4: Contemporary Cinema and the Neoliberal Social Margins

1. Aguilar sees *Elefante blanco* as an example of what he calls the "cine global de miseria" (global cinema of misery), although he is careful to point out that Trapero's film politicizes those excluded from society, unlike the internationally successful Brazilian film *Cidade de deus* (2002), in which the protagonist manages to find success and leave the slum to presumably enter the middle class (Aguilar *Algunas películas recientes sobre las villas miseria*).

2. These factors are described in great detail in Falicov's *The Cinematic Tango: Contemporary Argentine Film* (115–146).

3. Berlant further develops the concept of cruel optimism: "All attachments are optimistic. When we talk about an object of desire, we are really talking about a cluster of promises we want someone or something to make to us and make possible for us. This cluster of promises could seem embedded in a person, a thing,

an institution, a text, a norm, a bunch of cells, smells, a good idea—whatever. To phrase 'the object of desire' as a cluster of promises is to allow us to encounter what's incoherent or enigmatic in our attachments, not as confirmation of our irrationality but as an explanation of our sense of *our endurance in the object*, insofar as proximity to the object means proximity to the cluster of things that the object promises, some of which may be clear to us and good for us while others, not so much" (23–24, emphasis in original).

4. In *Los Marziano* the use of free-indirect discourse is limited to this shot, and does not make up any larger formal strategy that might engage with sensorial perturbation, such as that we will see in the next film analyzed.

5. Taylorization refers to the "scientific management" of workflow at a steel factory carried out by Frederick Winslow Taylor, and the resulting theoretical basis he set out in *The Principles of Scientific Management* (1911). Taylor's main goal was that of the economization of time in a factory process. He measured the amount of time the task assigned to each individual worker on the assembly line should take, and on the basis of this, designed the factory as a machine, of which each human worker functioned as a mechanical part. This extreme version of the modern division of labor became widespread, and its influence is acknowledged in such diverse contexts as Soviet economic management, the "corporate reengineering" of the late twentieth century, and in current marketing techniques, in which the individual's capacity to consume commodities is studied in order to maximize it.

6. Paradoxically, in many modern Latin American urban films, from *Los olvidados* onward, the lumpenproletariat characters that inhabit the streets could be said to experience a postcivilization "return to the jungle" in which their corporeal sensorium returns to a fully functioning *aesthetica naturalis*, open to detect opportunity and/or danger in their dysfunctional urban surroundings.

7. See Ruiz for an enlightening take on what he calls "central conflict" in film.

8. Falicov (2007, 146–148) formulates an illuminating comparison of Solanas's films of the early 2000s with his earlier militant work.

9. Much has been written on the subjective or first-person documentary. See Nichols, Renov; Bruzzi; and for the specific Argentine case, Piedras (2014).

10. Piedras traces the appearance of Solanas in the first-person in his work to specific sequences of *Memoria del saqueo* (2011, 666). Piedras refers to this kind of use of the first-person as the "modalidad epidérmica" (epidermic modality), in which there is "una relación menos necesaria, esencial y cercana entre el cineasta, el mundo representado y los sujetos que lo habitan. Dicho de otra manera, la inscripción de la primera persona en estos films no implica una puesta en cuestión de la experiencia, la interioridad y los afectos del cineasta" (a less necessary, essential, and close relationship between the filmmaker, the world represented, and the subjects who inhabit it. Put in another way, the inscription of the first person in these films does not imply a questioning of experience, interiority, and the affects of the filmmaker) (2014, 80).

11. In some cases these strategies are questionable, such as the use of the widely seen video of the salt-dome cave-in at Bayou Corne in Louisiana, which

Solanas implies happened as a result of fracking. While the Bayou Corne episode is due to the actions of the hydrocarbons industry, its direct cause is more often attributed to the collapse of an underground salt dome used to store crude oil. But here, as in his *Cine Liberación* period, Solanas's privileging of spectacularity over credibility does not necessarily make his films less rhetorically effective.

12. Marcone writes of a general lack in documentary film of the representation of indigenous understandings of "human and other-than-human interactions" (223).

13. For a theorization of the concept of "cine villero" and several examples (including the work of Julio Arrieta), see Bosch.

Works Cited

Abel, Richard. *The Ciné Goes to Town: French Cinema 1896–1914*. Berkeley: U of California P, 1998. Print.
Acree, William. "Cultura visual cotidiana y el consumo de imágenes de la patria en el Río de la Plata (1880–1910)." *Hispanófila* 176 (January 2016): 137–158. Print.
Aguilar, Gonzalo. "La representación de las villas en el cine." *Informe escaleno* (enero 2013). Web.
Aguilar, Gonzalo. "Algunas películas recientes sobre las villas miseria." *Informe escaleno* (enero 2013). Web.
Aguilar, Gonzalo. *Otros mundos: Un ensayo sobre el nuevo cine argentino*. Buenos Aires: Santiago Arcos, 2006. Print.
Alberdi, Juan Bautista. *Bases y puntos de partida para la organización política de la República Argentina*. Buenos Aires: W.M. Jackson Editores, 1946. Print.
Altamirano, Carlos, "Introducción al *Facundo*." *Para un programa de historia intelectual y otros ensayos*. Buenos Aires: Siglo XXI, 2005: 25–61. Print.
Andermann, Jens. "Estilo austral: paisaje, arquitectura y regionalismo nacionalizador en el Parque Nacional Nahuel Huapi (1934–1943)" *Artelogie* 10 (2017). Web.
Andermann, Jens. "Exhausted Landscapes: Reframing the Rural in Recent Argentine and Brazilian Films." *Cinema Journal* 53.2 (Winter 2014): 50–70. Print.
Andermann, Jens. *New Argentine Cinema*. London: I.B. Tauris, 2012. Print.
Andermann, Jens. "Expanded Fields: Postdictatorship and the Landscape." *Journal of Latin American Cultural Studies* 21.2 (June 2012): 165–187. Print.
Andermann, Jens. *The Optic of the State: Visuality and Power in Argentina and Brazil*. Pittsburgh: U of Pittsburgh P, 2007. Print.
Ballent, Anahí. "Kilómetro Cero: La construcción del universo simbólico del camino en la Argentina de los años treinta." *Boletín del Instituto de Historia Argentina y Americana Dr. Emilio Ravignani* 27 (2005): 107–137. Print.
Ballent, Anahí, and Adrián Gorelik. "País urbano o país rural: La modernización territorial y su crisis." In Cattaruzza, Alejandro, ed. *Nueva Historia Argentina*. Buenos Aires: Sudamericana, 2001: 143–200. Print.

Bazin, André. *What is Cinema? Volume II*. Trans. Hugh Gray. Berkeley: University of California, 1971. Print.
Beckman, Ericka. *Capital Fictions: The Literature of Latin America's Export Age*. Minneapolis: U of Minnesota P, 2013. Print.
Bergson, Henri. *Matter and Memory*. Trans. Nancy M. Paul and W. Scott Palmer. New York: Doubleday Anchor Books, 1959. Print.
Berlant, Lauren. *Cruel Optimism*. Durham, NC: Duke UP, 2011. Print.
Bernini, Emilio. "La transposición política: la literatura en el cine argentino de los años treinta." In *La década infame y los escritores suicidas (1930–1943)*. Ed. David Viñas. Buenos Aires: Fundación Crónica General, 2007: 121–131. Print.
Bernini, Emilio. "El documental político argentino." In *Imágenes de lo real: La representación de lo político en el documental argentino*. Ed. Josefina Sartora. Buenos Aires: Libraria, 2007: 21–34. Print.
Bernini, Emilio. "Un estado (contemporáneo) del documental: Sobre algunos films argentinos recientes." *Kilómetro 111* 5 (November 2004): 41–57. Print.
Birri, Fernando. *La escuela documental de Santa Fe*. Rosario: Prohistoria, 2008. Print.
Bogue, Ronald. *Deleuze on Cinema*. New York: Routledge, 2003. Print.
Bogue, Ronald. *Deleuze on Literature*. New York: Routledge, 2003. Print.
Bordwell, David, Janet Steiger, and Kristin Thompson. *The Classical Hollywood Cinema: Film Style & Mode of Production to 1960*. New York: Columbia UP, 1985. Print.
Bosch, Carlos Luis. "La discursividad del Cine Villero." *Imagofagia* 15 (2017). Web.
Brakhage, Stan. "Metaphors on Vision." *Essential Brakhage*. New York: McPherson and Company, 2001: 12–71. Print.
Bruzzi, Stella. *New Documentary*. New York: Routledge, 2006. Print.
Buck-Morss, Susan. "Aesthetics and Anaesthetics: Walter Benjamin's Artwork Essay Reconsidered." *October* 62 (Autumn 1992): 3–41. Print.
Burton, Julianne. "Democratizing Documentary: Modes of Address in the New Latin American Cinema, 1958–1972." *The Social Documentary in Latin America*. Burton, Julianne, ed. Pittsburgh: U of Pittsburgh P, 1990: 49–84. Print.
Butler, Judith. "Torture and the Ethics of Photography." *Environment and Planning D: Society and Space* 25 (2007): 951–966. Print.
Chamosa, Oscar. "Criollo and Peronist: The Argentine Folklore Movement during the First Peronism, 1943–1955." *The New Cultural History of Peronism: Power and Identity in Mid-Twentieth-Century Argentina*. Karush, Matthew B. and Oscar Chamosa, eds. Durham, NC: Duke UP, 2010: 113–142. Print.
Cook, David A. *A History of Narrative Cinema*. New York: W. W. Norton & Co., 1990. Print.
Couselo, Jorge Miguel. *El 'Negro' Ferreyra: Un cine por instinto*. Buenos Aires: Grupo Editor Altamira, 2001. Print.
Cuarterolo, Andrea. "El cine científico en la Argentina de principios del Siglo XX: Entre la educación y el espectáculo." *Historia da Educação* 19.47 (2015): 51–73. Print.

Cuarterolo, Andrea. "Ciencia y espectáculo. Algunas reflexiones sobre el temprano cine científico argentino." *La pantalla letrada: estudios interdisciplinarios sobre cine y audiovisual latinoamericano.* Torello, Georgina and Isabel Wschebor, eds. Montevideo: Espacio Interdisciplinario de la Universidad de la República, 2016: 33–47. Print.

Cuarterolo, Andrea. *De la foto al fotograma. Relaciones entre cine y fotografía en la Argentina (1840–1933).* Montevideo: CdF Ediciones, 2013. Print.

Cuarterolo, Andrea. "Imágenes de la Argentina opulenta: una lectura de *Nobleza gaucha* (1915) desde el proyecto fotográfico de la Sociedad Fotográfica Argentina de Aficionados." Lusnich, Ana Laura, ed. *Civilización y barbarie en el cine argentino y latinoamericano.* Buenos Aires: Editorial Biblos, 2005: 19–34. Print.

Cuarterolo, Andrea. "El viaje en la era de la reproducibilidad técnica. Discursos etno-geográficos en los primeros *travelogues* argentinos." *Cine Documental* 3. 2011. Web.

Cuarterolo, Andrea. "El arte de 'instruir deleitando.' Discursos positivistas y nacionalistas en el cine argentino del primer Centenario. *Iberoamericana* X (2010): 197–210. Print.

Cubitt, Sean. "Film, Landscape and Political Aesthetics: *Deseret.*" *Screen* 57.1 (Spring 2016): 21–34. Print.

Dabove, Juan Pablo. *Nightmares of the Lettered City: Banditry and Literature in Latin America 1816–1929.* Pittsburgh: U of Pittsburgh P, 2007. Print.

De Certeau, Michel. *The Practice of Everyday Life.* Trans. Steven Rendall. Berkeley: U of California P, 1988. Print.

Deleuze, Gilles. *Cinema 2: The Time-Image.* Trans. Hugh Tomlinson and Robert Galeta. Minneapolis, U of Minnesota P, 1989. Print.

Deleuze, Gilles. *Cinema 1: The Movement-Image.* Trans. Hugh Tomlinson and Barbara Habberjam. Minneapolis: U of Minnesota P, 1986. Print.

Deleuze, Gilles, and Félix Guattari. *A Thousand Plateaus: Capitalism and Schizofrenia.* Trans. Brian Massumi. Minneapolis: U of Minnesota P, 1986. Print.

Derbyshire, Philip. "Imaginar en el aire: reflexiones sobre el cine de Jorge Prelorán." *Estudios sociales del NOA/Nueva Serie* 12 (2012): 5–17. Print.

Di Núbila, Domingo. *Historia del cine argentino.* Buenos Aires: Ediciones del Jilguero, 1998.

Doane, Mary Anne. *The Emergence of Cinematic Time: Modernity, Contingency and the Archive.* Cambridge: Harvard UP, 2002. Print.

Dorsky, Nathaniel. *Devotional Cinema.* Berkeley: Tuumba Press, 2005. Print.

Drajner Barredo, Tamara. "¿Cosificación o uso político? *Carne* de Armando Bo-Isabel Sarli." *Imagofagia* 14 (2016). Web.

Duncan, Ian. "The Provincial or Regional Novel." Brantlinger, Patrick and William Thesing. *A Companion to the Victorian Novel.* London: Wiley-Blackwell, 2005: 318–335. Print.

Eseverri, Máximo, and Fernando Martín Peña. *Lita Stantic: el cine es automóvil y poema.* Buenos Aires: EUDEBA, 2013. Print.

España, Claudio. "Emergencia y tensiones en el cine argentino de los años cincuenta." *Nuevo Texto Crítico* 21/21 (1998): 45–73. Print.

Falicov, Tamara L. *The Cinematic Tango: Contemporary Argentine Film*. London: Wallflower Press, 2007. Print.

Falicov, Tamara L. "Argentine Cinema and the construction of national popular identity, 1930–1942." *Studies in Latin American Popular Culture* 17 (1998): 61–78. Print.

Félix-Didier, Paula. "Introducción." *Generaciones 60/90: Cine argentino independiente*. Peña, Fernando Martín, ed. Buenos Aires: Malba, 2003: 11–21. Print.

Félix-Didier, Paula. "La crítica de cine en los 60." *Generaciones 60/90: Cine argentino independiente*. Peña, Fernando Martín, ed. Buenos Aires: Malba, 2003: 328–335. Print.

Félix-Didier, Paula. "Soñando con Hollywood: Los estudios Baires y la industria cinematográfica en Argentina." *Studies in Latin American Popular Culture* 21 (2002): 77–103. Print.

Fontana, Patricio. "*Suburbio*: nadie sale vivo de aquí." *Informe escaleno*. (Noviembre 2012). Web.

Foster, David William. "Las lolas de la Coca: El cuerpo femenino en el cine de Isabel Sarli." *Karpa* 1.2 (Summer 2008). Web.

Garcete, Horacio. "Luis Brandoni: Entrevista." *Esto no es una revista*. n. date. Web.

García, Viviana. "Lautaro Murúa." *Generaciones 60/90: Cine argentino independiente*. Peña, Fernando Martín, ed. Buenos Aires: Malba, 2003: 204–209. Print.

García Melero, Rodrigo. "Palito Ortega cumple 75 años preparando su biografía y sin ganas de jubilarse." *Agencia EFE*. March 7, 2016. Web.

García Falcó, Marta, and Patricia Méndez. "Recuperación de las salas cinematográficas porteñas. 1896–2010." García Falcó, Marta, Patricia Méndez and Julio Cacciatore, eds. *Cines de Buenos Aires: patrimonio de siglo XX*. Buenos Aires: CEDODAL, 2010: 47–89. Print.

Gionco, Pamela C. "Después de 1955: Entre clasicismo y modernidad, entre revolución y resistencia." *Una historia del cine político y social en Argentina (1896–1969)*. Lusnich, Ana Laura and Pablo Piedras, eds. Buenos Aires: Nueva Librería, 2009: 269–295. Print.

González, Leandro. "Apuntes para una historia de la industria cinematográfica argentina: la etapa silente (1896–1932). *AsAECA Congreso Internacional 2016*. Web.

Gunning, Tom. "The Cinema of Attractions: Early Film, Its Spectator and the Avant-Garde." *Early Cinema: Space, Frame, Narrative*. Thomas Elsaesser and Adam Barker, eds. London: British Film Institute, 1990: 56–62. Print.

Halperin, Paula. "'With an Incredible Realism that Beats the Best of the European Cinemas': The Making of *Barrio Gris* and the Reception of Italian Neorealism in Argentina, 1947–1955." *Global Neorealism: The Transnational History of a Film Style*. Giovacchini, Saverio and Robert Sklar, eds. Oxford: UP of Mississippi, 2012: 125–140. Print.

Halperín Donghi, Tulio. *Historia contemporánea de América latina*. Madrid: Alianza, 1993. Print.
Hansen, Miriam Bratu. "Introduction." *Theory of Film*. By Siegfried Kracauer. Princeton, NJ: Princeton UP, 1997: vii–xlv. Print.
Hardouin, Elodie, and Lilian Laura Ivachow. 2011. "Eva, la atrevida." *El Amante Cine* 231 (August 2011): 48–50. Print.
Harvey, David. "The 'New' Imperialism: Accumulation by Dispossession." *Socialist Register* 40 (2004): 63–87. Print.
Hernández, José. *Martín Fierro*. Buenos Aires: Losada, 1995. Print.
Hernández, José. *The Gaucho Martin Fierro*. Trans. Frank Gaetano Carrino, Alberto J. Carlos and Norman Mangouni. Albany: SUNY Press, 1974. Print.
Karush, Matthew. *Culture of Class: Radio and Cinema in the Making of a Divided Argentina, 1920–1946*. Durham, NC: Duke UP, 2012. Print.
Kelly Hopfenblatt, Alejandro. "Manuel Romero y el aburguesamiento del cine argentino: la puesta en tensión de una visión." *AsAECA* (2016). Web.
Kelly Hopfenblatt, Alejandro. "Un modelo de representación para la burguesía: La reformulación de identidades y espacios en el cine de ingenuas" *Imagofagia* 10 (2014). Web.
Kelly Hopfenblatt, Alejandro and Jimena Trombetta. "Características de la censura entre 1933 y 1956." *Una historia del cine político y social en Argentina (1896–1969)*. Lusnich, Ana Laura and Pablo Piedras, eds. Buenos Aires: Nueva Librería, 2009: 251–267. Print.
King, John. *Magical Reels: A History of Cinema in Latin America*. London: Verso, 2000. Print.
Kittler, Friedrich A. *Discourse Networks 1800/1900*. Trans. Michael Metteer. Stanford, CA: Stanford UP, 1990. Print.
Kohen, Héctor R. "De Fresco a Perón: La aventura cinematográfica de Miguel Machinandiarena." *Secuencias: revista de historia del cine* 10 (1999): 8–22. Print.
Kracauer, Siegfried. *Theory of Film: The Redemption of Physical Reality*. London: Oxford UP, 1960. Print.
Kriger, Clara. *Cine y Peronismo: el estado en escena*. Buenos Aires: Siglo Veintiuno Editores, 2009. Print.
Kuhn, Rodolfo. *Armando Bó, el cine, la pornografía ingenua y otras reflexiones*. Buenos Aires: Editorial Corregidor, 1984. Print.
Lefebvre, Henri. *The Production of Space*. Trans. Donald Nicholson-Smith. Oxford: Blackwell, 1991. Print.
Lefebvre, Martin. "Between Setting and Landscape in the Cinema." *Landscape and Film*. Lefebvre, Martin, ed. New York: Routledge, 2006: 19–60. Print.
Lefebvre, Martin. "On Landscape in Narrative Cinema." *Canadian Journal of Film Studies* 20.1 (Spring 2011): 61–78. Print.
López, Ana M. "Early Cinema and Modernity in Latin America." *Cinema Journal* 40.1 (Fall 2000): 48–78. Print.

López, Ana M. "An 'Other' History: The New Latin American Cinema." *New Latin American Cinema, Volume One: Theory, Practices, and Trnascontinental Articulations*. Martin, Michael T., ed. Detroit: Wayne State UP, 1997: 135–156. Print.

Losada, Matt. "Before Bemberg: Eva Landeck, *Gente en Buenos Aires* and the Gendered Division of Labor in Argentine Cinema. *Revista de Estudios Hispánicos* 50.3 (October 2016): 711–728. Print.

"Los nombres prohibidos de la dictadura." 2013. *Página/12* (Nov. 16, 2013). Web.

Lugones, Leopoldo. *El payador y antología de poesía y prosa*. Caracas: Biblioteca Ayacucho, 1979. Print.

Lugones, Leopoldo. "El hermoso día." *El libro de los paisajes*. Buenos Aires: Otero y García Eds., 1917. Print.

Lusnich, Ana Laura. "Los relatos de frontera en el cine argentino: estrategias narrativas y textuales." In *Civilización y barbarie en el cine argentino y latinoamericano*. Ana Laura Lusnich, ed. Buenos Aires: Editorial Biblos, 2005: 35–42. Print.

Lusnich, Ana Laura. *El drama socia-folclórico: El universo rural en el cine argentino*. Buenos Aires: Biblos, 2007. Print.

Mafud, Lucio. "Nación y ficción: Mariano Moreno y la Revolución de Mayo en el contexto previo al Centenario de la Independencia." *Cine mudo latinoamericano: inicio, nación, vanguardias y transición*. De los Reyes, Aurelio and David M.J. Wood, eds. México: UNAM, Instituto de Investigaciones Estéticas, 2015: 153–174. Print.

Mahieu, Agustín. "La obra de Fernando Birri." *Lyra* 20.186–188 (1962): (n.p.). Print.

Manrupe, Raúl, and María Alejandra Portela. *Un diccionario de films argentinos (1930–1995)*. Buenos Aires: Corregidor, 2001. Print.

Mansilla, Lucio V. *Una excursión a los indios ranqueles*. Buenos Aires: Agebe, 2006. Print.

Maranghello, César. *Breve historia del cine argentino*. Barcelona: Laertes, 2005. Print.

Maranghello, César. "La guerra gaucha." *Tierra en trance: El cine latinoamericano en 100 películas*. Elena, Alberto and Marina Díaz López, eds. Madrid: Alianza, 1999: 63–67. Print.

Marcone, Jorge. "Filming the Emergence of Popular Environmentalism in Latin America: Postcolonialism and Buen Vivir." *Global Ecologies and the Environmental Humanities: Postcolonial Approaches*. DeLoughrey, Elizabeth, Jill Didur and Anthony Carrigan, eds. New York: Routledge, 2015: 207–225. Print.

Marrone, Irene. *Imágenes del mundo histórico. Identidades y representaciones en el noticiero y el documental en el cine mudo argentino*. Buenos Aires: Editorial Biblos, 2003. Print.

Martínez Estrada, Ezequiel. *Radiografía de la pampa*. Buenos Aires: Losada, 2001. Print.

Montaldo Graciela. *De pronto, el campo. Literatura argentina y tradición rural*. Rosario: Beatriz Viterbo, 1993. Print.

Moretti, Franco. *Atlas of the European Novel: 1800–1900*. London: Verso, 1999. Print.

Moretti, Franco. *Graphs, Maps, Trees: Abstract Models for a Literary History*. New York: Verso, 2007. Print.
Mulvey, Laura. "Visual Pleasure and Narrative Cinema." *Narrative, Apparatus, Ideology: A Film Theory Reader*. Rosen, Philip, ed. New York: Columbia UP, 1986: 198–209. Print.
Nichols, Bill. *Introduction to Documentary*. Bloomington: Indiana UP, 2001.
Nixon, Rob. *Slow Violence and the Environmentalism of the Poor*. Cambridge, MA: Harvard UP, 2013. Print.
Nouzeilles, Gabriela, and Graciela Montaldo. *The Argentina Reader: History, Culture, Politics*. Durham, NC: Duke UP, 2002. Print.
Orquera, Fabiola. "*El camino hacia la muerte del Viejo Reales*, de Gerardo Vallejo: la lucha por su proyección, su inscripción en medios gráficos y la emergencia del 'zafrero tucumano' en el espacio público." *Entrepasados. Revista de Historia* 38–39 (2012): 185–209. Print.
Page, Joanna. *Crisis and Capitalism in Contemporary Argentine Cinema*. Durham, NC: Duke UP, 2009. Print.
Paranaguá, Paolo Antonio. "Of Periodizations and Paradigms: The Fifties in Comparative Perspective." *Nuevo Texto Crítico* 21/21 (1998): 31–44. Print.
Pasolini, Pier Paolo. "The 'Cinema of Poetry.'" *Heretical Empiricism*. Trans. Ben Lawton and Louise K. Barnett. Washington, DC: New Academia Publishing, 2005: 167–186. Print.
Peluffo, Ana, and Sánchez Prado, Ignacio M. "Introducción." *Entre hombres: masculinidades del siglo XIX en América Latina*. Peluffo, Ana and Sánchez Prado, Ignacio M., eds. Madrid: Iberoamericana-Vervuert, 2010: 7–20. Print.
Peña, Fernando Martín. *Cien años de cine argentino*. Buenos Aires: Biblos-Fundación OSDE, 2012. Print.
Peña, Fernando Martín, and Carlos Vallina. *El cine quema: Raymunod Gleyzer*. Buenos Aires: Ediciones de la Flor, 2006. Print.
Pérez Llahí, Marcos Adrián. "Las razones de Jorge Prelorán." *Una historia del cine político y social en Argentina (1969–2009)*. Lusnich, Ana Laura and Pablo Piedras, eds. Buenos Aires: Nueva Librería, 2011: 97–104. Print.
Pérez Llahí, Marcos Adrián. "La voluntad del individuo: El cine de Jorge Prelorán." *Una historia del cine político y social en Argentina (1969–2009)*. Lusnich, Ana Laura and Pablo Piedras, eds. Buenos Aires: Nueva Librería, 2011: 307–312. Print.
Pérez Llahí, Marcos Adrián. "La tierra es del que la ha perdido: A propósito de Raymundo Gleyzer y Jorge Prelorán." *Una historia del cine político y social en Argentina (1896–1969)*. Lusnich, Ana Laura and Pablo Piedras, eds. Buenos Aires: Nueva Librería, 2009: 395–402. Print.
Philip, George. *Oil and Politics in Latin America*. Cambridge: Cambridge UP, 1982. Print.

Pick, Zuzana. *The New Latin American Cinema: A Continental Project.* Austin: U Texas P, 1996. Print.

Piedras, Pablo. *El cine documental en primera persona.* Buenos Aires: Paidós, 2014. Print.

Piedras, Pablo. "Fernando Solanas: esplendor y decadencia de un sueño político." *Una historia del cine político y social en argentina (1969–2009).* Lusnich, Ana Laura and Pablo Piedras, eds. Buenos Aires: Nueva Librería, 2011: 651–674. Print.

Piedras, Pablo. "Las relaciones permeables entre historia y cine documental argentino: del testimonio a la militancia." *The Colorado Review of Hispanic Studies* 8 (Fall 2010): 11–26. Print.

Piglia, Melina. "El ACA e YPF: La construcción de la primera red nacional de estaciones de servicio (1936–1943)." *IV Jornadas de Historia Política,* 2009. Web.

Podalsky, Laura. *Specular City: Transforming Culture, Consumption, and Space in Buenos Aires 1955–1973.* Philadelphia: Temple UP, 2004. Print.

Podalsky, Laura. "Cityscapes and Alienation: Buenos Aires in the Argentine Cinema, 1950–1960." *Nuevo Texto Crítico* 21/22 (1998): 77–92. Print.

Poggi, Marta, Bernardino Pacciani, and Matías Emiliano Casas. "Los 'perseguidos' en vías de 'rehabilitación': Las representaciones del gaucho y del indio en las escuelas argentinas, 1930–1950." *Cadernos do Aplicação* 27/28.1/2 (2014/2015): 11–20. Print.

Prelorán, Jorge. "Conceptos éticos y estéticos en cine etnográfico." *El cine documental entobiográfico de Jorge Prelorán.* Rossi, Juan José, ed. Buenos Aires: Ediciones Búsqueda, 1987: 72–116. Print.

Ramos, Julio. *Divergent Modernities: Culture and Politics in Nineteenth-Century Latin America.* Trans. John D. Blanco. Durham, NC: Duke UP, 2001. Print.

Renov, Michael. *The Subject of Documentary.* Minneapolis: U of Minnesota P, 2004. Print.

Rocha, Carolina. "Introduction." *Modern Argentine Masculinities.* Rocha, Carolina, ed. Chicago: Intellect, 2013: 3–16. Print.

Rodríguez, Fermín A. *Un desierto para la nación: La escritura del vacío.* Buenos Aires: Eterna Cadencia Editora, 2010. Print.

Romero, Luis Alberto. *Breve Historia Contemporánea de la Argentina.* Buenos Aires: Fondo de Cultura Económica, 1995. Print.

Romero, Luis Alberto. *A History of Argentina in the Twentieth Century.* Trans. James P. Brennan. Buenos Aires: Fondo de Cultura Economica, 2006. Print.

Rossi, Juan José ed. *El cine documental etnobiográfico de Jorge Prelorán.* Argentina: Ediciones Búsqueda, 1987. Print.

Ruffinelli, Jorge. "Jorge Prelorán." *Cine documental en América Latina.* Paranaguá, Paolo Antonio, ed. Madrid: Cátedra, 2003: 164–178. Print.

Ruffinelli, Jorge. "Bajo cinco banderas: el cine multinacional de Carlos Hugo Christensen." *Nuevo Texto Crítico* 21/21 (1998): 277–325. Print.

Ruiz, Raúl. *Poetics of Cinema 1: Miscellanies.* Trans. Carlos Morreo. Paris: Éditions Dis Voir, 2005. Print.

Russo, Vito. *The Celluloid Closet*. New York: Harper & Row, 1987. Print.
Sala. Jorge. "Conflictos sociales y tránsito a la modernización en tres films de ambientación rural." *Una historia del cine político y social en Argentina (1896–1969)*. Lusnich, Ana Laura and Pablo Piedras, eds. Buenos Aires: Nueva Librería, 2009: 297–310. Print.
Sarmiento, Domingo F. *Facundo: Civilización y Barbarie*. Buenos Aires: Edicol, 2006. Print.
Sasiaín, Sonia. "En clave local. Ciudad y territorio en el cine argentino (1930–1955)." *Cine Documental* 16 (2017). Web.
Schroeder Rodríguez, Paul A. *Latin American Cinema: A Comparative History*. Oakland: U of California P, 2016. Print.
Sebreli, Juan José. "La categoría de lo típico y el cine argentino." *Lyra* 20.186–188 (1962): (n.p.). Print.
Silvestri, Graciela. "Postales argentinos." *La argentina en el siglo XX*. Altamirano, Carlos, ed. Buenos Aires: Ariel, 1999: 111–135. Print.
Smith, Neil. *Uneven Development: Nature, Capital, and the Production of Space*. Athens: U Georgia P, 2008. Print.
Solanas, Fernando and Octavio Getino. "Towards a Third Cinema." *New Latin American Cinema: Volume 1. Theory, Practices and Transcontinental Articu-lations*. Martin, Michael T., ed. Detroit: Wayne State UP, 1997: 33–58. Print.
Sorensen Goodrich, Diana. Facundo *and the Construction of Argentine Culture*. Austin: U of Texas P, 1996. Print.
Spadaccini, Silvana. "Carlos Alberto Pessano, de la opinión a la gestión." *Imagofagia* 5 (2012). Web.
Spence, Louise, and Vinicius Navarro. *Crafting Truth: Documentary Form and Meaning*. New Brunswick, NJ: Rutgers UP, 2011. Print.
Stam, Robert. "The Two Avant-Gardes: Solanas and Getino's *The Hour of the Furnaces*." *Documenting the Documentary: Close Readings of Documentary Film and Video*. Grant, Barry Keith and Jeannette Sloniowski, eds. Detroit: Wayne State UP, 1998: 254–268. Print.
Steiner, George. *Martin Heidegger*. New York: Penguin, 1982. Print.
Stites Mor, Jessica. *Transition Cinema: Political Filmmaking and the Argentine Left since 1968*. Pittsburgh: U of Pittsburgh P, 2012. Print.
Svampa, Maristella. *La brecha urbana: Countries y barrios privados*. Buenos Aires: Capital Intelectual, 2004. Print.
Svampa, Maristella. "Commodities Consensus: Neoextractivism and Enclosure of the Commons in Latin America." *South Atlantic Quarterly* 114.1 (January 2015): 65–82. Print.
Szeman, Imre. "Crude Aesthetics: The Politics of Oil Documentaries." *A Companion to Documentary Film*. Juhasz, Alexandra and Alisa Lebow, eds. United Kingdom: Wiley-Blackwell, 2015: 28–42. Print.

Taquini, Graciela. "Los documentales de Jorge Prelorán: un cine antropomórfico." *El cine documental entobiográfico de Jorge Prelorán*. Rossi, Juan José, ed. Buenos Aires: Ediciones Búsqueda, 1987: 30–41. Print.

Taylor, Frederick Winslow. *The Principles of Scientific Management*. New York: Cosimo, 2006. Print.

Taylor, Lucien. "Introduction." *Transcultural Cinema*. MacDougall, David. Princeton, NJ: Princeton UP, 1998: 3–21. Print.

Terán, Oscar. *Vida intelectual en el Buenos Aires fin-de-siglo (1880–1910): Derivas de la "cultura científica."* Buenos Aires: Fondo de Cultura Económica, 2000. Print.

Thompson, Currie K. *Picturing Argentina: Myths, Movies, and the Peronist Vision*. New York: Cambria Press, 2014. Print.

Thompson, Kristin and David Bordwell. *Film History: An Introduction*. New York: McGraw-Hill, 1994. Print.

Tranchini, Elina. "El cine argentino y la construcción de un imaginario criollista, 1915–1945." *Entrepasados* 18–19. (2000): 113–141. Print.

Tranchini, Elina. *El cine argentino y su aporte a la identidad nacional*. Buenos Aires: Fundación Argentina de la Industria Gráfica y Afines, 1999. Print.

Trelles Plazaola, Luis. *Cine y mujer en América Latina: directoras de largometrajes de ficción*. Río Piedras, P.R.: Editorial de la Universidad de Puerto Rico, 1991. Print.

Truglio, Marcela. "Fernando Birri." *Generaciones 60/90: Cine argentino independiente*. Peña, Fernando Martín, ed. Buenos Aires: Malba, 2003: 66–83. Print.

Werner, Louis. "Cineast of the Human Angle." *Américas* 54.4: 46–53. Print.

White, Patricia. *Women's Cinema, World Cinema: Projecting Contemporary Feminisms*. Durham, NC: Duke UP, 2015. Print.

Filmography

Los afincaos. Dir. Leónidas Barletta, 1941.
Amalia. Dir. Enrique García Velloso, 1914.
Barrio gris. Dir. Mario Soffici, 1954.
Buenos Aires. Dir. David José Kohon. 1958.
El camino hacia la muerte del Viejo Reales. Dir. Gerardo Vallejo, 1971.
Carne. Dir. Armando Bó, 1968.
Cochengo Miranda. Dir. Jorge Prelorán, 1975.
Con el diablo en el cuerpo. Dir. Carlos Hugo Christensen, 1947.
Contracampo. Dirs. Rodolfo Kuhn and Manuel Antín, 1958.
Detrás de un largo muro. Dir. Lucas Demare, 1958.
Estrellas. Dirs. Federico León and Marcos Martínez, 2007.
Gente en Buenos Aires. Dir. Eva Landeck, 1973.
La guerra del fracking. Dir. Fernando Solanas, 2013.
Hermógenes Cayo. Dir. Jorge Prelorán, 1969.
La hora de los hornos. Dirs. Fernando Solanas and Octavio Getino, 1968.
Los inundados. Dir. Fernando Birri; Prod. Escuela Documental de Santa Fe, 1960.
Juan sin ropa. Dirs. José González Castillo, Camila Quiroga, Héctor Quiroga, Georges Benoit, 1919.
Kilometro 111. Dir. Mario Soffici, 1938.
Los Marziano. Dir. Ana Katz, 2011.
Los muertos. Dir. Lisandro Alonso, 2004.
La mujer sin cabeza. Dir. Lucrecia Martel, 2008.
El nexo. Dir. Sebastián Antico, 2007.
Nobleza gaucha. Dirs. Humberto Cairo, Eduardo Martínez de la Pera, and Ernesto Gunche, 1915.
Pajarito Gómez. Dir. Rodolfo Kuhn, 1965.
Paula cautiva. Dir. Fernando Ayala, 1963.
Petróleo. Dir. Arturo S. Mom, 1940.
La rubia del camino. Dir. Manuel Romero, 1938.

Shunko. Dir. Lautaro Murúa, 1960.
Suburbio. Dir. León Klimovsky, 1951.
Tire dié. Dir. Fernando Birri; Prod. Escuela Documental de Santa Fe, 1956–1960.
El trueno entre las hojas. Dir. Armando Bó, 1958.
El último malón. Dir. Alcides Greca, 1917.
Yo tengo fe. Dir. Enrique Carreras, 1974.
Zafra. Dir. Lucas Demare, 1959.

Index

accumulation by dispossession, 16–24, 100–106, 153–165
Acree, William, 167n4
actors, non-professional, 16–24, 145–153, 163–165
afincaos, Los, 36, 38–39, 95
Aguilar, Gonzalo, 64, 112, 131, 135, 176n1
Alberdi, Juan Bautista, xii–xiii, 29, 59, 167n2
Alcón, Alfredo, 70, 71, 174n13
Alias Gardelito, 96, 173n6
Alonso, Lisandro, xxi; *Fantasma*, 144–153; *La libertad*, 145; *Los muertos*, 144–153
Altamirano, Carlos, 152, 153
Amadori, Luis César: *Puerto Nuevo*, 64, 67, 172n19
Amalia (film), 8, 9–10
Amorim, Enrique, 50
Andermann, Jens, xvi–xvii, 27–28, 132, 133, 135, 140, 145, 146, 150, 151, 167n3, 167n5
Anderson, Wes, 140
Antico, Sebastián: *El nexo*, 163–165
Antín, Manuel: *Contracampo*, 80–82
anti-Semitism, 43–44
Apold, Raúl Alejandro, 34
Argentina latente, 132

Argentina, mayo de 1969: el camino a la liberación, 109–110
Arrieta, Julio, 163–165, 178n13
Asmodeo, 61
autonomy, xviii, 7–8, 29–54, 76–79, 168n3
autotelia, 137–138
Ayala, Fernando: *El jefe*, 71; *Paula cautiva*, xxi, 92–95
Ayerza, Francisco, xiv, 4–5, 10–11, 26

Badinter, Elizabeth, 58
Balbín, Ricardo, 81
Ballent, Anahí, 41, 42, 45–46, 48–49, 50, 170n9
Barletta, Leónidas: *Los afincaos*, 36, 38–39, 95
Barrio gris, 64, 66–67, 92
Bazin, André, 89
Bases y puntos de partida para la organización política de la República Argentina, xii–xiii, 29, 59, 167n2
Beckman, Ericka, xv
Bemberg, María Luisa, 107
Bergson, Henri, 88
Berlant, Lauren, 136–137, 140–141, 142, 143, 176n3
Bernini, Emilio, 156, 158, 169n3, 172n1

Bielinsky, Fabián, 132
Birri, Fernando, 79–80, 119, 133;
  Tire dié, xx, 77, 80, 82–85, 97; *Los inundados*, xx, 82, 85–92, 173n8
blacklist (under the dictatorship of 1976–1983), 173n13
Blanes, Juan Manuel, xiii–xiv
Bo, Armando, 116; *Carne*, xxi, 117–122; *Fuego*, 118; *El trueno entre las hojas*, 117–118, 119, 175n17, *Una viuda descocada*, 117
Bo, Víctor, 121
Bogue, Ronald, 88
Borel, Fernando, 47
Bosch, Carlos Luis, 178n13
Borges, Graciela, 70, 71
Brakhage, Stan, 150
Brandoni, Luis, 106, 108, 173n13, 175n15
Bringing Up Baby, 57
Buck-Morss, Susan, 137–138
Buenos Aires, 15, 78, 79, 80–81, 173n6
Butler, Judith, xvii

camino hacia la muerte del Viejo Reales, El, xxi, 78, 98–100, 124, 128
Cámpora, Héctor, 98–100, 106–115, 122–129
Campos, Susana, 68
Cancela, Arturo, 42
El cañonero de giles, 33
Carne, xxi, 117–122
Carreras, Enrique: *Yo tengo fe*, 122–129
Carri, Albertina: *Los rubios*, 156
Celluloid Closet, The, 57, 58, 59, 60
censorship, 31–35, 106–108, 122, 124, 173n3, 173n13
ciénaga, La, 140
Cine de la Base, 97
Cine Liberación, Grupo, 73–74, 97–100, 158, 159, 178n11

cinematic free indirect discourse, 141
Chamosa, Oscar, 63
Christaller, Walter, 52
Christensen, Carlos Hugo: *Con el diablo en el cuerpo*, xx, 57–63, 172n17
Chucalezna, 103
Cochengo Miranda, 104–105
Con el diablo en el cuerpo, xx, 57–63, 172n17
Contracampo, 80–82
Cordobazo, 110–111
Cosimi, Nelo: *Mi alazán tostao*, 170n8
country, the, xxi, 136–140
Couselo, Jorge Miguel, 165
Crónica de un niño solo, 95
cruel optimism, 136–137, 140–141, 142, 143, 176n3
Cuarterolo, Andrea, 4–5, 7–8, 10–11, 36, 167n5
Cubitt, Sean, 36
Dabove, Juan Pablo, 1, 6, 11, 13, 22

de Certeau, Michel, 37, 83, 84, 100
del Carril, Hugo, 106
de Filippis Novoa, Francisco: *Flor de durazno*, 8
Deleuze, Gilles, 88, 91
Della Valle, Angel: *La vuelta del malón*, 16
Demare, Lucas, 2, 170n5; *Después del silencio*, 68, *Detrás de un largo muro*, 64, 67–70, 81; *La guerra gaucha*, 2, 27; *Pampa bárbara*, 2, 27; *Zafra*, 70–71
Derbyshire, Philip, 100
Desanzo, Juan Carlos, 107
De Sica, Vittorio: *Umberto D*, 89
Después del silencio, 68
Detrás de un largo muro, 64, 67–70, 81
di Chiara, Roberto, 110–111
dignidad de los nadies, La, 132

di Núbila, Domingo, 12, 15, 33, 34, 44, 47–48, 167n2
dispossession, 134–135, 154–162
Doane, Mary Ann, 89
Dorsky, Nathaniel, 145
Duffau, María Esther, 115
Duncan, Ian, 53

Echeverría, Esteban, 167n2
Elefante blanco, 132, 176n1
Escuela de Cine, Universidad de la Plata, 79
Escuela Documental de Santa Fe, 77, 80, 82–92
España, Claudio, 66, 67
Estrellas, 162–165
ethnographic documentary, 16–23, 100–106
extractivism, 153–165

Faena, 15, 120, 148
Falicov, Tamara L., 132, 170n5, 176n2, 177n8
Fanon, Frantz, 109
Favio, Leonardo, 174n13; *Crónica de un niño solo*, 95
Fantasma, 144–153
Feldman, Simón, 79
Félix-Didier, Paula, 75–76, 77, 168n5, 169n2, 170n7, 173n2
Ferreyra, José Agustín: *Una noche de garufa*, 165
film d'art, 9–10, 168n7
Flaherty, Robert: *Nanook of the North*, 20, 147
Flor de durazno, 8
folklore: as state policy under Perón, 63
formal conventions: of classical cinema, 35–38
Foster, David William, 117
Fregonese, Hugo: *Pampa bárbara*, 2, 27

Freyre, Susana, 58, 63, 92
Frondizi, Arturo, 81
Fuego, 118
Fuera de la ley, 33

Garcés, Delia, 51, 174n13
García Viviana, 95, 207
García Falcó, Marta, 167n1
García Velloso, Enrique: *Amalia*, 8, 9–10
Generación del 60 (Generation of 60), xxi, 77, 94–95, 112, 173n4
Gente en Buenos Aires, xxi, 75, 106–115, 174n14, 175n15, 175n16
Getino, Octavio, 73–74, 78, 97–98, 106, 153, 169n2, 174n13; *La hora de los hornos*, 15, 73–74, 97, 99, 106, 109, 113, 124, 148, 153, 155, 172n1, 173n10, 173n11
Gionco, Pamela C., 67, 68, 172n20
Gleyzer, Raymundo, 78, 105; *Ocurrido en Hualfin*, 101; *Quilino*, 101, 103; *Swift*, 97
Gomes Bas, Joaquín, 66
Gorelik, Adrián, 41, 42, 45–46, 48–49, 170n9
Grant, Cary, 51, 57
Greca, Alcides: *último malón, El*, xix, 6, 8, 16–24, 40, 71
Guattari, Félix, 91
Gunche, Ernesto, 11; *Hasta después de muerta*, 8; *Nobleza gaucha*, ix, 4, 8, 10–13, 17, 23, 36–37, 44
guerra del fracking, La, 153–165
guerra gaucha, La, 2, 27

Halperín, Paula, 67
Halperín Donghi, Tulio, 21
Hardouin, Elodie, 108, 174n14
Harvey, David, 114
Hasta después de muerta, 8
Hepburn, Katharine, 57

Hermógenes Cayo, 104
Hernández, José, 2, 4–5, 7, 11–12, 99, 157
"hermoso día, El," ix–x
Historia de la literatura argentina, 27–29
Historias breves, 132, 140
hora de los hornos, La, 15, 73–74, 97, 99, 106, 109, 113, 124, 148, 153, 155, 172n1, 173n10, 173n11
hydrocarbons: production and distribution in the cinema, 41–44, 48–54, 153–165; Yacimientos Petrolíferos Argentinos (YPF), 41–42, 154

indexicality, 30, 170n4
inundados, Los, xx, 82, 85–92, 173n8
Irigoyen, Hipólito, xi, 8
Ivachow, Lilian Laura, 108, 174n14

jefe, El, 71
jóvenes viejos, Los, 94
Juan sin ropa (film), 8, 13–16, 17, 24, 40, 82, 119, 148
Juárez, Enrique: *Ya es tiempo de violencia*, 109

Katz, Ana: *Los Marziano*, 135–140, 177n4
Karush, Matthew, 25–26, 29, 44, 45, 47, 56
Kelly Hopfenblatt, Alejandro, 30, 31–34, 63, 169n1
Kilómetro 111, 41, 48–54, 68
King, John, 106
Kittler, Friedrich, xi
Klimovsky, León: *Suburbio*, 64–66, 128
Kohon, David José, 74, 92, 97, 133; *Buenos Aires*, 15, 78, 79, 80–81, 173n6; *Prisioneros de una noche*, 94

Kracauer, Siegfried, 30, 147
Kriger, Clara, 34–35, 65, 66, 168n3
Kuhn, Rodolfo: 79, 118–119; *Contracampo*, 80–82; *Los jóvenes viejos*, 94; *Pajarito Gómez*, 95, 125
Kuleshov, Lev, 129

Landeck, Eva: *Gente en Buenos Aires*, xxi, 75, 106–115, 174n14, 175n15, 175n16
Lefebvre, Martin, 91, 117, 145
León, Federico: *Estrellas*, 162–165
Ley de cine de 1957 (Cinema Law of 1957), 77
Ley de cine de 1994, Nueva (New Cinema Law of 1994), 132
libertad, La, 145
López, Ana M., 74, 170n6
López Rega, José, 106
Lugones, Leopoldo, ix–xii, xiv, 5, 7, 8, 12–15, 28, 70, 147; "El hermoso día," ix–x, 167n1; *El payador*, 1–3
Luppi, Federico, 125, 174n13
Lusarreta, Pilar de, 42
Lusnich, Ana Laura, 38

Machinandiarena, Miguel, 42
Mafud, Lucio, 9
Mahieu, Agustín, 173n8
Manrupe Raúl, 63
Mansilla, Lucio, 17, 36
Maranghello, César, 63
Mármol, José, 9
Marcone, Jorge, 178n12
Marrone, Irene, 167n5
Martel, Lucrecia, xxi, 153; *La ciénaga*, 140; *La mujer sin cabeza*, 136, 140–144; *Rey muerto*, 140
Martínez, Marcos: *Estrellas*, 162–165
Martínez de la Pera, Eduardo: *Hasta después de muerta*, 8; *Nobleza gaucha*, ix, 4, 8, 10–13, 17, 23, 36–37, 44

Martínez, Estrada, Ezequiel, 49–50
Martín Fierro, El gaucho, 2, 4–5, 7, 11–12, 99, 157
Marziano, Los, 135–140, 177n4
Marzio, Duilio, 92, 115, 174n13
masculinity, 55–63, 119–122
Masacre de la Plaza Lorea (Massacre of Plaza Lorea), 1
Masacre de Trelew (Massacre of Trelew), 109
Memoria del saqueo, 132, 154, 156, 177n10
Méndez, Patricia, 167n1
Mentasti, Atilio, 123
Mi alazán tostao, 170n8
migration, internal, 14–16, 67–70, 81–82, 98–100, 122–129
Mocoví, 16–23
modernizing projects and the cinema, national, 39–54
Moglia Barth, Luis: *Tango!*, 31, 32
Mom, Arturo S.: *Petróleo*, 41–44, 49
Montaldo, Graciela, xviii, 3, 28–29
Morack, Irene, 108
Moretti, Franco, 52, 53
muertos, Los, 144–153
mujer sin cabeza, La, 136, 140–144
Mulvey, Laura, 117
Mundo grúa, 132
Murúa, Lautaro, xxi, 74, 93, 174n13; *Alias Gardelito*, 96, 173n6, *Shunko*, xxi, 95–96, 173n6; *La Raulito*, 115–116

Nanook of the North, 20, 147
Navarro, Vinicius, 157
nexo, El, 163–165
New Argentine Cinema, 132–153
Nichols, Bill, 30, 102, 103
Nixon, Rob, 103, 157–158, 160
Nobleza gaucha, ix, 4, 8, 10–13, 17, 23, 36–37, 44

noche de garufa, Una, 165

Ocupación militar del Río Negro bajo el mando del General Julio A. Roca, 1879, xiii–xiv
Ocurrido en Hualfín, 101
Olazabal, Tirso de, 81
Olivera, Héctor, *La Patagonia rebelde*, 106
Oliveri, Carlos, 50
Onganía, Juan Carlos, 96, 97–116, 117, 119, 122, 123
Ortega, Palito, xxi, 122–129, 156, 176n19, 176n20
Orquera, Fabiola, 98, 99
Oubiña, David, 140

Page, Joanna, 133–134, 135, 144, 155, 156
Pajarito Gómez, 95, 125
palo enjabonado, 60
Pampa bárbara, 2, 27
Pasolini, Pier Paolo, 141
Patagonia rebelde, La, 106
Paula cautiva, xxi, 92–94
payador, El, 2
Peluffo, Ana, 55, 58
Peña, Fernando Martín, 32–33, 63, 97, 123, 168n3, 172n18
Pérez Llahí, Marcos Adrián, 101, 173n12
Perón, Isabel, 106, 108, 115, 124
Perón, Juan Domingo, xx, 24, 34, 63, 66, 68, 77, 92, 106, 122–123, 126, 129; return of, 122–129, 176n19
Peronism, 33–35, 55–72, 97, 122–129, 176n19
Pessano, Carlos Alberto, 31–33, 86, 170n10
Petróleo, 41–44, 49
Philip, George, 42
Pick, Zuzana, 97

Piedras, Pablo, 177n9, 177n10
Podalsky, Laura, 80, 173n10
Politti, Luis, 115
Pondal Ríos, Sixto, 50
Portela, María Alejandra, 63
Prelorán, Jorge, xxi, 75, 78, 100–106, 173n12; *Chucalezna*, 103; *Cochengo Miranda*, 104–105; *Hermógenes Cayo*, 104; *Ocurrido en Hualfín*, 101; *Quilino*, 101
Prisioneros de una noche, 94
Prividera, Nicolás, 173n7
Puerto Nuevo, 64, 67, 172n19

Quebracho, 106
Quilino, 101
Quiroga, Facundo, 85, 153

Ramos, Julio, xviii, 6
Raulito, La, 115–116
Renán, Sergio: *La tregua*, 108
Renier, Jérémie, 132
Rey muerto, 140
Ríos, Humberto: *Faena*, 15, 120, 148
Roa Bastos, Augusto, 118
roadway network project, 44–48, 48–54
road movie, 44–48, 57–63
Rocha, Carolina, 56
Rodríguez, Fermín, xiii–xiv
Rojas, Ricardo, 27–29
Romero, Luis Alberto, 1, 110
Romero, Manuel: *El cañonero de giles*, 33; *Fuera de la ley*, 33; *La rubia del camino*, 41, 44–48, 56, 57; *Tres anclados en París*, 33
Rosas, Juan Manuel de, 10
Ross, Marilina, 115, 174n13
rubia del camino, La, 41, 44–48, 56, 57
rubios, Los, 156

Ruffinelli, Jorge, 101, 172n17
Russo, Vito, 57, 58, 59, 60

Sáenz Peña Law (Ley Sáenz Peña), xi, 30
Sala, Jorge, 95
Sánchez Prado, Ignacio, 55, 58
Sánchez Sorondo, Matías, 33, 86
Santos Vega, 14, 15, 82
Santos Vega vuelve, 82
Sarli, Isabel, xxi, 116–122, 175n17
Sarmiento, Domingo Faustino, 1–2, 21, 23, 59, 60, 84, 96, 135, 147, 150, 152
Sarquís, Nicolás, 79
Sasiaín, Sonia, 170n10, 173n9
Schroeder Rodriguez, Paul A., 40
screwball comedy, 44–48, 57–63
Sebreli, Juan José, 89–90, 91
Semana Trágica, La, 1, 13, 15
El secuestrador, 92, 95
Shunko, xxi, 95–96, 173n6
Silvester, Stanley, 97
Singerman, Paulina, 47
slaughterhouse: as setting, 13–16, 119–122, 148–149
slow violence, 153–165
Smith, Neil, xv–xvi, 80
Sociedad Fotográfica Argentina de Aficionados (SFA de A), xiv, 4–5, 10–11, 26
Sociedad Rural, La, 113
Soffici, Mario, 4, 36, 38, 71, 106, 170n5; *Barrio gris*, 64, 66–67, 92; *Kilómetro 111*, 41, 48–54, 68; *Puerto Nuevo*, 64, 67, 172n19
Solanas, Fernando "Pino," xxi, 73–74, 78, 97–98, 101, 105, 106, 119, 132, 153–162, 174n13, 177n8, 177n10; *Argentina latente*, 132; *La dignidad de los nadies*, 132; *La guerra del fracking*, 153–165; *La hora*

de los hornos, 15, 73–74, 97, 99, 106, 109, 113, 124, 148, 153, 155, 172n1, 173n10, 173n11; *Memoria del saqueo*, 132, 154, 156, 177n10; *Tierra sublevada: Oro impuro*, 154, 155; *Tierra sublevada: Oro negro*, 154
Sorensen Goodrich, Diana, 3–4, 168n10
Spadaccini, Silvana, 170n10
Spence, Louise, 157
Steiner, George, 147
Stites Mor, Jessica, 110–111
Suburbio, 64–66, 128
sugar industry, 70–71, 98–100, 124, 128
Svampa, Maristella, 114, 136, 158–159
Swift, 97
Szeman, Imre, 161–162

Tango!, 31, 32
Taquini, Graciela, 101
Tato, Miguel Paulino, 106, 124
Taylorism, 15, 148–149, 177n5
Teatro del Pueblo, 38–39
Thorry, Juan Carlos, 58, 60, 63
Tiempo, César, 57
Tierra sublevada: Oro impuro, 154, 155
Tierra sublevada: Oro negro, 154
Tire dié, xx, 77, 80, 82–85, 97
Torres Ríos, Leopoldo: *Santos Vega vuelve*, 82
Torre Nilsson, Leopoldo: *El secuestrador*, 92, 95
tourism development, 44–48
train: in early silent film, 170n6, use of in formal conventions, 36–39, shots filmed from, 81–92, 99–100, 103–106, 115–116, 124–125, 128–129
Tranchini, Elina, x–xi, xiv–xv, 55–56

Trapero, Pablo: *Elefante blanco*, 132, 176n1; *Mundo grúa*, 132
tregua, La 108
Trelles Plazaola, Luis, 107, 108
Tres anclados en París, 33
tres berretines, Los, 31, 32
Trombetta, Jimena, 30, 31–34, 63
trueno entre las hojas, El, 117–118, 119, 175n17
Truglio, Marcela, 86–87

último malón, El, xix, 6, 8, 16–24, 40, 71
Umberto D, 89
uneven development/uneven modernization, xv–xvi, 16–23, 36, 70–71, 80–81, 83–86, 98–100, 108–115, 129; lack of representation in classical cinema, 29–72; role of train in, 48–54
Uriburu, José Félix, xix, 6, 8, 40, 42

Vallejo, Gerardo, xxi, 79, 101, 105, 125; *El camino hacia la muerte del Viejo Reales, El*, xxi, 78, 98–100, 124, 128
Vallina, Carlos, 97
Vargas, Argentino, 146–153
Velloso, Enrique García, 9
Verbitsky, Bernardo, 64
viuda descocada, Una, 117

Werner, Louis, 102–103
Wullicher, Ricardo: *Quebracho*, 106

Ya es tiempo de violencia, 109
Yo tengo fe, 122–129
Yupanqui, Atahualpa, 71

Zafra, 70–71

www.ingramcontent.com/pod-product-compliance
Lightning Source LLC
Chambersburg PA
CBHW030652230426
43665CB00011B/1055